The Next Happy

"A bold, brave, and incredibly relevant book."

"Tracey delivers a much needed injection of nuance and reality into the otherwise overly cheerful conversation about following dreams. You'll be happier if you read this book!"

"The Next Happy is like the friend you call when your car is stuck in a ditch on a journey you never expected to take. From the moment you open this book, you'll begin to feel unstuck, and by the end, you'll find yourself moving forward in the right direction, toward your new happiness."

"In a world where we have been taught to chase our dreams no matter what, The Next Happy *will gently tap you on the shoulder, turn you around, and take you in a whole new and more joyful direction. Author Tracey Cleantis is generous, wise, and compassionate. When it comes to self-help books on finding happiness,* The Next Happy *is truly a game changer."*

"Knowing when to give up on a dream—and knowing how to do it—is a skill that could save us all from years of agony. If your dream is costing you too much, The Next Happy *could be the thing to save you."*

The Next Happy

Let Go of the Life You Planned and
Find a New Way Forward

TRACEY CLEANTIS

Hazelden
Publishing

Hazelden Publishing
Center City, Minnesota 55012
hazelden.org/bookstore

Library of Congress Cataloging-in-Publication Data
Cleantis, Tracey, 1965-
The next happy : let go of the life you planned and find a new way forward / Tracey Cleantis.
   pages cm
   ISBN 978-1-61649-572-5 (paperback) — ISBN 978-1-61649-576-3 (ebook)
   1. Happiness. 2. Self-realization. 3. Success. I. Title.
   BF575.H27.C58 2015
   158.1—dc23

                                                                      2014046630

Editor's note
Some names and details have been changed to protect the privacy of those mentioned in this publication. In some cases, composites have been created.
     This publication is not intended as a substitute for the advice of health care professionals.

18 17 16 15   1 2 3 4 5 6

Cover design: Terri Kinne

Dedication

To Karen Cohen, who made me see myself differently
while standing in line at McDonald's and ever after.

To Wendy West Brenninkmeijer for pushing me to do the
scary things, like a fierce, caffeinated, insistent mother bear.

And to Keith Dwyer for laughing wildly at my
self-imposed limitations. Seeing, pushing, laughing, and
loving made all the difference.

Contents

Foreword

In this country, most of us are reared under the high-flying banner of the American dream. From the moment we are born, we are told to "Go for it," "Never stop believing," "Dream big," and "Never give up." Our teachers are Disney movies, sports heroes, plucky characters from popular literature, and well-meaning adults who relentlessly cheer us on, promising that if we work hard enough and try hard enough, we will succeed. They never have to say out loud that failure is not an option, that failure is a weakness. We get that message loud and clear.

So what happens if going after the dream isn't going to lead to happiness? What if pursuing a dream at all costs is precisely the *unhealthiest* thing we could do for our soul? You are about to find out in the pages of this very timely and incredibly relevant book.

The bold and not-as-popular position that Tracey Cleantis takes in *The Next Happy* is exactly what many of us need to hear when we bump up against the truth about real life: that not being able to attain exactly what we want is simply part of the human condition. There are times in life when we must learn how to accept this, to grieve it, to sit with disappointment, and to move through it. *The Next Happy* gives us a road map for how to accomplish this difficult and necessary work, step-by-step.

Yes, going full throttle ahead can sometimes bring the happiness we're seeking, but at other times, the best way forward is to stop trying, to stop striving for the unattainable. How freeing to know that what lies just beyond "giving up" may be your next happy. A bold, brave, and incredibly relevant book.

Lee Woodruff,
New York Times best-selling author of *Perfectly Imperfect: A Life in Progress,*
with her husband, Bob Woodruff, and *CBS This Morning* contributor

Acknowledgments

Thanks to Keith Dwyer, my life mate, for entering into "the agreement" after lunch at Julienne's in San Marino. That agreement made this book possible. Thanks to Jennie Nash, my book coach, for her boundless encouragement and for being the kind of cheerleader who makes you think you can do anything and then gives you the infrastructure to show you that she was right; thanks to Wendy West, my dear friend, for pushing me to go to Harvard's CME Writing Conference and insisting that I pitch to everyone in the room; thanks to my incredible agent, Don Fehr, for making my publishing dreams come true; thanks to Sid Farrar, my editor, for his warm and gentle edits and easy can-do confidence and encouragement, which made what had seemed like mountains transform into something much more like molehills; thanks to Lee Woodruff for being an incredible role model of surviving difficult things and for her generous foreword; thanks to all the people who generously shared their stories with me (their names were changed to protect their privacy) and to Lisa Manresa and Stephanie Baffone for their enormous generosity of spirit and real and meaningful involvement—I can't imagine this book without you.

Thanks to Karin Thayer for helping me to realize I had something to teach on the topic. Thanks to Lisa Manterfield, Hannah Stephenson, and Karen Cohen for being gentle readers. Thanks to Leah Norris Jenner for having conversations with me on the topic that inspired me.

Thanks to Jamie Cat Callan for being the first writing teacher who made me think that one day I would be thanking her in the acknowledgments section of a book published by a real publisher that was in a real store; thanks to Tom Cleantis for seeing me as a writer before I did; thanks to my blog friends who helped me to tell this story before I knew what I was telling; thanks to my Facebook friends who endured a year of me asking questions about their grief, most especially Angie, Bonnie-Ann, Deni, Elatia, Elise, Jeanette, Jennie, Kate, Kirie, Leesa, Lisa, Lisa Ann, Linda, Lori, Lynn, Mardel, Marla, Rabia, Serena, Shefaly, and Susan; thanks to Loretta Shepherd and Pam Dixon for helping me when I needed it; and thanks to Wendy Cruz and Lily for all they did to help me through this time and for making my life a little more lovely.

Introduction

Let me guess: You wanted something very, very badly—so badly that you have done everything in your power and then some to get it, but you still didn't get it. You dreamed of this thing—this job or this partner or this baby or this house or this fame or this fortune—and it was so vivid in your mind that you could practically taste it. Maybe you can taste it, still. And not having it hurts in a hundred thousand very specific ways—psychically, spiritually, emotionally, socially, physically. It hurts when you get up in the morning and when you go to bed at night. It hurts when you see some undeserving person, standing there in line at the grocery store, who seems to be living *your* dream, all la-di-da and carefree about how all-giving and generous the universe is, when you know for a fact that life is unfair.

Well, let me say right now that I feel your pain, my friend. I am, in fact, a person who specializes in your pain, both on a personal level, as you will soon read about, and on a professional level. People come to me when the cost of never giving up has gotten to be too great. They come to me when, somewhere deep inside, they know they need to stop trying, and I not only give them permission to let the dream go, but I give them the lethal injection. Call me the Dr. Kevorkian of dreams, if you will. Many have. But I wear the badge proudly. Someone's got to tell it like it really is. Someone's got to raise her voice and say, "It's okay to give up, to give in, to cry uncle." And someone's got to speak the truth about what happens when you do.

This book is not about making the pain go away, because it isn't going to just magically go away. It's about making the decision to say adios and sayonara to your dream so that you can feel the true depth of the loss. Yeah, you read that right: It might hurt more before it hurts less. But I'm betting that you're tougher than you think, that you can take it.

How can I be so sure? Because you picked up this book. Even if some irritating, well-meaning friend or therapist shoved it into your unwilling hands, you still picked it up and opened it. We live in a never-never-never-give-up culture, and right now, some part of you knows that it might be time to say, "Well, screw that." Some part of you is thinking that it just might be time to tip your hat and ride out of town. And some part of you knows that you will be fine.

I'm here to help you on your way, because I know that what's almost certainly waiting out there is what I call "the next happy." Not happily ever after, mind you, because let's be honest: We all know that's BS. But there's some version of you being happy again—some new and unexpected and undreamed-of, even outrageous happy—and it's shimmering out there on the other side of impossible, just waiting for you to arrive. I know, because I've helped an awful lot of people get there, and I have staked a claim in the next happy myself.

I said it might hurt, and that is true. This is no "make lemonade out of lemons" guidebook, because all that recipe does is add a little sugar to some bitterness to mask the pain. This is more like brewing a fantastic lemon liqueur. It's a more complex process, and it goes something like this:

- You accept the situation: I have lemons.
- You sit with your lemons; you grieve and cry a bit.
- You taste the bitterness of the fruit.
- You slice into them and see what they are made of.
- You start making an effort to do something with what is before you— add a pinch of courage, a dash of new perspective.
- Add some time and patience and watch something truly transformative emerge—an adult acceptance that can be sipped and savored.
- Drink up the delicious goodness of your next happy, of your new beginning.
- Repeat as necessary.

Sound good? Then let's get started.

chapter 1

Never Give Up

"Never, never, never, never give up."
>> Winston Churchill

One morning last year, before I had even sipped my first cup of coffee, I was innocently lounging in bed with my dog, Lily, and waiting for Al Roker to tell me what the weather was in my neck of the woods, when I heard one of the winners of *The Apprentice* saying words like *pregnancy, infertility, success,* and *baby.* I've never watched *The Apprentice* on purpose—okay, that is not entirely true; once I saw an episode in which Arsenio Hall had a screaming fit and attacked a housewife from New Jersey as Donald Trump looked on with his version of semi-horror on his face—but when I heard the spunky interviewer ask this Apprentice and his E! Entertainment wife what their advice was to people out there who were struggling with infertility, I snapped to attention. I wondered what a guy whom Donald hired and a woman who reported on the latest entertainment news might know about infertility that I didn't already know. You see, I know a lot. I spent five years trying to conceive on my own (with my partner's help) and another five years and more than $100,000 trying to conceive with a reproductive endocrinologist's help. I did four-and-a-half rounds of in vitro fertilization (IVF) and twenty or so rounds of intrauterine insemination (IUI). I did intracytoplasmic sperm injection (ICSI). And we moved on to doing IUI with a sperm donor. I didn't stop there. No, I was determined. I really wanted to get pregnant.

The Most Dangerous Advice Ever Given

I did things I thought I would never do—things that only sad and desperate people might try (which is the kind of judgment I might have made about others before I tried to get pregnant and couldn't). When I wasn't at my doctor's office enduring uncomfortable procedures and invasive ultrasounds, I was at my acupuncturist's office getting needled and chugalugging disgusting herbal tea with gusto, the way frat boys might down a bottle of beer. The black, tar-like medicinal concoctions that were supposed to make me a baby-making machine were (I swear) a mix of moldy earth, yak hooves, dried dung beetles, and the most noxious and unpleasant assortment of herbs that they could come up with. I had a fantasy about this tea. I had come to believe that the Chinese acupuncturists created this vile and bitter tea as a means of seeing if you *really* wanted to have a baby or not. If you could pass the test and drink the tea, then they would immediately give you the *real* remedy, which would taste of sugar and spice and everything nice (if you wanted a girl, and I did), and with a single sip you would immediately get the Gerber baby of your dreams. Even at the time, I knew my fantasy was absurd, and yet it was no more absurd than my refusal to look at the statistics that 70 percent of women who try IVF don't get pregnant, or my refusal to hear the doubt in the voice of the doctor when he told me that in the last round we had really "put the pedal to the metal"—and yet my egg production was still disappointing.

My trying didn't stop there. I hired a reputable feng shui guy, because if you are an unbeliever, you want to make sure that the feng shui guy you get has some street cred. Mine was famous for doing hotels and the homes of the rich and famous. Feng Shui Guy came into my home and tsked and took notes and told me in no uncertain terms how my couch was impacting my odds to conceive. I am a somewhat logical and pragmatic person, and this seemed ridiculous at the time, but *what if?* What if it could make a difference? What if replacing my couch meant I could have that baby that I had always dreamed of?

In my free time, I went to yoga, got massaged, and got back into therapy to manage the stress that trying to manage my stress was causing. With the help of my Jungian analyst, I looked at my psychological resistance to pregnancy and mothering and everything I could possibly be resistant to, and I explored how my mother complex might be making my womb inhospitable. I ate more yams than one human should (because a friend told me that her ultrasound tech told her that she sees lots of babies who were conceived due to excessive amounts of yam consumption) and turned to trying-to-conceive websites for tricks, tips, suggestions, and the pregnancy-inducing baby dust that the well-meaning message-board readers virtually sprinkled on each other. One woman my age who lived in Minnesota, with the pseudonym of "Fertile Myrtle," had managed to get pregnant without the use of assisted reproductive technology. I turned to her tips like they were pronouncements from Mount Sinai written on stony tablets and not just the writings of a woman on the instant message board of a trying-to-conceive Internet site. Fertile Myrtle claimed that her secret was a mix of cough syrup, pumpkin seeds, and keeping her legs up in the air for a half hour after coitus. I followed her directions to the letter. My ex-husband ingested more pumpkin seeds than you could find in an entire pumpkin patch, I filled my Viva Atlantic City shot glasses with Robitussin, and there were feet marks on my bedroom wall.

I got way in the deep end of "not my comfort zone," and I saw healers, energy workers, and Maori tribal chieftains who supposedly had the power to heal even the most profoundly infertile couples for the low price of $375 for a fifty-minute session. We were assured by psychics, astrologers, and all who loved us that there was a baby in our future. And even though I am a somewhat lapsed Episcopalian, I had friends and families saying prayers, rosaries, and masses for us. We were on prayer chains at more than a hundred churches. I wrote affirmations every morning and evening ("I easily and effortlessly become pregnant"). Instead, I had become, uneasily and with great struggle, *not* pregnant.

The madness all came to a crashing halt on December 17, 2008. I was shopping at Target in Highland Park, Illinois. My trip was interrupted by an un-ignorable urge to find the ladies' room. When I went into the bathroom and saw the evidence that another round of treatment had not worked—I wasn't pregnant *again*—I immediately went home, called the doctor's office, and, instead of scheduling yet *another* round, I told the nurse I was done. My voice was colder than the subzero Chicago temperature. "I'm done," I said. "No more appointments, no more procedures. Take me off the schedule." The nurse told me, even more dispassionately, "Okay"—and that was it. That was the moment I was done trying. I would no longer pursue any heroic efforts to conceive. I hung up and cried and cried and cried. I had howled and sobbed in disappointment before, but this time was different. This time there would be no "next time."

I knew that day, in a way that I had never known before, that I could keep doing this over and over and I still would not get pregnant. I knew it. All the king's horses and all the king's men weren't going to get me pregnant, no matter what kind of success rate they advertised or what kind of magic potion I choked down. Nothing anyone could tell me would change my mind. Just as the day before, and for years before that, no one could have told me that my dream *wasn't* going to come true; on that day, no one could tell me that it *was*. I had to give up because I knew that trying wouldn't make a difference, and continuing to try—when trying was hurting my mind, body, relationships, career, and finances—was not something I was willing to do anymore. That was the day that I *started* to move on with my life (emphasis on the word *started*—but more on that later).

Back to the Apprentice and his E! Entertainment wife and their advice for anyone facing the pain and heartbreak of infertility. Here it is, and it's pretty simple. You've likely heard it before from teachers and coaches, parents and friends, pastors and counselors, strangers and Oprah. It's "never give up." That's it. That was their advice. I am writing this book because those three little words are some of the most insidious words in the English language. They are some of the most dangerous, some of the most cruel, and, if you are holding on tight to a dream—be it a dream about children, or marriage, or occupation, or fame, or location, or even how you imagined your life would be—they just might be the one thing holding you back from a real happy ending.

The Dark Side of Optimism

The advice that the Apprentice gave to the *Today* show audience is a deeply embedded cultural cliché. "Never give up" is so beloved a philosophy that we dare not say out loud that we are actually letting our dream go—that we are no longer going to try to save the marriage or be a star athlete or be a mother or launch the start-up or get the corner office or achieve all the great things we set out to achieve. Seriously, there are some things you just can't say out loud: (1) You can't shout "Fire!" in a public place unless there really is something burning, and (2) you can't say you are giving up your dream unless you are willing to be seen as a complete and total failure. See for yourself: Google "give up on a dream," page through all the returns, and see what unwanted word appears again and again in the advice that people are giving. Yeah, that's right. Google and everyone else are telling you what you have already heard a million times before: Never give up on a dream. Never, never, never, ever give up on your dream—never! It is standard advice. It is an answer of hope and optimism, which is lovely on the one hand, but here's the thing that isn't often said about the other hand: Sometimes hope is sadistic, sometimes optimism is dangerous, and sometimes this annoying thing called reality really must be faced if you are to preserve your sanity.

When patients come to my office and sit across from me with tears in their eyes and their heart breaking because their marriage fell apart, or their desire to have children has been unfulfilled, or they were unable to realize a long-held career dream, there is usually a component of shame to their story. They most often tell me their story as if they are admitting a terrible secret. If they dare admit it at all, they may not look me in the eye; they may whisper the words. Often they go with the Sour Grapes Method of coping and pretend that they never had the dream to begin with. We've all employed this method a thousand times: "I really didn't want to win"; "I'm actually relieved it didn't work out." We resort to this tactic because it saves us from actually having to admit defeat. If we didn't even really want it to begin with, then we don't have to feel ashamed of our failure.

Here's a news flash: Deciding to stop pursuing something that is not working for you, and that may in fact be destructive for you, does *not* mean you are a quitter or a loser. You might want to read that last sentence again. I know there is a part of you that knows that you are not a quitter, but there are other voices that may be masking this knowledge. Maybe you had a dad who told you that just because you didn't keep up with guitar lessons you were a quitter, or maybe you had a coach tell you that because you decided not to go out for the varsity team you were a quitter. Those voices live in your head, too, and maybe they are shutting down the voice that knows it is time to let go of your dream. It took me some years and a whole lot of therapy to tune in to the voice that could calm and soothe me and help me look at things in a rational way, but now I can call up that voice just like a station on the radio. The voice sounds a lot like Glinda the Good Witch. Listen carefully, and you can hear your version of that voice, too: *Giving up on your dream does not make you a failure or a quitter.*

Books like *The Secret* tell us that all we have to do is imagine a goal clearly and really want it, and it will then automatically, naturally, and easily happen for us. But what does it mean when it doesn't? Are we a bad person? Did we not really want it? Did we not visualize clearly enough? Is it our fault that we didn't get it? Or is the real secret that there are some things in life that are just simply beyond our control? Embedded in that last question is a hard truth that many people go through a lot of suffering trying to deny: *There are some things in life that are just simply beyond our control.*

I wanted a baby so desperately. Giving up that dream was harder than anything I did in my entire life—and yet, I *had* to. You hear people say that the definition of insanity is continuing to do the same thing over and over, expecting different results. My moment of giving up was a moment of mental health, even though it hurt like a son of a bitch—and even though it might have looked like quitting to people on the outside.

The Self-Blame Game

Why do we blame ourselves for our dreams not working out the way we'd hoped? It's the same reason that the patients I see with traumatic childhoods tend to blame themselves rather than their abusers: If you blame yourself, there is more of an illusion of a locus of control and a sense of agency or ability to impact the situation. If the trauma or loss was caused by others or by events outside of your control, then you feel more out of control, which is not a comfortable feeling. As the British psychoanalyst Ronald Fairbairn said, "It is better to be a sinner in a world ruled by God than to live in a world ruled by the Devil."[1] Fairbairn wasn't literally talking about God and the Devil. He was using that analogy to explain why children, and adults for that matter, take on all the responsibility and make themselves bad as a means of coping with abusive or destructive traumas.

I know I did this with my own inability to conceive. I came up with what, in hindsight, were irrational narratives about how this was further evidence of my inability to get what I want and proof that therefore something must be wrong with me. I looked to my past for evidence for this irrational argument, and I found it. You see, I needed that evidence; I needed this to be at least partly my fault because, in a strange way, that was more tolerable than the outcome just being random and chaotic. Because how exactly do you impact random and chaotic? I needed to believe that I was a "sinner" and that my not being able to get pregnant was my fault. It's probably easy for anyone, including you, to look at my story and see that it *isn't* my fault. I don't know you, and I don't know where you are in your quest to fulfill your dream, but I can bet that it would be easy for me to look at your story and see all the ways you're not at fault in not fulfilling it as well. We tend to be very good at seeing when other people's situations are beyond their control—even as they desperately try to manage the outcome—but are much less skilled at seeing it in ourselves.

Positivity as a Means of Avoiding Reality

The problem with always looking at the bright side and ignoring the reality of the situation is that we have to employ a fair amount of denial along with denial's ugly stepsisters, minimizing and rationalizing. They are kind of the shapewear of emotional life. You put them on so that you can look better and cover up what really is going on. Have you met them? I have. They are on my speed dial. We are close personal friends. They like to send me instant messages and tell me that my pain is not that big of a deal compared to some other people's pain, and that I should just suck it up and stop complaining. You've probably sung their favorite songs, too: "Everything happens for the best" or "I shouldn't be sad as I have my health, and there are people much worse off than me." People minimize and rationalize even as they are clearly and undeniably in the midst of active grieving for a genuine loss: the realization that something that was vitally important to them simply isn't going to happen. They feel that they don't deserve to express their pain (because they shouldn't be feeling it), and therefore they repress it.

Being told or pretending that your pain isn't that big of a deal is never helpful. Your pain is your pain, and it hurts you—it hurts, and it sucks to have put your heart and soul into making a dream a reality and have nothing to show for it but a pile of receipts, a divorce decree, some headshots, or a bankruptcy.

The people I see in my practice have had all kinds of dreams. They wanted their marriage to work so badly that they endured all kinds of bad behavior and self-esteem-sucking situations. They wanted to be an actor so much that they sacrificed ten years waiting tables, and all they have to show for it is one commercial for a gas-relief medication and a bit part in an off-Sunset production that no one has ever seen. They were so *sure* that they were going to have children that they let all the other good, strong relationships in their life wither on the vine. Their business was going to be such a success that they were willing to go bankrupt trying to make it work. These people, still clinging to a dead dream, use positivity and optimism as a means of not looking at things as they really are. The cycle they are stuck in now—the never-give-up cycle—can be exceedingly damaging. Continuing to try—even as it hurts their relationships, their mental and physical health, and their finances—is only possible if they can cling to the delusion that "if I only believe hard enough, my dream will come true."

When people tiptoe around talking about the nature of their grief, I find that I just want to throw my arms around them and tell them that it's okay, that they are safe here, and that this is a place where they can drop the clichés and spew their anger or scream or sob and take off their emotional shapewear or do whatever it is they need to in response to their pain. I tell them, "This is a place where your feelings are okay, and not just the positive kind . . . the ugly and messy and stinky kinds are really welcome here, too. Feel free to express whatever you're feeling: You can cry until you howl, until your face looks like an abstract watercolor painting, and until you have used up all my Kleenex." That is not something that people who have been long pursuing an impossible dream hear a lot. The attitude that most people want to see in those grieving a dream is positivity and blind-eyed optimism and glass-half-full thinking with a chaser of can-do spirit.

Other People's Good Cheer

Patients employing the "It's Not So Bad" school of coping were probably raised by some version of my mother. My mother is a bit of a self-described Pollyanna. Her favorite phrase was "If you can't say anything nice, don't say anything at all." I know she developed her "think positive" and "look on the bright side of life" attitude as a means of dealing with a difficult life, but I can tell you that there were times when I turned to her during hard moments in my life, and I just wanted to hear "This sucks big time" and not "Turn that frown upside down. Everything happens for a reason." There are plenty of things that don't happen for a reason, and being told that they do feels a bit like having sunshine blown up your sundress, if you will.

As someone who worked her tushy off to make a dream come true and had it all come to naught, I know all too well that feeling of being compelled to take care of other people and not overwhelm them with your grief. I was *really* good at that. Whenever I would tell someone that we just failed at another IVF round, I would muster all the cheeriness I could manage and end the sentence with an upbeat aphorism. I didn't do this because I wanted to; trust me, I didn't. I did it because when I told the truth about my pain, people would tell me that horrible thing that someone on Donald Trump's reality TV show *The Apprentice* said or even something worse. Their response was always some version of "Stop your whining and stay positive. It will eventually work out." I used to think that people said that just for me, that they were really and truly trying to encourage me, and while that was often the case, I do believe that something else was often at play, which is other people's fear.

My belief is that when people hear about a dream that didn't come true, they panic and start to think of all the things *they* yearn for and all the things *they* are striving for, and they have a flash of fear that these things might not happen either, no matter how hard they try. We all know somewhere deep inside the truth that not everything is in our control. It's a scary thought, and so when your pain pings that place deep within someone, they often lob back encouraging words—"It will all work out okay in the end! Don't give up!"— and by uttering that one phrase, they have eliminated their own anxiety, or at least pushed it back down to the place where they keep hidden all their fears about their marriage, their career, and their own lives. No matter how other people react to your decision to take care of yourself and let go and move on, please remember that you are not responsible for their fears. Recognize their response for what it is, and then go on feeling the grief that you feel.

> > >

So how do you face the dangers of "never, never, never give up"? With the Movie Rx and the steps below, you're going to determine if it's time to give up your dream or if there's more to be done. If you truly believe that there's more to be done, this book probably isn't for you—and that's entirely okay. If, however, you've begun to suspect that it might really be time to give up—to declare that the dream is dead—then I hope this book can be a lifeline for you.

Movie Rx: An Explanation

I prescribe movies and books as much as, or more than, I ever refer to psychiatrists, and I will be doing so throughout this book. Here's why: Stories, both fictional and factual, contain an element of truth that is applicable to us all. Stories work when they are both personal and archetypal. As we watch a film, we know if it feels real, even if it is a story about a princess on another planet who is unwillingly rescued by her brother (who she doesn't know is her brother) and a couple of robots. The *Star Wars* films work not because of Princess Leia's dazzling hairdo, but because they do what all successful films do: They tell a mythic story that speaks to us on a deep level. We turn to the cinema the way ancient Greeks turned to Homer and his *Odyssey* and the adventures of the cast and crew of those wacky Greek mythologies. These characters and stories endure and have the longevity that they do because they mirror our personal experience, even if in exaggerated ways. Like mythology and literature, many of today's films give us opportunities to be mirrored and give us a sense of the universality of our experience. They also allow us the chance to experience ourselves as people who are able to overcome obstacles that we might not yet have managed to overcome in our personal life.

One reality that shows up a lot in film is the experience of dreams coming true. Moviegoers love a happy ending. You know why? Because they don't happen in real life as much as we'd like them to, and we really, really, really want to believe that a happy ending is possible. We live in the land built on dreams—the American dream. It is a land where hard work and a can-do attitude can make anything happen, right? Well, actually, hard work and a can-do attitude are often not enough. Just ask the approximately two million people whose homes were foreclosed on in 2008,[2] or the 700,000 women who lost their husbands this year,[3] or the couples in the 41 percent of first marriages that ended in divorce.[4]

If you want to find a film where the hero succeeds and gets the girl, all you have to do is go down to the local theater, and there will be at least five versions of this scenario playing at any given time. What is less likely to show up at your AMC theater is a film about a character who struggled and labored and worked his buns of steel off and still didn't get the girl. This is a motif that is more likely to show up at the art house theater with uncomfortable seats that plays foreign films, low-budget indies, and documentaries.

At dinner the other night, I was asking a friend for her favorite films about dreams that don't come true even after heroic efforts. She thought for a moment and began to list: *Rudy, The Untouchables, Norma Rae, Million Dollar Baby, The Shawshank Redemption, The Girl with the Dragon Tattoo, Rabbit-Proof Fence,* and *Whale Rider*. "No, no," I interrupted. "No. I am not asking about films where the hero triumphs; I am asking about films where the character has to *give up* their dream." My friend went silent. After a brief pause, she asked me to pass the bread, and we transitioned to another topic. Over dessert she blurted out, "*The Piano*. That's one." And then we want back to talking about her latest dating triumph.

―――――――――――――――――――――――――――――― Movie Rx

SILVER LININGS PLAYBOOK[5]

Because I am a therapist, when I tell someone I like a movie that has a therapist in it, they always say, "Of course you like that movie; there's a therapist in it." But I swear, I am not recommending *Silver Linings Playbook* because there is a therapist in it (and yes, there is a therapist in it). I am recommending this movie because it may in fact be the best movie ever made about the importance of giving up on a dream. This film is a must-see for anyone who may suspect that "never, never, never give up" just may not be working for them.

When a doctor writes a prescription, she never just gives you the medicine; she also gives you instructions on how to take it. The same is true for *Silver Linings Playbook*. Here's how to "take it": First, get yourself some "homemades" and "crabby snacks." I don't really know what these are, but they sound good, and they are things that the main character's mother is always making to comfort people. I know that this film might trigger some intense feelings about dreams and shame and failure and pain, so having some carb-laden treats might be helpful. If it were me, I might prepare one of my culinary self-care specialties, which is Velveeta Shells & Cheese (yes, I am quite the cook). I add some overcooked frozen broccoli (to make it healthy and give it some fiber) and cut-up precooked chicken (for protein, for emotional endurance). Any comfort food of any variety will do.

Once you get the food issue resolved, it is time to make sure you have a full box of Kleenex, just in case this film activates unexpected and uncontrollable secretions from your tear ducts. Now sit back and watch the show. Once you have seen the film, feel free to read the following—otherwise, *spoiler alert!*

Silver Linings Playbook begins with Pat, our hero, just getting out of a psychiatric hospital. Why was he there? His wife had an affair, he caught the couple in the shower, and he was so enraged that he nearly killed the guy. The reason that he went to a psychiatric hospital and not prison was that he was diagnosed with bipolar disorder. Now Pat is out of the hospital, and a restraining order keeps him away from his wife. But she's all he wants. His dream is to get her back. As the movie begins, he is not even in the precontemplation stage of letting go of his dream—he is in the "never, never, never give up" phase. Elisabeth Kübler-Ross, the author of the classic text on grief, *On Death and Dying*,[6] would likely classify Pat in the stage of denial, as he hasn't accepted the state of this marriage. (Kübler-Ross's stages are denial, bargaining, anger, depression, and acceptance.) Pat is also in the bargaining phase—he is trying to finagle his way back into the marriage he dreams of. Pat's plan for getting his wife back is to become the man she wanted him to be. Toward that end, he is going to do two things she always wanted him to do: read every book on her high school English class's syllabus and lose weight.

Tiffany, the other protagonist, is in the depression phase. Her husband is dead, she has lost her job and her reputation, and there is no finagling left for her to do. Tiffany managed her grief by becoming what she imagined her husband wanted her to be (a highly sexual person), and she had sex with everyone in her office in order to deal with her guilt and grief. When she meets Pat, her grief is recognized, and that triggers a desire for something new. (This new desire is a sign of her moving through the stages of grief.) She wants a dance partner. She wants to enter the dance competition with Pat, and he agrees, but only as a means of getting his wife back. Wouldn't she *love* to know he learned how to dance?

Both characters are facing a reality that life didn't turn out the way they planned. They also have in common a kind of emotional honesty that they don't see reflected in their worlds—they feel less alone in their experience as soon as they meet each other because no one else has been willing to talk about their pain. Their friends and family are afraid to speak about the death of their dreams, but by seeing each other honestly, they are able to start moving through their stages of grief.

What Pat and Tiffany eventually do is give up and move on. It's an act of bravery and courage, not an act of failure and defeat.

SELF-HELP SUGGESTIONS

☐ When you hear the advice "never give up," what's your reaction? Does it make you want to throw a cup of coffee at an Apprentice's head? Be honest with yourself, because I'm not going to judge you.

☐ What have you tried? You might want to write out a list of all the things you have done in order to make your dream work. Take a look at that list and be proud of your tenacity. Looking at all of the actions I took in order to conceive makes me feel really good about myself. I see myself as incredibly tenacious. I almost feel like that list of actions should be on my curriculum vitae, as it says more about my determination and stick-to-itiveness than anything else on my résumé. As you look at your list and see *all* that you did to make your dream work, what qualities do you see in yourself that you might not have realized you have? Did you know you were tenacious, long-suffering? Was that part of your self-concept before?

☐ Are you like Pat in the *Silver Linings Playbook* and think that maybe there is more you need to do? Maybe if . . . ? Well, what are the maybes? I have zero regret about all the trying I did. Yeah, sure, I wish I had the $100,000-plus I spent trying to have a baby, but I think I would have been filled with regret if I didn't feel like I gave it my all. But your mileage may vary. What your *all* is will be different than my *all*. Don't let anybody tell you otherwise. Your limit is your limit, and only you can know what that is. I am a believer in trying everything that you think might make your dream come true until you just can't try anymore. Now, if you think there is anything left that you could still do to make that dream happen, write out a list of what this might be. Not every kind of dream has that; for example, Tiffany in *Silver Linings Playbook* couldn't bring her husband back. But if you believe that there is something you can still do to make your dream come true, and you feel inclined to do it, then go ahead. It's okay if there are twenty things or zero things (yes, it's even okay if you realize there really is nothing left to do). This gives you more information about where you are.

☐ What does the committee in your head say about you letting go of the dream? The voice of your mother, father, brother, Aunt Joan, Uncle Fred, your favorite teacher, your best friend, your inner critic, and your inner Glinda the Good Witch—they all are in there, and they all are impacting your ability to let go of your dream. You might want to make a list of all the people whose opinions matter to you, then ask yourself what they might say when they hear that you are letting go of your dream. Is it someone else that you are really pursuing this for? Is it their opinion and imagined disappointment or criticism that is haunting you?

☐ How do you feel about other people's ideas for what else you can do? Notice how you react to people's suggestions. Trust me, they'll have them. It's not a bad thing: After all, they are on your side, and they want you to have what you want. It's simply a good thing to notice. See if you are open to suggestions or if you aren't.

☐ Plan comments to have at the ready should people start in with the "never give up" advice. When I first came to the end of my baby dream, I felt sad, bad, and angry when people suggested I shouldn't give up. My impulse sometimes was to tell the person who insisted I hadn't done enough and that I needed to get embryo donors or a surrogate that they go and *&%# themselves, but I didn't. I'd smile at their Pollyanna perspective. When they went on to ask me if I had sacrificed a goat on a full moon, I would stop and for just a moment think *maybe I should,* but then I would remember my truth. My truth was that I knew I couldn't try anymore. And I would say, "I get how much you want this for me, but I did *everything* I could do, and I can't try anymore." So, let's come up with some things you can say when people start in with their suggestions. How about "I appreciate your suggestions, but I have hit my limit with trying, and I need you to support that." Or "I'm not giving up; I'm moving on." Or "You can't create the future by clinging to the past." Come up with five of your own and have them ready. You will need them when that well-meaning friend begins to tell you that you can't give up. You might be gobsmacked by their insensitivity, but you will have your answers all ready to turn to. And if the well-meaning person keeps with the suggestions, I would suggest changing the subject. "This is a hard topic for me, and I'd rather talk about something more cheerful, maybe global warming or the strength of the euro."

How do you know when it's time to stop trying? This one is tough, but I would say there are some clues: In *Silver Linings Playbook,* it was being *seen* that helped Pat and Tiffany move through the stages of grief. Who sees your grief? Who can say it like it is? Who dares to tell you that they see your suffering? Who can *really* listen to your pain and not be afraid of it? If your answer is "No one," it is time to seek out a therapist or a support group who can accept you for who you are. Therapy was *vital* for me. I needed someplace to come every week where I didn't have to worry that I was being too intense or overwhelming. I didn't need to assure my therapist that I was okay. She could take all of my grief, even if it was mean and angry and ugly. And, actually, really feeling those mean, angry, and ugly feelings helped me to move fully into other feelings—surprising feelings like joy, happiness, and laughter.

chapter 2

Why Did the Chicken
Push the Rock up the Hill?

A Cautionary Tale of What Can Happen If You Don't Give Up

*"We would rather be ruined than changed.
We would rather die in our dread
Than climb the cross of the present
And let our illusions die."*

>> **W. H. Auden,** *The Age of Anxiety*

If you have, like me, spent a little too much time in the self-help section of the bookstore, and/or misspent some of the glowing days of your youth listening to infomercial gurus promising you that you can have it all in thirty days if you only purchase their transformational program for three easy, low payments of $49.95, then you have likely heard two bits of contrary advice that are at the heart of many self-help pitches—and at the heart of many of the problems people encounter when they refuse to give up on a dream.

Bit One is a quote that has been misattributed to Albert Einstein, Benjamin Franklin, Mark Twain, and Tony Robbins, and still no one knows exactly who uttered it first: "The definition of insanity is doing the same thing over and over and expecting different results." While that is not actually the definition of *insanity,* I know what they are getting at, and I am betting you do, too. It has become a cultural platitude that we accept as true the minute we hear it. "Oh, yeah, I keep dating the same kind of guys and it never works out," we say, or "I continue to make the same self-destructive choices over and over, and it takes me further away from where I want to be." Clearly, it's foolish/foolhardy/not entirely wise of us to do the same thing over and over and expect different results. True enough. I am good with this. I take no issue with this.

However, often in the same self-help speech, same infomercial, same book (and sometimes even in the same *chapter*), we are given Bit Two, which is a story like the famous one about Colonel Sanders (you know, the guy responsible for bringing you the delicious yet nutritionally questionable KFC Original Recipe fried chicken), and which flies in the face of the advice given in Bit One. When the self-helpers drag out a story like the Colonel's, it is always to teach us the importance of tenacity and inspire us to never, never, never give up. The Colonel was sixty-five years old, retired, and broke, with a small house, a beat-up car, a coronary-clogging yet highly delicious recipe for fried chicken, and of course—*of course*—a dream. As the story goes, the Colonel went to more than a thousand restaurants and offered them his secret recipe for only a small commission on every order of chicken. The Colonel was told "no" more than a thousand times, yet he undauntedly persevered and ultimately succeeded beyond his wildest expectations. We are supposed to be impressed by his perseverance. Yet his perseverance is a direct contradiction of the "definition of insanity" deal.

Okay, so which is it? Is it Bit One, "The definition of insanity is doing the same thing over and over and expecting different results"? Or is it Bit Two, "Never, never, never give up"? How can it be both? Yes, I see the point of tenacity; however, we don't often see the *costs* of tenacity. We don't hear about the price the Colonel paid in never giving up. And there is always a price. Maybe the price wasn't high for the Colonel. Maybe he didn't ruin his marriage, mortgage his health, lose his friendships, and sell out a chicken farm that had been in his family for three generations. I certainly hope not. He seems like a lovely man (I base that entirely on his kindly countenance as depicted on the side of the family-size bucket). Whatever the truth, we may never be privy to it because of the "all's well that ends well" attitude that defines his story. We *love* these kinds of stories because they give us hope, but they also require us to ignore the consequences of "never give up." For many people, there are real hurts and consequences that come from doing something over and over that isn't working for them, and it is useful to examine these costs.

Lessons from the Tabloids

Every age has its never-never-give-up celebrities who show us by example the high cost of refusing to stop. Elizabeth Taylor never gave up on marriage, despite seven divorces. President Nixon was so committed to his dream of a second term that he broke the law and ultimately lost the presidency he wanted so much. Countless success stories ended in something entirely different than success. Franz Kafka, Virginia Woolf, Christina Stead, Emily Dickinson, Marie Curie, Bobby Fischer, Jane Austen, Elvis Presley, Tennessee Williams, William Faulkner, Eugene O'Neill, Marilyn Monroe, Frank Sinatra, Ava Gardner, Orson Welles, John Ford, Judy Garland, Joan of Arc, Sylvia Plath, Muhammad Ali, Michael Jackson. All of these people paid a heavy price for their dreams.

The poster boy for our time in the never-never-give-up mythology and its ugly consequences is Lance Armstrong, the seven-time consecutive winner of the Tour de France. Lance offers the perfect cautionary tale for the self-destruction that can happen when we don't face reality. Lance liked to say, "Pain is temporary. Quitting lasts forever." Lance's body aged like everyone else's body does, and he suffered setbacks, injuries, and illness like all other humans, only he didn't have the courage to face the reality (like you are doing, courageous you), and he didn't grieve the reality that his body would no longer allow him to compete at the same level he had previously enjoyed. Instead, Lance ignored this reality and lied, cheated, and injected his body with dangerous and illegal drugs. Yes, he was able to compete, but when his transgressions were discovered, he was publicly disgraced and stripped of his seven titles, banned for life from the sport he loved, and sued by the Department of Justice and the U.S. Postal Service. Had he bowed out gracefully after his initial extraordinary success (one victory in the legendary race? Two? Three?), Lance Armstrong would have lived his life as a revered sports legend. You can imagine him lighting the Olympic torch, riding on a float in the Rose Parade. Was his relentless pursuit of the dream worth the fall from grace? I think not.

And yours may not be, either.

APER 2

The Statistics of Dreams

Let's look at the cold, hard reality of the statistics behind the most common dreams. You might want to eat some Original Recipe fried chicken before you read on, as these are tough statistics to take on an empty stomach.

The dream of a long-term marriage? As noted earlier, according to the U.S. Census Bureau, 41 percent of first marriages end in divorce. Sixty percent of second marriages and 73 percent of third marriages also end in divorce. Every thirteen seconds, a marriage ends and a dream dies. The average age of those going through a first divorce is thirty.[1]

The dream of parenting? The Centers for Disease Control and Prevention report that there are 6.7 million people with impaired fecundity. There are 1.5 million women who are infertile. One out of every five couples is involuntarily childless.[2]

Career dreams? In 2010, the Center for College Affordability and Productivity conducted a study that concluded that almost 50 percent of American college graduates were underemployed, meaning that they were working at jobs that were low paying and low skilled.[3] Richard Vedder, Jonathan Robe, and Christopher Denhart wrote a report on the aforementioned study entitled "Why Are Recent College Graduates Underemployed?"[4] In this study, they concluded that the rate of college graduates to the rate of jobs that require a college degree is disproportionate; hence, there are many bartenders with BAs. According to Deloitte's Shift Index survey, 80 percent of people are dissatisfied with the jobs they have.[5]

The dream of being the next Brad Pitt or Angelina? The Screen Actors Guild–American Federation of Television and Radio Artists (SAG-AFTRA) has 160,000 actors as members. According to the Screen Actors Guild, the unemployment rate for its members is about 85 percent.[6]

Want to be a dancer? Only .001 percent of graduates from dance programs end up becoming professional dancers.[7]

Athletic dreams? Heather Robinson of Howard University wrote in 2009, "Of the 18.4 million students that attended college last year, 400,000 were student-athletes, and only one out of every 25 went on to compete professionally."[8] In her article, she quotes a 2008 study done by Peter-Danton de Rouffignac, a sports counselor, in which he concluded that "less than .00007

20

percent (roughly 50 individuals) successfully made it to the NBA." The study also found that one out of every 460,000 in black communities went on to compete in the NFL, NBA, or MLS. However, 43 percent of young black athletes believed they would turn pro.

The dream of being a business owner? Fifty percent of businesses fail in their first year; 56 percent fail in the next five years.[9]

The dream of homeownership? In 2011, 2,698,967 homeowners lost their dream home to foreclosure.[10]

Okay, I know that was tough to read. Trust me, it was tough to write. I feel like I just killed the Tooth Fairy, the Easter Bunny, and Santa Claus in one fell swoop. I am not trying to be a pessimist. I am trying to be a realist. I don't want to kill your dreams. I just don't want your dreams to kill you. I don't want you to hear the Colonel Sanders story and say, "Well, if Colonel Sanders can do it, I can do it, and so I'd better keep on trying and trying and trying regardless of the costs."

There are people who would tell you that because Colonel Sanders made it, you shouldn't give up, and I want to tell those people that just because one person won the lottery, it doesn't mean you should plan your financial future on the Powerball.

I want you to see that if you didn't become Brad Pitt or Michael Jordan or succeed in your marriage or have a baby, it isn't because you didn't want it enough. You did. Don't let the Colonel Sanders myth keep you on a treacherous and destructive path. If there are a million kids who *really, really, really* want to be professional basketball players and only two hundred jobs in the world, should the 999,800 other kids just keep trying endlessly? No, they should not. They should come to a point where it makes sense to stop, mourn their dream, and figure out something else that can give them the essence of what they want.

The Consequences of Not Giving Up

It's your decision how long you hang on to your dream, but the consequences can negatively impact nearly every aspect of your life—physical, psychological, financial, relational—and they can even threaten your integrity and spiritual well-being.

Physical Costs

If your dream involves the physical body—athletics, modeling, dancing—the physical costs of pushing too hard for what you want are direct and obvious. As Diego explains:

> I was training in tae kwon do six days a week, sometimes twice a day. In the couple of years I was living with this intense workout regimen, I suffered various physical injuries: a couple [of] concussions, a strained back, soft tissue damage on the top of one foot, and various other strains, bumps, and bruises. The style I trained in is not meant to be so taxing on the body, but I pushed the limits. I trained more than anyone else I knew, so that upped the chances of getting hurt. . . . So accidents would happen.

Diego eventually had to stop altogether, and was bereft.

The surprising news about the physical costs of unattainable dreams is that they are not just paid by athletes such as Diego, Lance Armstrong, and Muhammad Ali. Holding on too tightly to your dreams can cause significant consequences to your physical health. According to a study by Gregory Miller and Carsten Wrosch,[11] not quitting could make you seriously sick! How, you ask? Well, Miller and Wrosch claim that chronic states of frustration, ambivalence, and exhaustion impact our autonomic nervous system and ultimately our health. People who don't let go of unachievable dreams have higher levels of inflammation, which, if they persist, could cause real physical illnesses such as diabetes, osteoporosis, and atherosclerosis.

Their study suggested that those who don't disengage from unachievable goals likely suffer sleep disturbances, which increases your risk for all the aforementioned health concerns. In other words, if your dreams aren't coming true, then you likely aren't dreaming at night, and if you aren't dreaming at night, you are likely putting your physical health at risk. Almost everyone who I interviewed for this book named sleeplessness as a cost of not getting their dream, and sleeplessness is not just annoying—it is harmful to your health. Sleeplessness causes accidents and injuries. It impacts memory, judgment, and cognitive functioning. It can affect our capacity to learn, and it can aggravate depression. Chronic sleeplessness puts you at risk for heart disease, stroke, high blood pressure, and diabetes. Not getting enough sleep can also kill your libido and cause weight gain.[12]

"I used to wake up feeling like I was running in a marathon, my heart was beating so fast," says Betty, a woman who dreamed of owning a hotel and casino in Atlantic City. "I turned to antianxiety medicine." Others turn to sleep medication to deal with the lack of sleep.

It was my bias prior to doing the research that those who were perseverant, tenacious, and relentless would likely have better health than those who weren't. I imagined that tenacity and resilience had biosocial and evolutionary payoffs that our body might like. Once I digested the research, I changed my mind. I could now see why letting go of your dream might actually be better for your health than holding on to a dream beyond all reason. Miller and Wrosch explain: "When people are faced with situations in which they cannot realize a key life goal, the most adaptive response for mental and physical health may be to disengage from that goal."[13] Those who do disengage from unattainable goals have more normal levels of cortisol secretion and fewer physical symptoms than those who don't disengage. This is all to say that giving up on your unattainable dream can be good for your health.

Psychological Costs

As mentioned in the section on physical costs, those who haven't disengaged from a dream that isn't working tend to have feelings of frustration, ambivalence, and exhaustion. When I was pursuing my dream and not getting it, I suffered significant clinical depression. Hopelessness, helplessness, anxiety, and an overriding sense of being unable to make something happen made me lose my sense of efficacy. I lost interest in other things. I isolated, which exacerbated my depression and made me feel like the only thing that could make me happy was the dream coming true.

Another psychological issue is the cost to self-concept. The more we pursue something that doesn't work, the more we take on the identity of a failure. Our self-concept changes. We see ourselves differently; we may edit out any achievement, accomplishment, or success from the past and define ourselves solely by the failure to achieve this dream. At the height of my grief, when I lamented that "nothing works out for me" and "I don't get what I want,"

I objectified myself in this one aspect of my life and ignored many areas of my life where things worked out even better than I imagined.

"There was a great cost to my mental health," Diego says of his pursuit of tae kwon do perfection. "It is only in the last year, after a decade of doctors, therapy, and grief, that I feel I am really beginning to put the pieces of myself back together. My sense of self was lost. Before the injury, I only defined myself as a martial artist. Having that stripped from me was crushing."

Cassandra, who fantasized about one perfect house and spent years trying to get it, says something almost identical: "My sense of self was all wrapped up in whether my offer for the house would be accepted. I felt a real decline in my self-esteem every time I felt that I was losing the dream. I felt that I would have a new identity if I were to move into the new neighborhood. I felt unsuccessful because I did not have more money saved up to buy and fix up the 'dream house.'"

Financial Costs

As I mentioned earlier, I personally spent more than $100,000 on a dream that led to nowhere. I have no baby, but I have a huge box filled with receipts. I stopped when there was no more money to spend on trying to conceive, but there are people who don't quit there. I know people who took out loans and second mortgages in order to do another round of in vitro fertilization, and they *still* didn't get pregnant. Now every month they are paying a debt for something that didn't happen. And there are certainly dreams with even higher price tags, such as losing your home to foreclosure or spending ten years and many hundreds of thousands of dollars on an advanced degree that you will never use (or never complete).

The truth about money is that the more we invest (be it energetically or financially), the harder it can be to let the dream go. *But I have come this far,* we say. *I have spent this much. I can't give up now. I am too far in. I'm in too deep.*

Let the gal who has trouble balancing her checkbook give you some financial advice: Putting out money you don't have for a dream that isn't happening is simply a bad investment. There is an economic concept called "sunk costs" that explains why we keep throwing good money after bad. A sunk cost is a cost that has already been invested and that you can't get your money back from. According to economists, we shouldn't make economic decisions based on sunk costs. If you were to tell Ben Bernanke, "Hey, Ben, so I have already spent $75,000 on something that has showed no return on its investment, and I am thinking I shouldn't pull out of the investment and that I should keep putting more money into it," it is likely that Ben would pull out the little hair he has left on his head and advise you not to let the sunk costs keep you in a bad investment. He would say that it is simply madness to make financial decisions based on what you have already spent.

Even though Bernanke and other economists would advise you against having sunk costs influence your decision, they would likely understand that it is human nature not to want to walk away from our investment. We are by nature risk averse (well, most of us are), and yet we manage not to see the long-term risk of letting sunk costs determine our continued investment in a dream that is high on cost and low on reward. The bottom line is that draining your savings, spending your inheritance, and mortgaging out your future does not make good economic sense.

Relational Costs

When we are putting all of our eggs into one basket, whether that basket be a career, a marriage, a desire to have children, or to beat a world record, the truth is that we only have so much energy to spend, and if the bulk of our energy has gone toward that dream, then there are likely relational costs. Are your only relationships the ones that are about pursuing this dream? If so, that makes it even harder to give up on the dream—and if your dream was actually about a marriage or a relationship, it can be harder still. You may have withdrawn from other relationships; you may be ashamed of not achieving what you set out to do; you may feel very alone.

This happened to Cassandra over her dream house. "Since I needed to constantly talk about the possibility of getting my dream," she says, "loved ones lost their patience with me. I could not really feel connected to my husband unless we were speaking optimistically about getting the house. I also felt a sense of shame that kept me from seeking out new relationships as well as participating in current friendships. I felt alone; I wished that somehow I would have a benefactor who would rescue me."

Being forced to stop tae kwon do left Diego very alone. "Without my sport, I was pretty lost and brokenhearted," he says. "I had a string of destructive relationships. I'm not sure I was capable of having any other kind."

Betty, who dreamed of owning an Atlantic City resort, puts it simply and clearly: "Some of my friends became frustrated with my 'stuckness,' and they walked away from me."

Look around at the people who love and support you. Are they starting to get weary of your dream? Are they begging you to stop? These may be signs that the relational cost of your dream has gotten too steep.

Integrity Costs

Sometimes, people want a dream so badly that they are tempted to do things that compromise their integrity. Remember Lance Armstrong and Richard Nixon. If you feel yourself on this slippery slope—lying, cheating, stealing—then your dream is costing you way too much. No dream is worth betraying your core values. Even if you get the dream, you will be stuck with the costs to your sense of self. This is a cost that is never worth paying. Get help now.

Spiritual Costs

Not getting what you wanted most and what you hoped and prayed for can lead to a crisis of faith; it did for me. Losing hope can change your worldview or understanding of how the world works. I went from having a belief system in which I was sure that "everything works out for the best" to believing in chaos. I am happy to report that with some time and work, I have managed to get back to believing that ultimately everything works out for the best—even if it wasn't what I wanted or expected at the time.

The Inside Story

BIG GAMBLE, BIG LOSS

Betty, a woman in her mid-fifties, and her husband of twenty-five years had a shared dream—a *big* dream. Betty's eyes get brighter than a Vegas billboard when she talks about all the plans they had to create a theme hotel in Atlantic City. They had it all mapped out—the shows, the restaurants, and the merchandise they'd sell in the gift shop. She shows me with a great deal of pride the prospectus and all the plans and renderings they had for their dream. She recounts a list of investor names that sounds like the *Who's Who* list of people you'd most like funding your dream. She speaks these big names to explain the viability and value of their big dream. These big names promised to back their venture. The couple dedicated themselves single-mindedly to their dream for ten years. Betty laughs easily as she speaks of it: "We gambled big on Atlantic City, and we lost everything. We lost it all. It ruined us financially." Her voice is light, but the reality is very dark: The couple lost their home and their savings and all that she had inherited from her family. They lost friendships, a strong family bond, and even a sense of self-worth.

When I ask Betty why she wanted this dream so much, her sparkling eyes dim. "I wanted to give my family security. I wanted to give my girls security." The irony isn't lost on Betty: The thing she wanted to give them the most was lost by pursuing the dream.

As Betty talks on about why she wanted the hotel so much, she discovers that this dream is connected to a frustrated desire from her past: "I wanted to be a singer, but my father dissuaded me by telling me how few singers make it. Him telling me about those odds crushed my dreams." So in a way, by attempting to do this *big* thing, she was showing her father that she could beat the odds and do something important.

Another unexpected aha moment comes for Betty as we talk further. "As a teen, I wanted to shop at the high-end store Contempo, but my dad was very conservative (even though there was money), so we shopped at the discount store Zody's." Doing something splashy and showy would have been vindication for this slight. Furthermore, Betty explains, "I was shy in high school. I wasn't part of the cool group of kids. I felt like I was on the outside. And maybe part of the desire to have the hotel was that I would be where the party was. I would be the 'cool' kid in the middle of the action." Betty seems saddened by her insight.

In order to keep pursuing the dream, Betty utilized a whole host of psychological coping mechanisms. "I was in denial. I ignored signs. I ignored dreams at night that told me that this wasn't going to work. . . . The economy was failing; I ignored that."

Beyond losing their savings and home, there were myriad other costs. Her biggest regrets are about how the pursuit of the dream impacted her children. "I regret all the time that I didn't spend with them. I feel like I failed them. We should have put $100,000 away for their education," she says. There were also significant consequences in her marriage. As Betty begins to speak of this, tears overtake her. She still cannot voice this loss, but she goes on to talk about how relationships with friends grew distant. She felt like she couldn't be entirely honest about what was going on, and so she withdrew from friendships. She also admits that for many years, "We were the ones who paid when we went out to dinner, and when we couldn't do that anymore, the friendships changed."

Betty reports significant psychological costs: anxiety, depression, loss of self-confidence, anger, and lots of self-blame. Her self-concept changed: "I no longer know that I am a person who can get stuff done."

She worries that, due to the amount of stress she was under, there might be physical consequences. "I had insomnia, so I had to go on Ambien. I gained a lot of weight. My teeth are bad." At the time of the interview, Betty's physician informed her that her uterus was enlarged. Betty fears that it may be fibroids or cancer.

Since losing their home and letting go of their dream, Betty and her husband have been struggling to find jobs, and they have had to stay with friends and family. All of their things are in storage. Betty has been forced to pawn off her jewelry to pay for food and gas. She worries that she might not get a job and be able to get her jewelry out of hock. "I don't want to lose [that], too."

The Therapy Couch

THE MYTHS WE LIVE BY

In this section, we will look at some of the underlying psychological motivations that lead us to do the same thing over and over even as we don't get a different result. And I am going to start by talking about a myth, and no, not the kinds of myths that you read about in *Prevention* magazine— "Ten Myths About Fat Burning" or "Ten Myths About Green Veggies." I am talking about the kind of myths that Joseph Campbell, the acclaimed mythologist, talks about—you know, like the Greek myths you studied in freshman English. According to C. G. Jung, the Swiss psychologist, myth is collective psychological phenomena that are projected out into stories: our inner world made visible in stories, literature, and even mythic movie motifs (like *Star Wars*—or maybe more like the *Diagnostic and Statistical Manual of Mental Disorders* [*DSM-5*] told in story version).[14] As Joseph Campbell says, "Myths are public dreams; dreams are private myths."[15] The enduring stories of our time tell us about who we are as people. And the story I am about to tell you, I believe, tells us a lot about those of us who have a hard time giving up on our personal dreams.

Remember old King Sisyphus from your twelfth grade English class? He was a king who lied and defied and otherwise aggravated Zeus, the grand pooh-bah of the Greek mythic pantheon who was infamously ill humored about mortals who tried to mess with him—which never worked out well for anyone (ask Prometheus). When punished, Sisyphus was taken to the underworld to be killed by Death (a.k.a. Thanatos). Instead, wily Sisyphus captured Death and locked him up in chains so that he could never kill another human being again. The gods really didn't appreciate this, as they wanted to continue to corner the market on immortality, so when Thanatos got free and it was Sisyphus's turn to die, he did all he could to escape Death. This only further infuriated the gods, so they decided to create a special punishment for him that would last for all of eternity. Sisyphus's eternal task was to push a rock up a mountain. Once the rock would reach the top, it would roll down again, never to get to where he was trying to get it—never, ever, ever to be done.

I am sure you are thinking, *Well that is all terribly sad for Sisyphus, but what on earth does that have to do with me and my life?* Whatever you keep trying relentlessly to achieve, I believe, has Sisyphus's name all over it. And I believe that this just may be the dominant myth of our time. It's the myth that makes the somewhat counterintuitive point that it's not so much whether you win or lose as long as you keep trying—relentlessly. It's a myth that tells us we can't ever stop and smell the roses, that we have to keep single-mindedly pushing that rock up the hill, or taking the chicken recipe to the restaurants, or working on that marriage, or striving toward that big career achievement. It's the myth that we can't be happy or have a meaningful life where we are now and that we have to keep striving and becoming. All of this, I believe, is a metaphorical way to escape death, as it was metaphorically for Sisyphus.

I think our culture cares more about never quitting than it does about actually achieving. Our age idealizes someone on the hot pursuit of success (rock pushing) more than it does achieving (getting the rock to the top of the hill). As soon as someone manages to get on top of the mountain, no matter the cost, the media looks for clues of why they don't really deserve to be on the mountaintop and what they are doing that is evident of their unworthiness.

However, I am sure that if Sisyphus were able to stop his rock rolling for a minute, he would be happy to tell you that he would love to give up his life of rock and roll for an ordinary life free from the search for fame and fortune and immortality. He would, I am sure, tell you there is nothing heroic in living a life that is all about effort and potential and endless, fruitless trying.

How Death Anxiety Might Be Fueling Our Dreams

I am sure that as surprised as you are to learn how much you may have in common with a Greek myth, you might be even more surprised to learn that fear of death could in some way relate to the goal you have been pursuing with such determination and singular focus. Sometimes when we ignore the realities that are smacking us upside of the dream (or head; your location may vary), it can be because of the psychological need to see ourselves as a hero. To illustrate these points theoretically, let's look at the work of Ernest Becker, the author of the classic psychological text *The Denial of Death*,[16] and see how it may explain how death anxiety can impact our desire to never, never, never give up.

Becker's work is largely concerned with the dual nature of human life: We have physical bodies that are destined to die, but we have minds that are capable of imagining immortality. We love to do things that make us feel as though we are immortal—e.g., having children, writing books, or undertaking any kind of "immortality project" that we hope will go on long past our own brief lives. Becker contends that we don't do these things just *because,* or just for *fun,* or even because we're egotistical dolts. We do them as a way to deny death, as a way to make it possible to live with the stark reality that we are, in fact, going to die. We do them, in other words, as a hedge against the truth, as a way to feel that our lives will end up having some meaning and immortality.

You can see where this is going: Wanting to be a hero is, in effect, wanting not to die. Never, never, never giving up is a cry for immortality, a hedge against death. So no wonder it's so difficult to walk away.

On a psychological level, we are, perhaps, like Sisyphus: Through pursuing our dream, we are trying to prevent death (literal or metaphoric). Yes, I know that you know that you literally can't triumph over death, but there is something about the "I can do anything if I try hard enough" mythology that gives us some illusion of control in our lives. If we can make our dream a reality and control our fate, then maybe we can even beat death. Obviously we really can't, and no matter if we achieve all of our goals, we are still going to die. And by becoming an actor, becoming an astronaut, writing a screenplay, becoming the next Oprah, or, in my case, even becoming a mother, we feel that we are creating a *causa sui* (immortality project) and conquering death (like Sisyphus tried and failed to do again and again).

Movie Rx

You know how some prescription bottles have warning labels on them? Movies, too. Imagine that *The Wrestler* is covered with bright, colored warning labels that should not be ignored. This movie is tough to take, and you might want to have smelling salts standing by in case it takes you down for the count. I prescribe it if you are having trouble facing the truth about the consequences of your dreams, but the warnings are in bold type: May cause nausea, the physical and/or the existential variety. May make you shriek in shock and horror. May make you wonder why you are watching it, even though the message is an important one for those who need to be reminded of the consequences of not giving up on a dream that is not working out. All of these side effects may be heightened by an extreme sensitivity to blood, violence, and masochism. That said, this may be one of the best movies to demonstrate the consequences of not ever giving up on a dream, and that is why I am recommending it—but don't say I didn't warn you.

The Wrestler is about Randy "The Ram" Robinson, who had known success in the 1980s as a professional wrestler.[17] He had it all—video games, action figures, big-time pay-per-view events, legions of fans—and then he lost it. Randy lost not only fame, but also his health and his youth. In the movie, he's broke, he's injured, he's been kicked out of his trailer, he works part time in a grocery store so he can do weekend wrestling events. He uses hundreds of dollars' worth of drugs in order to continue pursuing his dream. He has few friends and no family—only an estranged daughter, some wrestling buddies who are not real friends, and an exotic dancer whom he confides in. He is so lonely that he plays Nintendo with kids in the trailer park, and even they don't want to play with him.

There is a particularly brutal wrestling match in which Randy allows himself to be attacked with a staple gun. (I could only half-watch this scene. Remember the aforementioned warning about this movie causing nausea? All the saltines and ginger ale in the world would not have settled my stomach to take this masochistic moment.) After this match, Randy has a heart attack followed by bypass surgery. He is given strict instructions by his doctor not to continue wrestling. When hearing that his dream cannot be a reality, Randy, like all of us, experiences some denial. He asks the doctor if he can just go easy on his training. The doctor makes it clear that if Randy trains the way he has and wrestles again, his heart can't take it. "You almost died—maybe next time you won't be so lucky," he says. Randy ignores the doctor, goes for a run, and collapses. Slowly, Randy comes to accept the reality of the situation and relents. "I'm retiring. I'm done. I'm retired." He cancels his matches and reluctantly gives up the dream.

This, for me, is the most important part of the movie. When Randy gives up on his dream of getting back into the big time, he gets a full-time job in the grocery store's deli section. Of course, this isn't his dream—this feels like failure, humiliation, and a *huge* step down to him. Randy has to put his long Samson-like locks into a hairnet in order to work behind the deli counter and suffer the further humiliation of wearing a name badge with his birth name—Robin—instead of his wrestling name. But I see in this scene a possibility of some real happiness for Randy. He kibitzes and wisecracks with the customers as he gets them chicken breasts, smoked ham, and egg salad. He is connecting with people. He laughs and enjoys making the customers laugh. In hitting bottom and letting go of the dream, something new starts to emerge: real connection with people. At this time, he reaches out to his daughter, and he also has some hope about entering into a romantic relationship. There is a glimpse of the joy he could have if he made those choices. But when he struggles to make life outside of the ring work (he lacks life skills because *all* of his energy has gone into succeeding in the ring), he goes back to the area he knows how to feel good in: wrestling. He willfully ignores himself and the realities of his situation, and he participates in a match. He gets sucked back into the dream and pays the price. We don't know for sure if he paid the ultimate price, but we certainly can imagine another ending in which he lets go of the dream and accepts the reality and is able to find meaning and satisfaction in other ways.

Randy sacrificed so much for his dream that he didn't know how to live without it. He didn't invest energy into work, a romantic relationship, friendships, or anything besides wrestling. In the end, that is what did him in.

SELF-HELP SUGGESTIONS

☐ How are you holding in your mind the paradoxical thoughts of the Colonel Sanders story and the "definition of insanity"? Do you have your own version of the Colonel Sanders story that you tell yourself? Do you keep following it even though it is destructive? How do you keep yourself going even though the dream is not manifesting? How many times is enough to prove that you really gave it your best?

☐ You just don't have the energy to keep trying, but you also don't know how you can stop. Continuing to try is costing you too much. Your relationships are hurting. You can't financially afford to keep trying. Trying is hurting you psychologically. The continued efforts are causing anxiety and depression or other symptoms. You no longer have any identity other than "I can't have my dream." If any of this describes you, is the cost worth it?

☐ How many times do you need to try before the decision to keep trying starts to feel like insanity? How much more effort would it take for you to define your efforts as "insane"? How does this feel like insanity to you?

☐ What are the statistics on your dream? Do you know them, or do you ignore them? I know that when I was going through infertility treatment, I purposefully ignored the statistics. I didn't want to hear them. I was inflated enough (or deluded enough) to think that the statistics didn't apply to me. I am, to be honest with you, ashamed to admit that. Have you ignored the statistics? If I asked you to find out the cold, hard facts of your dreams, would you find that you don't want to know? Face the statistics. You, dear one, are not a failure. Yes, Colonel Sanders made it, but do you know how many restaurants go out of business each year? Statistics help you see the reality and help you stop driving yourself crazy with Colonel Sanders stories.

☐ What toll is this pursuit having on your relationships? Take a real look at this: Have relationships with friends and family suffered because of this pursuit? Do you spend less time with friends and family because you have spent all your time pursuing your dream? Are you isolated? Lonely? Are there relationships that you would like to put more time and energy into that you haven't in the name of your dream? Can you see that letting go of your dream might actually give you more of what you really want? Let me remind you of Randy, the wrestler. It looked like his dream was to be a famous wrestler, but the truth is that what Randy really wanted was to be loved. He sought love and approval from his fans. However, he had real love from his daughter and his almost-girlfriend, but he pushed away those who *really* loved him in an effort to get lots of "feels like love" from people who didn't really know him.

If we asked your friends and family this question, would they have a different answer? What price would they say that they have paid for your dream?

☐ What have the costs been to your body? Are you aware of how the tenacious pursuit of your dream has impacted your physical health? Do you have stress-related illnesses? Have you sacrificed taking good care of your body (diet/rest/exercise/trips to the doctor)? Have you postponed taking care of yourself? Do you tell yourself, "When I achieve my dream, I will then take care of me"?

☐ What is the bottom-line financial cost of this dream? How much money have you actually spent? What expenses do you incur that you might not be aware of? (Randy in *The Wrestler* not only didn't have a job that paid well, but he also spent money on hair color, tanning cream, and gym membership.) Have you said no to other opportunities for income because you are waiting for the big thing to happen? Where would your finances be if you let go of the dream? How much more money would you have for other things if you let go of this dream? The irony for Cassandra and her dream house was that she wanted the house to give her a feeling of connection with family. But in order to have it, she would have to give up time with her family. Quite a catch-22. Are there further costs you would have to pay if you achieved the dream that you haven't thought through? Did you minimize the future costs of the dream?

☐ What are the costs to your mental health? Are you suffering depression? Anxiety? A sense of hopelessness? Despair? Is your sense of self-worth entirely, or mostly, determined by this dream? Do you no longer see yourself as you really are? Has your dream impacted your ability to see your successes, accomplishments, talents, and abilities? Has the pursuit of this dream ravaged your self-esteem?

☐ Has there been a cost to your faith? Your religion? Has the pursuit of your dream changed the way you see the world? Did you go from an "everything happens for a reason" person into a pessimistic nihilist whose favorite expression is "shit happens" and who can no longer see the good? If so, that is a significant cost. It can certainly be difficult to feel like your deepest and dearest prayer went unanswered, and the impact on one's faith can be significant. What has it cost you, faith-wise?

☐ Have there been any integrity costs for your dream? Have you done things to make this dream a reality that you don't feel entirely good about? If the dream is requiring you to betray your values and morals, it needs to be seriously reevaluated.

☐ Has the pursuit impacted your ability to see the good in your life? Is it obfuscating your vision? I know that when I was trying, and failing, to conceive, it clouded my thinking on everything.

☐ What happens if you give this dream one more year? What about five more years? Ten more? What if you never give up? Then how will the costs be different? How will the prices you pay for the dream rise?

☐ If you keep taking action on your dreams, or don't let go, what serious consequences might you face? Maybe the consequences aren't as dire as Lance Armstrong's or Randy the wrestler's, but there are likely consequences. This is the time to be honest with yourself.

☐ How might you benefit by giving up on the dream? What good can come of it? Depending on where you are on the journey, this question can be really difficult to answer honestly. We can see so clearly how Lance Armstrong, Richard Nixon, or Randy would have benefited if they gave up, but what about us?

☐ If this were a movie, what would the audience be saying? Would they scream "Stop!" at the television (like I did when watching *The Wrestler*)? What would the audience see in your story that you aren't seeing?

☐ As with *The Wrestler*, Lance Armstrong, or Sisyphus, is there something mythic or heroic in your pursuit? How might your dream metaphorically make you immortal or give you the illusion that you are triumphing over death? How did this dream, or the pursuit of it, give you the illusion that you would be *more* by having it?

chapter 3

The Dr. Kevorkian of Dreams

"Il faut savoir quand s'arrêter. (One must know when to stop.)*"*

>> **French proverb**

"If at first you don't succeed, try, try again. Then quit.
There's no point in being a damn fool about it."

>> **W. C. Fields**

Do you remember Dr. Jack Kevorkian? If you weren't around back in the heyday of his infamy, let me refresh your memory. Dr. Kevorkian was an advocate of physician-assisted suicide for terminally ill patients. He was given the unfortunate title of "Dr. Death," but he practiced euthanasia medicine, and the word *euthanasia* means, in Greek, "good death." In his practice, Dr. Kevorkian helped more than a hundred patients to choose the time of their death and end their suffering. When I told Keith, my boyfriend, that I saw myself as a sort of "Dr. Kevorkian of Dreams" in writing this book, he recoiled in horror. "No, you're not," he said, pushing away the notion more quickly than he rejects the notion of enrolling in ballroom dance classes. People don't tend to have a warm and fuzzy reaction to a guy known as "Dr. Death," and, in fact, Dr. Kevorkian was a figure who stirred up all kinds of emotion and controversy. I get that being the "Dr. Death of Dreams" is not likely to get one invited to a lot of parties, but I also know this: When I was coming to the end of my dream of having a child, I would have *loved* to have somebody help me through the end stages of my dream, walk me through the process, tell me what to expect, comfort and console me, and help me come

37

to a compassionate decision to call it a day. And when I began to dare speak about the death of dreams, people came out of the woodwork to thank me. There were a lot of people like me, and they needed help.

Hoping against Hope

The first time I spoke about the death of dreams was at the Fertility Planit show in Century City, California, in January 2013. I was invited to be on the panel "Letting Go: How to Let Go and Move On from the Hope of Biological Children." I was a nervous wreck before the show. I felt like the skunk at the garden party or, perhaps more aptly, the divorce attorney at the wedding expo. This wasn't a topic that I imagined many people who were actively trying to have a child would want to hear about. I was terrified. I was sure that no one who was trying to conceive would want to attend a panel on such a topic. I imagined that the producers of the event would put our panel in the bowels of the hotel basement, we would have to sit on cases of canned foods instead of chairs, and no one would attend, other than a blogging journalist who was there to write a story on why on earth the Fertility Planit people would feature such a silly topic. Turns out I was wrong; people wanted to know.

The room was filled with men and women who were still trying to conceive and yet simultaneously trying to imagine how they would go on if it didn't work out. Not only were there people in attendance who wanted to hear about this, but there were also more than 25,000 people who were watching the panel online (and to date, 500,000 people have viewed it). People wanted to know, "How did you do it? How did you let go and move on?" "What do you do if your dream doesn't manifest?" "How do you go on?" "Can you be happy if your dream doesn't come true?" I saw in their faces, their tears, and their heartfelt questions that these people wanted assurance that they could go on if they didn't get what they wanted most. The amazing thing was that I had answers to their questions. I knew what worked; I had gotten through this and had gone from total despair at the death of my dream to a completely unexpected happy ending.

After the event, people in the audience came up to me and thanked me for sharing my story. They heard in my story that I wanted it as much as they did and that I had clear and definite things that helped me let go, move on, and find a new happy ending. I gave them hope even as I was talking about the very thing they were hoping against. I do the same thing with patients I see who are grieving their marriages, their careers, their dream homes, financial stability, or whatever their dream was. And I truly hope that I am able to help you come to a good ending with the help of this book. I believe strongly that if our dream is dying, our life is limping along because of its pursuit, and we are not fully functional because of it, we should bring the same sense of compassion to our dreams as we would to an animal we love. I want very much to help you let go of this terminal dream and to live fully and happily without it. When we do this with animals and with human life, it's called *compassion*. You deserve to give your dream that same level of compassion.

Moving Forward

So, how best to proceed with the delicate task of ending your dream? As controversial as Dr. Kevorkian's practices were—and this is certainly a complex issue that people have differing opinions on—there's good evidence that when he agreed to help someone, he didn't do so willy-nilly. He wanted to be sure that they were appropriate candidates. He said no to plenty of people. He asked people lots of questions. He wanted to be sure that there were no other options and that the suffering was so great that assisted suicide was the most compassionate choice: "As a medical doctor, it is my duty to evaluate the situation with as much data as I can gather and as much expertise as I have and as much experience as I have to determine whether or not the wish of the patient is medically justified."[1] In the last chapter, we took a hard look at the costs of your dreams, and I hope you are now clear about whether and why it is time for your dream to have a "good death" or whether it is time to put this book down and continue pursuing it. Like Dr. Kevorkian, I want to make sure this is the right choice, as it is one with significant consequences for your life. Not all dreams are to be let go of, and some most definitely are. I hope that three chapters into this book you have a good sense of which kind of dream yours is. And if it is time to call in "Dr. Death," the first step in the process is to say that out loud.

Calling the Time of Death

As hard as it is to call the time of death, it is important and necessary and can give some sense of control. The alternative is waiting until someone else tells you that there is nothing else that can be done, or waiting until something truly catastrophic happens, which comes with its own set of difficulties. But just because you chose to quit trying doesn't mean quitting will be easy. It won't be. I had people in my life, both strangers and beloved friends who had seen all of the Herculean effort I had undergone, respond to the news that I was done trying to have a child with the strangest advice: 101 ways I could become pregnant. You know, relax; go on vacation; adopt; buy the ultimate "you can do anything if you only believe hard enough" self-help book, *The Secret*; use a surrogate; sacrifice a goat. Some even bluntly told me that if I really wanted it, I wouldn't be giving up now. I don't remember what I said back to them; all of my brainpower had to go into preventing myself from physically attacking them.

And as hard as it was to hear those words from others, it would have been harder if I said those words to myself—if I, instead of crying uncle, began listing all the options that my ex-husband and I hadn't exhausted, and set about trying to accomplish each one. We hadn't done embryo donors. We hadn't hired a surrogate. We could have done more—but we were so battered, bruised, and bankrupt that it would have been damaging to continue. We really couldn't afford to do anything else. We just couldn't. It was the right time for us to quit.

I wrote a little about the time of death of my dream in chapter 1, but it bears expanding upon here. I had no idea when I woke up that morning that it would be the last day I would pursue my dream of having a child, and if you had told me at 8 a.m. on that day, I wouldn't have believed you. When I realized that once again I didn't get pregnant, I just knew that I was done. I knew it. I didn't realize it at the time, but I had actually already done an inventory of costs. It was not a proper inventory, which I highly suggest you do. It was unconscious. But still, I had reconciled the insanity of "doing the same thing over and over and expecting a different result" and the perniciousness of never giving up. I knew that I couldn't keep taking action on something that was depleting my physical health, mental health, finances, relationships, and sense of self. And maybe if I had been asking myself throughout the process about the costs of the dream, I wouldn't have felt like Alice in Wonderland, falling down the rabbit hole with no sense of security that I would ever land. I knew I had to stop, and I called the time of death right then and there.

When I said, "I choose to quit," it was the first time in a long time that I did not surrender my life to my fate, my body, my insurance company, or the cell quality of our embryos; this was me taking some control back. I didn't know how important it was at the time, but with the wisdom of hindsight, I now know that it was *huge*. I am not sure what gave me the ability to do it. Maybe it was my gut or my higher self or wisdom gleaned from all my therapy and/or from my training as a therapist, but whatever it was, I managed to make a choice. I just somehow knew that it was better to choose to stop than it was to keep hitting my head against the wall. It was me saying to myself, *I see your suffering and I am not going to make it worse for you. You, dear Tracey, have suffered enough, and I am not going to put you through more of this. Your quality of life has been diminished by the endless pursuit of this dream. It is time to end it. It is time to let this die.* This action allowed there to be a good death of my dream, or as good as was possible under the circumstances.

For some people, the moment a dream dies is equally as clear. Flores desperately wanted to become a diplomat and remembers the exact moment she gave up on her dream: "13 July 2010, 4:30 p.m., in Paris," she recounts. "I met my former boss, and I asked her what else I could do. What did the others have that I didn't? The things she mentioned—connections, money, degrees from Ivy League universities to which I had been accepted but that I hadn't been able to attend for financial reasons—were all part of a past I couldn't change, and over which I had had no control. I realized, there and then, that no one could see nor cared about potential, passion, or drive, and that I was never going to get it."

If you are staring your dream in the face and seeing that it is time to quit, I urge you to call the time of death right now. You can sit here with this book in your hand and do it, or climb to a mountaintop and shout it, or write it on a message in a bottle and throw it out to sea. However you do it, *do* it. I can guarantee that there is life on the other side of impossible. And naming the time of death is an important process in moving on, letting go, and getting to the other side.

Even If It Wasn't up to You, Declare That You Are Done

I know that some of you aren't able to choose the time of the death of your dream. Maybe you got fired, you got left behind, or there is nothing left for you to do or to try. For others, the end of the dream is a little fuzzier. "I did not have an exact moment when I knew the dream was over," says Margaret, a woman who lost her dream of earning a master's degree in art history and becoming a teacher. "It was a much slower, more gradual process for me. Some of this was because there were people who, when hearing my story, would insist there was more I could do. Someone I had not yet called, met with, etc. So I felt I could not say with total certainty that I was not going to get my degree. If I said that, I was not trying my hardest, fighting the good fight. I was letting the bad people win. I was giving up. I felt I would be letting people down by accepting that I was never going to get my degree from this school." Margaret was stuck in a dream limbo state. Limbo is no fun, and I am not talking about the Caribbean-inspired party dance; I am talking about the kind of limbo in which you can't move forward and there is no going back. This is a horrible, stuck feeling in which you feel as if you have no choices. Have you ever had that nightmare in which you are frozen and you can't move and maybe you can't even be heard? Maybe you're screaming for help and no one hears you? That is the emotional state of dream limbo. Choosing to let go of the dream, as hard as it is—and it is *hard*—begins to give you some choices, some movement. Saying "I am done" is a way to get your voice back and get out of limbo.

Even if that is the case, you can still create a good death for your dream and take some bit of power back by calling the moment of death. Declare that you are done. Even if all there is to do is to say to yourself, "I am done; this is over," that can be enough. Cassandra, the woman who nearly gave up everything in an effort to buy her dream home, did not choose the time of the death of her dream. It came in the form of a phone call. She remembers it with great clarity. "I can see myself sitting in my office [at home] and answering the home phone line in there. The call was from Connie, my realtor. She told me that my 'dream house' was sold to another buyer, who was not a contingent buyer. She shared this news bluntly with me. I felt enraged and profoundly depressed. I am a fighter when it comes to dreams, so I was shocked that it did not work out. Unfortunately, a day later, we had to go to Louisiana to see my in-laws. I cried the whole way. When I was with my in-laws, I took Xanax to control my inner feeling of hysteria."

Cassandra entered a severe depression and experienced months and months of complicated grief. She got over it in time. People do. "Every once in a while, I like to go back to the fantasy and replay it in my head," she says, "When I do, it just does not have the same energy. The magic is gone." But how much better off Cassandra would have been had she come to a point where she could have made the declaration for herself: *That house is gone; this dream is over.* My guess is that the shift in energy would have come all that sooner.

Stages of the Death of a Dream

Just because you have called the time of death and are no longer trying to make it happen doesn't mean that the dream is *really, really, really* dead. I know I said that it is important to name it, and it is—it's vital—but I thought it best to warn you that it can take a surprisingly long time to let the dream go, even if we are saying "I am done" or if we can clearly see that there is, in fact, nothing left to be done. Saying "I am done" and naming the time of death is just the beginning of the death of the dream, but that alone doesn't end it. It's not quick. It's a process. And, dear one, it can be a slow and painful process.

Nils B. Jostmann and Sander L. Koole write about different aspects of goal disengagement in their paper "When Persistence Is Futile: A Functional Analysis of Action Orientation and Goal Disengagement."[2] They suggest that goal disengagement can be decomposed into different aspects of disengagement: motivational, behavioral, cognitive, and affective. I have seen in my work and in my personal experience that, when going through the death of a dream, we go through similar phases of disengagement.

Motivational: In the death of our dream, an early stage of death might show up in the death of motivation or energy for the pursuit of the goal. We no longer have the energy and the enthusiasm that we once did. We might still be taking action, we might still want it to happen, and we are most likely thinking about it, but we just don't have the motivation for it anymore. This is where I most started to disengage: I lost the motivation even before I stopped taking actions. I still very much wanted it, and I had a whole lot of feelings about not having it—I just lost the drive I previously had, even before I called the time of death.

Behavioral/action: The death of "life force" or energy for the dream leads to behavioral death, in that we are no longer taking any actions on making it happen. For me, the stopping of action felt like the most difficult stage, probably because it was the most concrete. To no longer act on making the dream happen made it seem final. Yet even as we may not be acting on it, nor have any motivation around it, the dream may still be very much alive in our thoughts and feelings, and there can be a whole lot of feelings and thoughts that are activated when we are neither acting or motivated to do so.

Thoughts/cognitive: Even if we are no longer taking any action on our dream, we may still be thinking about it a lot; cognitively, the dream remains alive. Thoughts paired with emotions can bring us back into acting and can impact our motivation for the dream both positively and negatively. I know that for me, once I lost motivation and stopped taking action, the thoughts remained alive, and to some degree still do intermittently today. Thoughts about the dream will likely never leave us—and that is to be expected. However, in time, thoughts about the dream move from rumination to more casual, intermittent thoughts.

Affective/emotional: When the motivation is finally gone, we are no longer taking action to try to make our dream a reality, and it is no longer primary in our thoughts; our affective or emotional attachment to the dream will gradually diminish. This stage, I believe, is the stage that Elisabeth Kübler-Ross would call acceptance. When we've reached this stage, we find that we're beginning to be able to talk about the dream without it hurting so profoundly.

What to Expect When You Call the Time of Death

I remember the pain of my dear friend having to put down a dearly beloved dog, Bear. The vet told us the stages of Bear's death so that we would know what to expect. It was hard to hear that the death wasn't going to be immediate and that Bear might seem to struggle with it, but knowing helped. I wish I could be that specific about the death of a dream. I wish I could tell you that just saying "I am done" would end the pain and make things easier. I can't, but calling the time of death should offer you a little comfort—at least it is my sincere hope that it does. I don't know how long it will take, but once you say, "I am done," your motivation is already gone. Sure, you might get a burst of motivation to make it happen again long after you have worked through all of the stages of death, but trust me: In my personal and professional experience, the process of letting the dream go is much faster the second and third and tenth time you find yourself inclined to revive the dream. I have lost track of how many times I have had dream revivals (for example, every time in the last five years that my period was late), but letting the dream go again took a matter of days or, on occasion, even a couple of hours, whereas the first time it took almost three years to get from "I'm done" (motivational and behavioral death) to cognitive and emotional death.

I don't think about my dream much at all anymore, and when I do, it doesn't hurt like it did. I can think and talk about the dream now, mostly, without too much emotional upheaval. Sure, there are notable exceptions (put me on a stage and ask me to talk about all of this, and I might get a bit choked up). And even though there is no motivation, no hope, no action, and very little thought about my dream, there are times when the emotional or affective part of the dream remains very much alive.

Sally, who gave up her dream of a relationship with a certain man, explains how this works for her: "The biggest thing I learned and have come to accept is that letting go isn't just a onetime action. You can't just wipe your hands of something or someone that you have loved and be done. It's a decision that you have to make again and again. I read a great quote sometime in the last year and I don't remember where it was . . . but it basically said, 'You don't have to let go. You simply have to not hold on.' And that subtle distinction made great sense to me and gave me great relief. I didn't have to do anything special or big to let go. I just needed to not hold on so tight."

Recently, Keith and I were watching a funny film in which a forty-year-old woman was pregnant. I didn't expect to have an emotional reaction, as if I were watching *Love Story* or *Terms of Endearment,* but I did. Everyone else in the theater was laughing and yukking it up, and I was crying as if I were watching an entirely different movie—and I suppose to some degree, that is exactly what was happening. I tell you this so you know to be patient with yourself. Perhaps a part of your dream will always be alive for you the way mine is for me. But that doesn't mean you can't let go and move on and find a new happy ending. You can!

What is called for in the death of a dream is patience. Your process may not be fast, and it may not be easy, but it's your process. Declare the death of your dream, and then be gentle with yourself as the stages unfold.

The Inside Story

Alex had a dream of starting his own business. He came from a long line of entrepreneurs: His grandfather had been a woodworker, his father was a fisherman, and his mother ran a business teaching afternoon enrichment classes to local elementary schools. In high school, he started an entrepreneur club that sold pencils, notebooks, T-shirts, and other school spirit gear on the quad at lunch. In college, he elected to go to a school smack in the middle of Silicon Valley, the center of the universe for startup entrepreneurs. He studied economics so he could understand business, and sociology so he could understand people. While on campus, he played for his school's varsity soccer team and worked a variety of odd jobs to build up his savings. He was, at times, a DJ, a music blogger, a coconut water spokesperson, and a soccer referee for the local American Youth Soccer Organization (AYSO) league. During the summers, he interned for start-ups who needed free labor to run their social media campaigns, hand out fliers, stand on street corners, and answer the phones. "I didn't mind working for free," Alex says, "because I knew I would one day be the guy with the million-dollar idea. I was just paying my dues and waiting for my eureka moment."

It was the part-time soccer gig that gave him his big idea. For each game, parents would bring snacks for the kids—cookies and juice boxes, sometimes oranges—and after the sugar crash, they always became sluggish on the field. He had refined his own nutritional needs and knew that the body needed a more sustainable kind of energy. Why couldn't there be an energy food that the kids loved that helped their energy stay up for the remainder of the game? He began to scour the Internet for information on nutrition, food businesses, and recipes. He filed for a food service license, found a certified kitchen, found a factory who would make his healthy sports jelly beans during their off hours, tested flavors on the kids and their moms, hired a logo designer and a packaging firm, and worked tirelessly on his prototype. After graduation, he took a cheap apartment with his girlfriend not far from campus. He kept refereeing for AYSO and took a job at Home Depot to cover his rent and student loans, but it was a rough couple of years. He began to approach the venture capitalists he had met while interning. He got nowhere. He pitched himself for a television show where the winner got funding and lost in the final round. His best friends no longer wanted to hang out with him because he couldn't even afford pizza and beer. Soon he couldn't afford his half of the rent, and he had to move home.

Refusing to give up on his brilliant idea, he launched a Kickstarter campaign to get funding—and thanks to a last-minute heroic effort by his college roommate, he got the money. He raced to get production time, ordered his packaging, and began to pound the pavement trying to get sales. Within days, the disastrous news became apparent. Jelly Belly, the massive jelly bean company, had just announced a sports-based jelly bean, and no one would even consider a no-name start-up.

He wallowed in agony for weeks, calling in sick to Home Depot and quitting his soccer job.

His Dr. Kevorkian moment came when he approached his girlfriend, who had just gotten a promotion at a marquis Silicon Valley company, for a loan to try to ride out the Jelly Belly attack. He thought if he could rebrand his product and position it as a cheaper or healthier alternative, that he could still make his idea fly. "She not only said no," Alex explains, "She said no way and broke up with me on the spot. 'You're deluded, Alex, and you're the only one who doesn't see it.'

"Entrepreneurs are always talking about failing fast," Alex says. "But the truth was that I failed slowly, painfully, and completely."

The Therapy Couch

THE CHANGE IN TIME ORIENTATION AND THE IMPROVEMENT OF VISION

When people are sitting on my therapy couch, and we are talking about pulling the plug on their dream, I want to know a little bit about their vision. No, I don't pull out an eye chart and make them start reading for me. Rather, I want to know if they have been seeing distant objects better than objects at close range. Has their dream caused some farsightedness? Are they hyperopic? In a psychological sense, this is when we make choices based on what is perceived as better in the long term rather than what is better right now. This can be a good thing, but when in the pursuit of a dream, our hyperopia can go haywire, and we are unable to make decisions that benefit us in the here and now. And if we have long been sacrificing our *now* for an imagined dream that is not coming, then not only is our vision messed up, but our time orientation is, too. When you focus on the future at the expense of the present, it takes you out of the now and puts your happiness into the future, on layaway, if you will. "I am not happy now, but I will be when 'X' happens," we may say. Raj Raghunathan, PhD, in his article "The Art of Giving Up: The Importance of Disengaging from Goals," writes about how goal pursuit can make us hyperopic to a fault: "Most of us are constantly warned against being myopic: 'Don't be extravagant, save for the future,' or 'avoid unhealthy food for the sake of future health,' or, 'exercise regularly to be healthy,' etc. Perhaps as a result of exposure to such messages, many of us are habituated to thinking about the future consequences of our present actions."[3] However, there is a great sacrifice of present happiness that can come if we put all of our eggs in the future happiness basket. Ling, a woman who made an enormous personal sacrifice in pursuit of her acting dreams, explains that before giving up on her dream, "I was a future-oriented person, sacrificing my personal life for my dream." The maxim she lived by was "the best is yet to come."

Almost every person I interviewed for this book reported that when they let go of their dream, they changed their time orientation out of the future and into the present. Flipping this time orientation is one of the major and almost immediate benefits of letting go of our unmet dream, because it just may be that happiness is more likely to happen if we are living in the now. According to a study by Dr. Mark George, a psychiatrist and neurologist at the National Institute of Mental Health in Bethesda, Maryland, in a report published in the *American Journal of Psychiatry*, when people are happy, there is a *decrease* of activity in the regions of the temporoparietal area of the cerebral cortex, which is the area of our brain that spends its time planning and anticipating.[4] Dr. George saw in his study that when people are happy, this region shuts down. Ergo, happiness is seemingly as hard to manage while we are planning for the future as it is to simultaneously pat your head and rub your tummy.

There are other benefits that psychologists report seeing in patients who disengage from their unattainable goals. Miller and Wrosch's research offers evidence that giving up on a dream that isn't working is good for your body and mind: "People who can disengage from unattainable goals enjoy better well-being, have more normative patterns of cortisol secretion, and experience fewer symptoms of everyday illness than do people who have difficulty disengaging from unattainable goals."[5] They also say that if you disengage from the dream that isn't working, you are more likely to have the ability to move on to new goals—a concept we will talk about more in chapter 9. Particularly exciting is that the ability to form new dreams/goals is correlated with markers for well-being and health, and according to Miller and Wrosch, "it seems to be especially beneficial in people who cannot easily withdraw from goals that have become unrealizable."[6] What this means is that if you haven't been able to withdraw from this unachievable goal and now you are about to withdraw, you are likely to really benefit from this choice. If you are in the beginning stages of letting the dream go, I know that may not be a huge comfort, but knowing there's a possible reward can help when we're making hard decisions. Miller and Wrosch suggest that giving up on a goal can give us a whole host of psychological benefits: a higher level of subjective well-being than those who failed to disengage; increased resources for other goals (less time doing what doesn't work gives us more time to do something else); coming to "redefine the goals as not necessary for satisfaction in life." Another benefit that they cite is "avoiding accumulated failure experiences." I might say it another way: When we give up on our dream, we might initially feel like we failed, but in stopping the pursuit, there are fewer actual experiences of failure. Through giving up on the dream, the dream becomes less of a part of our identity—and that is important in moving on, letting go, and ultimately finding unexpected happiness.

Movie Rx

When you think about Hawaii and George Clooney together, you probably don't immediately think about death, dying, and loss. If you're a woman, you probably picture George spending a lot of time with his shirt off lying in the sun, sipping mai tais and offering to apply suntan lotion to your back— I mean, ahem, the costar's back. The first line of *The Descendants* tells us that we aren't in that movie: "My friends on the mainland think just because I live in Hawaii, I live in paradise. Like a permanent vacation. We're all just out here sipping mai tais, shaking our hips, and catching waves. Are they insane?"[7] So if you are dreaming of a movie that will allow you to escape, you might want to watch Elvis in *Blue Hawaii,* but as this is movie therapy, and I am prescribing this movie to help you come to a good ending to your dream, this will be a movie low on hula and heavy on heartbreak.

The Descendants is a story about Matt King, a middle-aged heir of Hawaiian royalty, who had been under the illusion that he was in a happy-ish marriage —even as he was disconnected, distracted, and emotionally unavailable; he hadn't really talked to his wife in months; he was something of a workaholic. Spoiler alert: If you haven't seen the movie yet, you might want to stop reading here and come back once you have quit crying and your bloodshot eyes are ready to read on, as I don't want to spoil this film for you.

The movie begins with an image of Matt's beautiful wife waterskiing and smiling, and then we are met with the hard reality that his wife, Elizabeth, was in a boating accident and has been in the hospital in a coma for the last twenty-three days. Matt is in denial. He tells us so: "I know it. It's not her time yet. She'll wake up, Scottie and Alexandra will have their mother back, and we'll talk about our marriage. I'll sell the land and quit my practice, and buy her whatever she wants—a big board, a house in France, a trip around the world, just the two of us. We'll get close again, like the early days. It's still in us. It must be." Then he strikes bargains and makes deals. "If you're doing this to get my attention, Liz, it's working," he says. "I'm ready now. I'm ready to talk. I'm ready to change. I'm ready to be a real husband and a real father. Just wake up."

The doctors inform Matt that she won't wake up, she'll never be like she was, and they are legally obligated to take her off the machines. She will die in the next few days to few weeks. With denial behind him, anger takes over when Matt learns that his wife has been having an affair, and then Matt begins to grieve the reality of his marriage. The anger literally moves him, as we see him running and flying and driving and running some more in order to confront his wife's lover, her friends who kept her secret, and the reality that his marriage was not the marriage he imagined it to be. In confronting the truth, Matt comes to terms with the reality and pulls the plug on the illusion.

When he says his good-bye to Elizabeth, he is no longer in denial, no longer angry at her. He says a good-bye that encompasses the reality of their relationship, and he realizes that there is nothing else to do but let her go (I challenge you to watch this scene and not shed a tear): "Good-bye, Elizabeth. Good-bye, my love, my friend, my pain, my joy. Good-bye. Good-bye. Good-bye." And then you see him in the hallway, his daughters going in to say their own good-bye to their mother.

We see that in losing his marriage and his wife, Matt reconnects to daughters from whom he has been essentially estranged; he is no longer the "backup parent," and in connecting to his girls, he is able to connect to his past. He makes the decision to pull the plug on a land deal that would rob his daughters' access to land that is their birthright.

As hard as it is to watch Matt struggle with the end of his dream and the end of Elizabeth's life, in seeing his process, his denial, his anger, and his very human reactions, we can give ourselves some empathy with our own reactions—our own long-held illusions, denial, deal-making, and anger.

The final scene of *The Descendants* is especially beautiful; there we are on our couch watching Matt and his two girls on their couch watching the documentary *March of the Penguins*. We can't see the TV. We can hear Morgan Freeman telling the story of the penguins. I see that scene as a sort of mirror. We see ourselves in that scene. The scene says, "You are in pain, you have had grief, just like Matt and his girls, and like the penguins, and you will endure. Something good will come from your loss. It will." I have no idea if that is what the filmmaker intended when he created that ending, but that is what I see. No matter your loss or your pain, if you let it go, if you pull the plug on what is hurting you and grieve it, you will emerge from it with the possibility of greater connection.

SELF-HELP SUGGESTIONS

☐ Have you ever had to put down a beloved animal? How hard was it? How did you come to the decision? How did you know it was the right thing to do? What can that experience teach you about how to approach the end of your dream?

☐ If you have read this far, it is likely that you now know that the right thing to do is to pull the plug on your dream. You know if it is time, don't you? How can you compassionately pull the plug? What does that mean for you? What would that look like? What are the specific actions necessary for you to do that? Will you need help in doing this? Or can you do it on your own? Only you know what is right for you—and you may change your mind, and that is okay, too!

☐ How might knowing what to expect help? How is hearing about others' experiences impacting you? Do you relate to these stories? If so, is there a way you can seek out more of them? We so rarely talk about the death of dreams in our culture, since we prefer to talk about success. If knowing more about the process will help, find a way to learn.

☐ Have you named the time of death? Is making the choice giving you any relief? Or is deciding to let it go making the pain more intense?

☐ Does making the choice feel better than not making this choice? Ask yourself: *Is making this choice giving me back some sense of agency?*

☐ Where are you with the death of the dream? Are you still motivated to act? Are you still taking action on the dream? Is the dream preoccupying your thoughts? Is it hard not to take action? Or is there little energy for action, but thoughts and feelings about your dream still remain? Take an assessment and see where the dream may have already died without you consciously knowing it.

☐ Like Matt King in *The Descendants,* are you ignoring certain realities? What are they? How, like Matt, are you still telling yourself a story about this dream that isn't true?

☐ What might you need to confront in order to move on and let go?

☐ We will see in chapter 5 how anger is an important part of grief, but can you see anger sneaking in as you call the time of death? Did you see how anger was important for Matt King in letting go of the dream that he had a good marriage?

☐ What are the benefits of your letting go of this dream? How will your health improve if you let this dream die? How will your mental health improve? How might your self-concept improve? How might your relationships improve? How might your finances improve?

☐ What would be the prenuptial for your dream, if you had written it? What would have been the terms of how long you would have pursued the dream? What would you want to walk away from your dream with if it didn't work out?

☐ Plan a funeral service for your dream. Why? Funerals serve as an important ceremony for our psyche; this is why there are cemeteries and mortuaries. We need to have a way to eulogize, memorialize, and publicly grieve our losses. There are no such services for our dreams. Only you can create one. You might want to create a ritual to memorialize your dream. There has been a death, and it deserves to be honored and remembered and eulogized. Funerals are meant to remember the life of something as well as to acknowledge the ending; your ritualizing this loss is to say that it mattered, and your dream did matter.

☐ Can you see that by letting go of this dream you may be making room for something else? It may be too soon to see this, and if that is the case, please don't use it as an excuse to beat yourself up about it. For Matt, it was the connection with his children; for Sally, it was opening to another relationship; and for me, it was completely unexpected happiness. Something new can't grow where something old is planted. As long as the dream is getting all of the attention, we can't expect something new to emerge.

☐ Can you see how your vision changed by pursuing this dream? Have you been farsighted? Has your focus been on the future? How might your vision get better just by giving up on the dream? What might giving up on this dream allow you to see more clearly?

☐ Have you been putting your happiness on layaway? Waiting for "X" to happen in order to be happy? How might giving up on that dream allow you to see some happiness that might be here right now?

☐ Can you look to the past years and see happiness that you didn't name or experience because the dream hadn't happened? Was there happiness that you missed out on?

☐ What is your time orientation now? Past, present, or future? Can you see that letting go of the dream might change that?

Let's Acknowledge
Just How Much This Sucks

"You cannot die of grief, though it feels as if you can. A heart does not actually break, though sometimes your chest aches as if it is breaking. Grief dims with time. It is the way of things. There comes a day when you smile again, and you feel like a traitor. How dare I feel happy. How dare I be glad in a world where my father is no more. And then you cry fresh tears, because you do not miss him as much as you once did, and giving up your grief is another kind of death."

>> Laurell K. Hamilton

When you decide that there is simply no more trying to be done, that is when the grief kicks in. Your reaction may not be this extreme, but when I really accepted that my dream was dead, the grief kicked me in the ovaries and my heart and then my ass, and it kicked and kicked again and again and I screamed and I cried and I screamed some more.

What Grief Feels Like

I felt anger, rage, guilt, shame, envy, despair, loss, hopelessness, sadness, jealousy, and back through the cycle again. I felt more than I felt I could take. And I felt that these feelings would never end and that I would *never* know peace or joy again. A varying mix of these feelings, with different degrees of intensity, is typically what happens when a dream dies. This is the natural order of things. You will probably feel all kinds of things that don't make sense—only they *really do.* Goodness gracious, you did everything you could to make it happen, you gave it your all, you worked your ass off, and you didn't get what you wanted—and the real honest-to-goodness truth is that the result of all that sucks. And feelings like anger, rage, shame, envy, guilt, helplessness, hopelessness, and an overwhelming sadness can eclipse any sun, so that you may find yourself making deals and promises and then crying in despair all over again.

This is normal. This is what happens when we lose someone or something we loved, be it a dream or a person. One of the things you might be telling yourself is that you don't deserve this grief, that it isn't like someone died—only it *is* exactly like that. It is a death of who you imagined you would be. It is a death of an imagined future. Your life and the life you imagined for yourself is not going to be as you thought it would, and that hurts. Pain is pain. Loss is loss, and this is a loss as real and valid as any other. If you start thinking that your grief is abnormal and wrong, that will only exacerbate your pain.

I have a Johnnie Cochran–like phrase that I use to make this point (remember the infamous lawyer from the O. J. Simpson team who came up with catchy phrases such as "If the gloves don't fit, you must acquit"?). Here's mine: "What you resist persists. What you embrace you erase." (Okay, I may not be the first therapist to coin this cheesy yet clever catchphrase. And I must warn you that the last bit about erasing is hyperbolic. Embracing the grief won't erase it, but it will change things and help you to feel what you feel, only that doesn't rhyme with *embrace.*) The point I am trying to make crystal clear to you is that trying to ignore your feelings *will not make them go away.* Ignoring your grief will make it worse in the long run. You need to feel this to get through it.

One important note before we continue to talk about grief: If you are concerned that your level of grief is *not* normal—that it's prolonged or especially intense, and that it is threatening your life or your mental health, please turn immediately to the end of this chapter, where I discuss what to do with what therapists refer to as "complicated grief." It's important that you get professional help in this case, especially if you're having thoughts of suicide.

What Grief Is

As a therapist, I often get the following phone call: "Hi, I think I need to start therapy. My (choose one) mom/dad/child/husband/wife/grandmother/grandfather/best friend died. And my friend/sister/boss told me I needed therapy. They say that I am not grieving. Or, they say I am grieving too much. They tell me I shouldn't be over it. Or they tell me I should already be over it. They tell me that my reaction to death doesn't seem right. Or, I can't let anyone know my reaction to death because I am so worried about appearing strong, and I don't want to overwhelm them." Very often the person calling will agree with the person who suggested that they seek therapy. They might know what their friend or family member meant, they know that they aren't functioning the way they used to, and they are feeling all kinds of horrible things that they can't manage on their own. They feel guilty for not grieving the way they think they should. They might even specifically seek me out for "grief work." And then they come into my office and sit on my couch and tell me how someone they loved has died and their story is unspeakably sad, and they tell me they are angry, sad, enraged, depressed—that they feel sick and can't eat and for some reason have sat and watched all six seasons of *The Gilmore Girls,* and they can't pay their bills or answer their phone, and then they ask me questions like, "Are my feelings normal? Aren't my feelings too much? Isn't there something wrong with me for feeling this way? Isn't this wrong? Shouldn't I feel something else? Shouldn't I be over it by now? How long is okay to grieve? Oh, and by the way, what exactly is grieving? And how do you do it?"

I want to reach over and hug these sweet souls. They are deep in grief and don't even know it. Many people don't truly know what grief is. For years before I went to grad school to learn about this stuff, I imagined the archetypal lady in black who is sending a sartorial message to the world that she has lost a loved one. This griever was always old and widowed and perhaps from Italy or Greece. I could see her looking sad and withdrawn and in a plain and lifeless black dress. I knew what she looked like when she was out in the world going into town and shopping for the black dress in the market. The picture was perfectly perspicuous for me; I might have even seen it in a movie. But I didn't know what this grieving widow did once she was home alone at night. And I didn't know that people who didn't look like her or dress like her could be in grief, too.

Like most people, I tended to think mostly of sadness when I thought of grief. Sure, sadness is part of grief, but it is by no means the whole enchilada. Grief is complicated. When I lost ten people in my family in one year, I didn't feel like I was grieving; I felt numb and checked out and in a state of enormous anxiety that someone else was going to die next, and I wondered who it was going to be. I didn't think I was grieving because I wasn't crying. And truth be told, I felt ashamed that I wasn't grieving the "right way," and I worried that it meant I didn't love the people who had died.

Grief is not just about tears and sadness. It's not even just about feelings. It's a very complicated process that is a bodily experience, a social experience, and a thought process. Grief manifests in your body, your mind, and your emotions. Somatically, we can experience grief as a physical ache, an emptiness or tightness in our chest, a pit in our stomach, a heavy heart, a closing of our throat, a sense of weakness, or lethargy. It can feel hard to walk, move, be around others, or do almost anything. It can be hard to sleep, eat, work, or do activities that we previously enjoyed. Uncontrollable crying and impaired memory can be part of grief. When we are grieving, we are often preoccupied with the loss and have difficulty focusing or thinking about anything else. We feel shock, a sense of surreal-ness, utter disbelief that this is really happening, and a whole host of emotions beyond sadness, such as guilt, shame, envy, jealousy, shock, loneliness, anger, rage, and numbness. Grief impacts our desire to participate in activities we love and can lead to isolation and withdrawal from social relationships. It can cause us to stay away from certain friends and family if being with them only exacerbates our grief.

I learned all this in school, but until I lost loved ones, I didn't know exactly what the experience felt like. Grief is something you can't explain, kind of like sex, only obviously very different. You can talk about it all day long, but if you haven't been through it, the conversation is purely academic. And when you find yourself in it, you may not have any idea what to do, and words seem inadequate to describe it.

How Grief Works

When I finally called the time of death on my dream of having a child, I didn't know how to grieve it. No one told me, "This is how you grieve a loss." I just did it; grief just happened; it took me over and had its way with me. It will probably do the same for you, so I am not here to tell you how to grieve. I am here to give you some guidelines on grief so that you can at least be clear about what is going on while you are going through it. Not all of what follows may apply to your situation, but take what works and leave the rest.

Remember That You Are Not Crazy

I am here to tell you that whatever you are feeling or doing is normal and that you will be okay. So many people who love us want us to feel better fast, and this makes a certain amount of sense. They love us, and they want us to be happy. They will give us platitudes and tell us we need to look at the bright side and that we should focus on all the good in our lives, and while there may be truth in what they say, this is not the time for doing any of that. You will get there, but until you do, all the talk of silver linings will only make you cry more, make you feel angrier, and even make you want to further isolate. I want to be the voice that tells you that it is okay not to look at the bright side right now. The bright side will be there when you're ready. Grief is a natural reaction to loss, and you have lost something major—you have lost the hope of this dream coming true. It is natural that you are feeling what you do, so go ahead and feel it.

Please Remember That Feelings and Facts Are Not the Same Thing

You may *feel* that your feelings about the death of your dreams are too much to bear. You may *feel* that you will *always* feel this way. You may *feel* sure that if you start to cry that you will never stop. You may *feel* that for the rest of your life this pain will be the first thing you think about when you wake up and the last thing you think about before you go to bed. You may *feel* absolutely certain that your life cannot be happy without this dream. I get it. I do. But this book is filled with stories of people who felt that way and no longer do. Such a person wrote this very sentence. Have the courage to feel it all. You will get through this, you will move on and through it, and you will get to the other side—you will.

Call Upon Your Good Mother

You have just had a major loss, and this is no time to internalize a General MacArthur stance of "suck it up, soldier." No, this is the time to call upon your internalized good mother and to treat yourself with tenderness, kindness, and compassion. If you don't have an internalized good mother, borrow one. I often recommend to patients who didn't have a particularly loving or kind or compassionate mother to borrow one from film or literature or even a friend who had a particularly kind and attuned mother, and imagine how she would treat them. If they can't imagine that, then I will ask them to imagine how they would treat their ten-year-old self. Very often, it is easy to be loving and kind to our younger selves. In my grief, I turned to Glinda the Good Witch from *The Wizard of Oz*. Glinda, in her sparkly white dress and singsong, soothing voice, was my companion in grief. And when the world told me to get over it, to get on with it, to stop grieving the loss of my dream because God had a plan for me or because I was meant to do something else, I conjured up the image of an all-good mother who would understand how I felt and wouldn't give me stupid advice and would, on occasion, turn into a cuss mouth to protect me from that world. I may have even, a time or two, imagined Glinda turning someone into a frog when they started to ask me if I had done enough to deserve to grieve. ("But did you adopt?" No, I did not, thank you very much. My dream was a biological child.) It was silly, but it somehow comforted me.

Having a Glinda, or any good mother, on your team can be an important counter to the "get over it" push that you may feel from yourself. Good mothers take our pain seriously. They are gentle and kind and they kiss our boo-boos and they know when to comfort and coo to us and when to tell us, "It's okay, you can go out to lunch with friends, and if it starts to hurt too much or someone tells you to start looking for a new man, new job, new dream, or new house, you can just tell them no." Your inner critic might find your inner good mother to be a bit gooey and overly attentive, but your inner critic can hold back on his or her criticism and his or her advice to "stop whining and get back on your horse and ride." That ain't what you need when you're grieving.

Watch for Pointy Fingers

When things don't work out as we hoped, we want to make sense of it. We look for a reason. We want to figure out the rules so we can emerge from confusion. We want to point a finger. We want to assign blame. Sometimes in my storytelling about my grief, I told the story of what the doctors did wrong and how this one was mean to me and that one didn't handle this right and the next one was on the edge of unethical. Blaming helped for a while, and then it didn't. Soon I saw that the blaming shifted.

I started to make the failure of my dream *my* fault, and yes, sometimes there are things we could have handled better. Goodness knows I would have been more likely to succeed if I had gotten my shit together before thirty-five so I could have started trying to conceive before I was already in the higher-risk-for-infertility pool, but as I was down and out and grieving that I would never be a mother, was it time for me to tear myself down and make me feel worse? Was that going to change anything? Was that going to get me through the grief more quickly? No. And actually the blaming sent a message to my psyche: "You don't deserve to be sad. This is your fault." Not helpful. Now is not the time for a cold, clinical analysis of what you did wrong. There may be a time and a place for that, and there may not be. However, that time is not now. You did everything in your power to make this dream a reality. And now you are letting it go. So, dear one, please don't beat yourself up.

Buy Good Kleenex; Don't Cheap Out

This is not a time to skimp. Get the good stuff. And have lots of it. Maybe a case from Costco. Keep a box in each room. Very often, patients apologize to me for crying so much and needing so much tissue. Do not apologize for your tears. Tears are healing. According to the research conducted by Dr. William Frey at the former St. Paul-Ramsey Medical Center in Minnesota (who describes himself as a student of "psychogenic lacrimation," or emotionally induced tears), emotionally driven crying contains protein and stress hormones, while tears that we cry because of an irritation (like dust particles or when cutting an onion) are mostly water.[1] Other research showed that crying activates endorphins, which is our body's natural painkiller. In other words, we feel better for having cried. So don't stop yourself from crying, and don't let anyone tell you not to cry. That said, if your grief is not activating tears, that is okay, too. If you don't cry, don't feel guilty. It doesn't mean you aren't hurting. Tear production is not a measure of how bad you feel. Some of our most painful moments are met by a horrible, flat, and icy emotionlessness that is more painful than any sob.

Eating Is Good

Grieving is not just an emotional process; it is a physical one, too. I remember crying so hard that I felt like I had just done a Spinning class. When I was done, I needed a towel, a shower, and a bottle of Gatorade to recover from the emotional workout. We therapists call grief that we are conscious of "active grief." Why? Because you aren't numbing it out, you are doing something, and it is something that takes a whole lot of energy to do. And because it takes energy, you need fuel—the best fuel you can give yourself. (Which is not, alas, Twinkies.) When you are grieving, it is common to either eat too much or not enough. This is really related to the self-kindness thing I mentioned earlier. Give yourself the best nurturing you can; it's hard enough to feel like crap because of grief, but you will only feel worse if you aren't sleeping, drinking water, taking your vitamins, getting a bit of sunlight, and exercising. It is rare that I have a grieving patient come in and report that she is doing all of the above. Most often I hear, "I just can't eat." Then how about a smoothie or some juice or a chocolate shake with maybe a scoop of protein powder and a Fred Flintstone multivitamin chaser? I know you know it is important to take care of yourself, but in grief, we can use a reminder to do these basic things. Treat yourself like you would a treasured friend, because you are.

Have Realistic Expectations with Yourself

You, like all human beings, have a finite amount of emotional, mental, and physical energy you can spend in a single day before you collapse into a blathering, nonfunctioning heap. Your energy will be impacted by the grief and the adjustment to not having the dream. And it is also likely you won't have the energy for other things the way you did before. Yes, I suppose with enough Red Bull and triple venti espresso mocha Frappuccinos, you can bypass some of those basic laws of metabolism; however, your homeostasis has been messed with. The dream that was taking all the energy is gone, and now the energy that was going into the dream is going into the grief. You may feel like you should be doing all the things you were doing before the death of your dream, that the death of a dream shouldn't impact your functioning. You may feel that you should be able to do more than a trip to the market before feeling the need for a nap. But the truth is that big feelings are tiring. I hear this all the time in session with patients. After doing a good bit of psychological work in which they confront their feelings, patients report being exhausted. Feelings felt fully (both the happy and sad kind) are energy expenditures. No, you won't find a calorie chart that gives you the energy expenditure for feeling anger, but every day I see the impact of feeling feelings fully. That said, I am equally sure it takes *more* energy to hold down feelings than it does to feel them. Once feelings are felt and you let them go, you will have energy for doing stuff again, I promise.

Use Self-Soothing Mantras

When I felt like I was being swallowed by grief, a memory of a conversation with a friend would flash into my mind. She is a gifted therapist, and one day, she tried to teach me to drive a stick shift. I was terrified. I was almost hyperventilating as she instructed me on the feel of the clutch. I panicked. I breathlessly told her, "*I cannot do this!* You've got to hear me. I cannot do this." My friend looked at me with sympathetic eyes and said to me calmly, "Your mother never taught you that bad things pass and that scary feelings don't last forever." She didn't pose it as a question; she saw it in my behavior—and she was right. My mother did not teach me that. I learned that anxiety was something to avoid and that if I felt something now, I would always feel it. In that moment, my friend gave me a huge gift, even though she didn't manage to teach me to drive a stick. I learned from her that I had missed an important life lesson: *feelings pass*. I knew it, but I didn't *know* it. At the end of our lesson, she gave me the prayer from the fourteenth-century Christian mystic Julian of Norwich: "All shall be well, and all shall be well, and all manner of thing shall be well," which in hindsight was a better lesson than learning to drive a stick shift.

This prayer may not be a comfort to everyone, but it definitely was for me. There was something in its vagueness that comforted me, a promise that I would be okay without a whole lot of specifics. I asked other people to share the phrases or words that comforted them during their grief. Here is what they offered:

- "Be gentle with yourself."
- "This sounds fatalistic and maybe not that positive, but to me it is. I tell myself, 'It is what it is.' I try to make that into kind of a Zen-like feeling, to accept what is and move on."
- "Knowing, thinking about, and believing that Bible verse that says Jesus will never leave us or forsake us, he's with us to the end of the world, has brought me great comfort in times of great sorrow and grief. It gives me an anchor of hope that I am not alone in what I am going through."
- "Remembering times when I thought I was going to die of grief or sorrow but lived through it and felt joy again. That's very helpful."
- "And this too shall pass."

Don't Make Big Decisions

When you are grieving, I would advise you to avoid making big decisions. You have already made a big decision in letting go of this dream or moving on after having this dream taken from you. The rule of thumb we learn in "therapy school" is not to make any big decisions for six to twelve months after a loss. There is already so much going on for you in adjusting to this loss that you, in the name of the aforementioned self-kindness, don't want to upset the proverbial apple cart when you already feel like your world has been smashed into applesauce by this loss. It is hard to make careful or nuanced decisions in the midst of grief. Sometimes our decisions are self-destructive and not in our own best interest. Letting go of a dream is already a big adjustment for you; don't add more to it by moving across the country, quitting your job, leaving your husband, becoming a Republican if you are a Democrat or becoming a Democrat if you are a Republican, or getting a tattoo on your face. If in a year's time you still want to get that tattoo, quit that job, leave that guy, and shave your hair off, then it may be the right decision for you.

Two of my favorite "death of dreams" books—*Eat, Pray, Love* and *Under the Tuscan Sun*—advise just the opposite.[2] Both stories tell of women whose dreams of happily ever after fell apart, and both women shook up their lives in a big way by switching continents. Travel as healer is a major motif of the memoir section of the Kindle store, so clearly there are times when this not only works out for people, but also results in a best-selling book, a film in which Julia Roberts plays you, and an appearance on *The Oprah Winfrey Show*, so who on earth am I to judge? I will tell you that a one-month trip was a part of my postpartum dream plan, but it's one thing to visit friends in San Francisco and Washington, D.C., or even to visit India, Italy, and Bali, and another thing to sell your house, sell all your possessions, and move to a country where you have no job, no community, and no support system. While it may be the right choice for some, I think there is something to be said for not adding to the uprooted, lost, and alone feeling by exacerbating it. At the very least, be sure to give big and somewhat irrevocable decisions time and space. Bali and Italy will always be there—well, except Venice. If it's Venice you want to go to, then maybe you'd better book the tickets.

One Thing Leads to Another

When we are grieving something, other grief is likely to get activated. Other losses from the past—other dreams, deaths, and disappointments—are going to come up, which can compound our grief, especially if we didn't fully allow ourselves to grieve the past. My grief was compounded by my looking at other losses and concluding that I was especially unlucky. I may have uttered the word *cursed* a time or two when I evaluated all the losses from my past. I would not advise this. It is not true and doesn't help. But when you are grieving, you can expect that all the other losses you haven't dealt with are going to rear their ugly heads. For me, all the grief around my emotionally absent dad and my lonely childhood came up, and they came up as anger and outrage and an endless chorus of "Life's not fair."

Watch for Addictive Behaviors

Oftentimes, the relentless pursuit of a dream takes on a kind of manic quality. There may have been an almost addictive relationship to action, where you conditioned yourself to believe that as long as you were actively trying to make the dream a reality, you were keeping depression at bay. However, now that the dream is dead, there is nothing you can do anymore. Your addiction to action may tell you that if you just take action—doing anything—you will feel better. In order to cope, you might turn to sex, exercise, shopping, video games, food, drugs, or alcohol, and you might do so to a dangerous degree. Addictive behaviors, like numbing, ultimately don't make the pain go away because we need to keep going back to that behavior again and again. Addiction and compulsive behaviors have zero power to heal grief and, in fact, only prolong the pain and exacerbate it. If you see you are filling the grief space with addictive behaviors, it is important to seek help.

How Long Does Grief Last?

First, let me answer that question honestly. The answer is, I don't know. Grief is unique to each person. There is a purpose to our grief, there are tasks that grief requires us to achieve, and there is no specific timeline to do these things. Once we call the "time of death" (which can take some time to really do), then we experience the feelings of grief that come with a death. And beyond that, we have to reorient our life without the dream. This is not easy stuff. Finally, we come to terms with the loss, say good-bye to the dream, and find some peace from the loss. The road from saying good-bye to finding some peace is long enough that you will want to pack a bag and some snacks. This isn't quick-fix territory. I know you want to know how long this process will take. My unsatisfactory answer is that it will take as long as it takes. I don't have a timetable to tell you how long your grief will last or a crystal ball to tell you when it won't hurt as much as it does today, but I can assure you that that time will come. Active grieving does end; for me, it was a year and a half before it wasn't the first thing I thought about in the morning and the last thing I thought about when I went to sleep. A therapist I saw to help me with my grief told me, "You will get through this," and I didn't know that when I walked through her doors. Now I see that the pain of that very grief has made me stronger and more able to risk, love, endure, and overcome—things I didn't really know how to do before. It will take as long as it takes. And in the meantime, you can't compare your grief to others' grief. Phrases like "But it only took Jennie a month," or "In five weeks Bob was dating again, so I should be back out there" have no place in your grief process. Comparison is of no value. You can't hurry through it. There are no shortcuts. There is no way through it but through it.

You have just given up something major, this is a big loss for you, and it is normal to feel sad, numb, angry, enraged. Don't let anyone tell you that it's not. But at a certain point, you should start to notice a change in the intensity and the pervasiveness of the feelings. If you don't, and the feelings of grief only intensify, then it is likely a sign that the grief has turned into complicated grief or something more serious that needs care and attention. We will discuss that more later.

The Inside Story

Margaret was a graduate student just a few classes away from graduating when the chair of her department made a pass at her, making it clear that he wanted a sexual relationship with her. When Margaret declined his advances, her hopes for finishing her graduate thesis were dashed. Margaret tried every avenue within her university to find another adviser, but nothing worked.

> I was at the mercy of an institution. No one there seemed to really care what had happened. They just wanted me to go away. After telling my story to the head of the department, then the associate dean, then the dean, then human resources, and then student services, I felt as if I had been assaulted over and over again. There was no one in my corner. And there would be no justice, either. That led to hopelessness. When I was finally told that the only way I could get my degree would be to suck it up and work with the professor who harassed me, I knew I would never get that degree. I was emotionally spent. There was no way I had it in me to start another art history program and do it all over again. I looked into trying to transfer credits to another institution, but because the school I was in was on a quarter system and most schools are on a semester system, most of my credits would not have transferred. It really did seem hopeless at that point.

Margaret turned to attorneys, but she was met with the unbearable news that there was nothing she could do and that if she wanted to get her degree, she would have to start all over again at another university. The grief that overtook her was paralyzing. She had invested years into her education, and if she wasn't going to graduate, what exactly could she do with this entire coursework? She was so paralyzed by the reality of the situation that she couldn't move.

Margaret was ashamed of her feelings and her situation. She blamed herself and was uncomfortable sharing her anger, rage, sadness, and depression with anyone. She attempted to repress her feelings, but the more she repressed them, the more depressed she grew. She cycled through her feelings over and over again. She turned to food as a source of comfort, thinking, *If I can't have what I want, I will give myself what I want.* "On any given day I could also feel deep sadness, anger, and a horrible sense of defeat," she says. "For me it was too much to bear some days (most days). I think the way I got through the early days of it was to not let myself feel too much for too long. I got through each day: I did what needed to be done (like feeding and walking the dogs, cooking dinner, doing laundry). But I didn't do much real living during that time. I was just surviving."

Margaret felt like she should be over it already. "It had been a year, and I still felt as sad as the day I withdrew from my school," she says. She isolated herself and then shamed herself for her perfectly natural feelings, wondering, *How could I have gotten myself into this situation? What did I do wrong? Did I encourage him in some way? Am I to blame? How could I have been so stupid, so blind?* This only aggravated her grief and ultimately prolonged the process.

I did what I could to feel better. I saw a variety of healers. I tried hypnotherapy. I went to regular therapy. I wrote in my journal daily. I also took a few classes (unrelated to art history). I watched my therapeutic TV (lots of British dramas). I also started doing Pilates and getting regular massages. It helped to have warm and nurturing people around me.

This grief was worse for me than deaths I had known. I was really, really sad when my mother died. And I miss her still. There is a quote that says, "Death ends a life, not a relationship." I still have so many happy memories of my mother. I feel her presence sometimes. I can find joy in knowing she was here and she lived a good life. The same is not true with the death of my dream.

The Therapy Couch

The norms around the duration of grief are extremely culturally sensitive. Monica McGoldrick et al., in *Living Beyond Loss: Death in the Family*, write: "Every culture throughout history has had its own ways of mourning. Over time and through immigration and contact between different groups in the United States, mourning patterns of groups have changed and continue to change all the time. Yet values and practices regarding bereavement still vary in profound ways, so clinicians should be careful about the definition of 'normality' in assessing families' responses to death."[3] McGoldrick et al. explain that an Egyptian mother's reaction to the loss of her child is to remain mute and withdrawn for seven years. A Balinese mother would do just the opposite; as a means of protecting themselves from illness and sorcery, the women would work to be as cheerful and upbeat as possible. In Greece and Italy, women who lose their spouses very often spend the rest of their lives wearing black, sartorially signifying their grief. Women in some regions of India have infamously thrown their bodies on top of their dead husband's funeral pyre. Latin Americans tend toward verbal and extroverted grief, while British families emphasize decorum and keeping their grief a private affair. McGoldrick et al. explain that "The dominant North American norm is that a certain, moderate level of expression, and even depression, is required, but that this should last only for a 'reasonable' period of time—perhaps a year or two for the death of a close relative.[4] In other cultural contexts, the rules for mourning are profoundly different."[5]

Monica McGoldrick and Froma Walsh believe that the following tasks are necessary for adaptation to a loss (a death) within a family:

1. Accept the reality of the loss and share it.

2. Have an experience of sharing the loss with others via rituals, such as

funerals and memorials, and put the loss into the context of the rest of your life.

3. Make the necessary shifts in critical roles in the family to compensate for the loss.

4. Find a way to reinvest in other relationships and in the future.[6]

You have the same tasks, even though your grief may not be about the loss of a loved one. You still have to accept the reality of the loss of this dream, share this loss, accept this loss into the context of your life, make shifts in your life, adjust and reformat your daily life without the dream taking the space it once did, and find new goals, interests, and hopes. Those things sound simple enough, and yet they aren't so easy to manage. Know that. Accept that. Give yourself time. Know that you will get there. And know that you aren't alone in this and that if you need help, there is help.

Acute Grief

If your grief is so pervasive and overwhelming that you aren't able to go to work or get dressed or eat or pay your bills or take care of yourself in basic ways, and you feel so locked into your mourning that you aren't able to do anything, your grief may have grown more complicated. You might be suffering from what we in the mental health field call "complicated grief" (which is a pretty lame name, as all grief is complicated) or "prolonged grief" (which is also a poor description, as there isn't one universal description of how long grief should last).

Acute grief is what happens immediately after a loss. It is the totally consuming and painful state that eclipses the ability to feel anything other than the loss. Over time, as the tasks of grief are accomplished, we begin to experience other emotions independent of the loss. Feelings of joy, happiness, and pleasure start to surprise us and sneak in. We might begin to feel relief that the dream is over and that the worst is behind us. We might start to have a sense of acceptance about the situation and begin to experience a desire to make meaning out of the loss. But for some of us, these changes do not come. And this kind of complicated grief makes it harder to move on.

A complicated grief response to a dream is likely to be characterized by an avoidance or refusal to be around anything that reminds you of your dream, a feeling that your life is totally devoid of meaning without your dream, or a withdrawing from relationships and activities that you had previously enjoyed. It may even include a feeling that life is not worth living without the dream. As I've already warned, if you are experiencing suicidal thoughts, it is extremely important to seek help, to share those thoughts with a trusted family member or friend, and to consult a mental health professional. If you feel you may act on those feelings, then it is time to call 911 or seek out emergency psychiatric care. Loss of a dream is devastating, and it can feel as if you will never feel differently, but if you hurt yourself, you can't get to the next happy—and, dear one, you deserve to get to the other side.

If you are feeling more and more grief, and it isn't lessening, and you are isolating more and more and not able to do things you need to do (work, pay bills, take care of yourself, sleep, or eat), then it is time to get some help. In chapter 6 (feel free to sneak ahead), I am going to talk about the importance of seeking help and support as a way of managing your grief even if you aren't experiencing complicated grief; however, if you are experiencing the following, it is important to get help right away.

- You are unable to think about anything other than the loss of your dream.
- The grief has made you isolate and you have no support system.
- Your grief has impaired your ability to care for yourself. If you feel like you just aren't coping well and aren't functioning well and are unable to take care of yourself, then it is time to ask for help.
- You feel that your life is not worth living without the dream.
- You are feeling hopeless.
- You have suicidal thoughts or fantasies.
- You have a plan to kill yourself.

As a therapist, I am not a big one for diagnosing. I think that the American Psychiatric Association's *Diagnostic and Statistical Manual of Mental Disorders (DSM-5)* has its place in the life of a clinician,[7] but when it comes to grief, I see the grief reaction as a crisis and *not* a diagnosis—even if your grief has gotten complicated. You are not sick or crazy or ill because your grief is stuck; it's just where you are. I am not telling you there is something wrong with you if you have any of these symptoms; I am just saying that if you are having trouble moving through grief—if you are in such despair that you can't function, if you are isolating absolutely, and if you have suicidal ideation or especially if you have a plan to kill yourself—it is time to get some help.

The Inside Story

HOW MY GRIEF GOT COMPLICATED
AND HOW IT GOT ME INTO THERAPY

The day when I said I was done trying to conceive was hard, but six months later, the grief really took over. It was a winter day when I sat in the parking lot of a shopping center with my Prius facing Rose Nail Salon, Peet's Coffee, and Pavilions grocery store when my grief moved from numbness into all the feelings I had been repressing. Instead of grabbing a cart and doing my shopping, I was frozen in the car. I started to cry. It was as if something had broken and I had sprung a leak, and I feared that I might not ever stop crying. Tears emerged like hiccups. Judgment was replaced by the fear that I would never stop crying. I called my then-husband, but my message went to voice mail. I looked at the names in my cell phone and wondered who would be home, up, and not working, and who wouldn't be too freaked out by the fact that I couldn't stop crying. The only person who met all of those qualifications was my friend Loretta, who had just moved to Sacramento and knew the pain of not having children come to you easily. And, I had racked up plenty of "it is my turn to cry" credits in the midst of all the hand-holding I did for her during her move.

"Hiya," my singsongy greeting belied my pain. "It's me. Are you busy?" I asked out of politeness knowing that even if she was busy, I was going to talk anyway. I could feel the start of a temper tantrum. For months I had held it together and acted like an adult, and I couldn't do it anymore. "I want what I want, and I don't want what I have. I thought I was going to get what I want, and I didn't want to come back here." Tears and snotty snorts punctuated my sentence.

"I, uh . . . I can't stop crying, and I am crying when I am out in public now. I can't seem to hold it in anymore. I am leaking and I am scared. I just can't do anything other than be sad."

"Oh, honey," Loretta cooed in a way that reminded me she *was* a mother. We sat in silence as I cried. Then she told me that she knew this pain and that maybe I should get some help. As a therapist, I knew she was right; I needed someplace to take my pain. You would think that the first place I would go with my pain was to a therapist—being one myself—but it wasn't. To tell you the truth, it didn't occur to me for a long time that I needed to talk to a professional about my pain and grief. You see, somehow I had mistakenly conceptualized *my* therapy as a way to deal with my past and how it was impacting my present. I didn't see grief in that category, so for some reason it didn't occur to me to go to therapy around my grief, and I dealt with it on my own. You've heard that one about how the cobbler's children have no shoes? Yeah, well, this therapist had no clinical support. When I hung up with Loretta, I immediately searched for a therapist who specialized in grief. I called her and told her, "I am not doing well. I can't stop crying. I can't do the things I need to do. I feel like I am falling apart."

The therapist responded warmly, "I understand. I can help. Can you come in today at ten?"

Movie Rx

First off, let me say I am a bit of a crier when it comes to movies. I don't just cry at *Love Story* or *The Way We Were* or epics that are intended to turn you into a sobbing idiot. No, I can, if in the right mood, cry at almost any film. I have even been known to cry during trailers. I am a sucker for that swelling music they use to hype up your hippocampus. I frequently cry at comedies. Some comedies even bring me to the crazy-face crying. You know the kind? It is the kind of crying where you don't just have a few tears rolling down your face, but rather you are making scrunched-up, ugly crying faces and may have completely destroyed all the eye makeup you put on for the evening. You don't even want to see me at the end of *My Big Fat Greek Wedding*. You remember when the Greek father gives the toast at the end?

I am a wreck at that point, sobbing not just at the father's love for his daughter, but also sobbing because my own father didn't toast me at my wedding. It takes me eight Kleenexes and a bottle of Lancôme eye makeup remover (or some Windex) to put myself back together after that scene. I know you may not be as cinematically sensitive or as prone to waterworks when watching *Tommy Boy* as I am, but even so, when you are in active grief, it is never a good time to watch a marathon of *Up, The Bridges of Madison County, Beaches, Bambi, Old Yeller,* and *Brian's Song.*

As I was preparing for this chapter, I watched *Steel Magnolias* and *Terms of Endearment,* thinking I was going to use them as examples of the stages of grief, and if you want to, I suppose you could watch them. These movies definitely do show the stages of grief. Sally Field and Shirley MacLaine earned those Oscars showing us what grief looks like: angry, sad, irrational, switching between denial and deal making and back to sad. But you know that. You have read this chapter, you are in grief, and the truth is, my inner Glinda the Good Witch would rather have you see movies that make you laugh and comfort and console you. So this chapter's film isn't really a film recommendation; it is more of a warning about being careful with what books you read, what films you see, and what TV shows you watch.

Even though I have come so far with my infertility grief, movies can still retrigger it. So, even though my grief is no longer active, I still am sensitive to this wound, and I do my very best to avoid films in which there are forty-somethings who accidentally and easily get pregnant. *This Is 40* was not a comedy for me, and films in which old infertile women are alone and sad because of their barrenness are not movies I should ever see. I would no more watch *The Odd Life of Timothy Green* or *Juno* than I would jump into a tank of hungry sharks. Why? I am not going to poke a flaming-hot stick into a healing wound. I just won't.

When dealing with the suckiness of grief, it is time be careful about what you watch. Remember how I advised you to be extra kind to yourself? This is what I mean. Find a movie review site, such as Rotten Tomatoes or Moviefone, and before you go to a theater, read the write-ups. The moment you read something that makes your throat choke and your eyes burn and your stomach clench, stay away. There is no purpose in watching films that are going to make you feel worse. Don't watch *Love Story, The Way We Were, Bambi, Revolutionary Road, Terms of Endearment, Steel Magnolias,* or *A Single Man.* Just don't. Instead try *Groundhog Day, Bridesmaids,* or *Best in Show.*

SELF-HELP SUGGESTIONS

- [ ] What did you believe about grief before you started to feel it?

- [ ] Which of the stages of grief are the easiest for you to accept? Denial, anger, negotiation/deal making, sadness, or acceptance?

- [ ] Which of the stages of grief are simply intolerable for you? Are you okay with sadness but not with anger, or vice versa? The ones you are not okay with are the ones you need to make special room for.

- [ ] Do you see how your grief moves and changes for you? How it is like the weather? It is helpful to notice how grief changes, and how from day to day it is not exactly the same. Grief is not a static state, and knowing that, you can see how you are moving through it and that where you are today will not be where you are next week or month or year. Where is your grief now? Where was it yesterday? How has it changed?

- [ ] If you aren't a journal keeper, this might be a good time to become one. Studies show that people who journal have higher immunity and more resistance to illness. However, that isn't the reason I am recommending it. It might be helpful to simply chart your process. How do I feel today? Chart it. Then look back and see how not every day is the same. It is important for you to see that the grief isn't locked in and unchanging.

- [ ] What is your belief about how long grief lasts?

- [ ] What is grieving the death of your dream teaching you about yourself? What are you discovering about yourself through grief that surprises you? Things like "I thought this would kill me, and it didn't."

☐ Do you have other losses that you endured? How is the grief with the dream different from other losses? How is it harder, easier, the same? For me, grieving the dream was harder, as I was grieving for things I hadn't known. Real joy, love, and tangible memories were a comfort for me as I grieved my grandmother; the same was not true for the dream of being a mother.

☐ Write up a eulogy for your dream. What was the life of your dream? What do you want people to know about it? What were the favorite or funny stories of your dream? Do you want to have a wake for your dream? Do you want to meet friends at a bar and tell your stories and toast to your lost dream? Do you want to write a letter to your dream and then burn the letter in the fireplace? If you were going to write up a memorial statement about your dream, what would you want people to know about it? What needs to be remembered? Do you want to create a ritual where you bury some symbol of the dream?

☐ Is there a blame story to your grief? You may need to tell that story over and over, and that's okay. If, however, the story gets into self-blame, then I'd like you to tell a new story, a story that includes "I did the best I could do."

☐ Is this grief bringing up old griefs for you? The reemergence of past losses, disappointments, and griefs not fully experienced is to be expected. When I grieved the end of trying to conceive, the grief around my childhood and around my father came back up to the surface. All of a sudden, I wasn't grieving just the loss of a child; I was starting to grieve my childhood. (Thank goodness for therapy for helping me to sort through all that.)

☐ Do you have a mythic, archetypal, imaginary "good mother" to call on to counter your internal General MacArthur? You need someone who might tell General MacArthur to shut up when he tells you to stop your bellyaching. Think of your favorite good mother features in your own mother, in literature, in a favorite aunt or grandmother, in film. If you don't have one to call on, create one.

☐ How are you being kind to yourself in your grief? What is your self-care treatment plan? How are you taking care of your body, heart, soul?

☐ Taking care of your physical self is important in dealing with the pain of grief. What good things are you doing for your body? What does your diet look like? It's hard to help a grieving brain on a diet of Skittles and Cocoa Puffs. Is there any small change you could make to take better physical care of yourself? Are you moving at all? Could you try a walk? Some yoga? A Pilates class? Are you receiving any physical touch? Try a massage, a bath, asking for some hugs or a hand to hold. Are you spending any time in nature? Are there any live plants or flowers in your space? Are you spending any time with animals?

☐ Are you setting reasonable and moderate expectations for yourself? How are you moderating your expectations? Are you tending to yourself and your broken heart the way you would to your ten-year-old self?

☐ Has a comforting/self-soothing mantra emerged for you as you grieve? It can't be someone else's platitude; it has to be yours, and it can't trigger a "that's bullshit" response in you. It might be something from your faith or a favorite phrase of a grandmother or friend.

☐ Are you having an escape fantasy? Do you dream of an *Eat, Pray, Love* or *Under the Tuscan Sun* getaway to soothe your grief? If you can't pull that off, a weekend away might be a good thing. Where would you want to go? What would you want to do when you got there? Even planning an imaginary trip on your favorite travel website can be healing. Looking at a desire to be in a different place is your psyche saying, "I don't want to stay in this pain forever. I want to move on and get to the other side." That's a good thing.

☐ Are you drawn to things that you weren't drawn to before? Are you thinking about getting a dog, reading different kinds of books, or watching different kinds of TV shows? This is important to notice. This is life creeping in. Don't make a big deal of it. Just notice— notice that something, even though it may feel totally inconsequential, is starting to emerge.

☐ If you are experiencing acute grief, do not try to manage it on your own. This is a time for you to get help from others. Please sneak ahead to chapter 6 to see how to find a therapist; if you feel you are in danger, let the therapist know that right away.

☐ If you feel you are in immediate danger, it is best to call 911 or go to the nearest emergency room and let them know that you feel unsafe.

chapter 5

The Ugly Stepsiblings of Emotions

Envy, Fear, Shame, and Other Stinking Thinking That Happens While You Are Minding Your Own Business and Trying to Move On and Let Go

"Unexpressed emotions will never die. They are buried alive and will come forth later in uglier ways."

>> **Sigmund Freud**

If life were fair, during your grieving you would be visited by angels, fairies, and unicorns to aid you in your agony, and they would come bearing a big vat of calorie-free yet taste-rich fettuccine Alfredo, a Greek chorus to sing you songs about how life is unfair, and a team of people to massage away the pain of that hard truth. What makes grief such a bitch is that what shows up instead are the Ugly Stepsiblings of Emotions: envy, fear, shame, sadness, and anger. We don't want the Ugly Stepsiblings of Emotions anywhere near us. They have warts, they smell bad, they have nasty teeth and hairs on their chinny-chin-chins. When they are with us, we feel like we have to hide, withdraw, and not let people see us. We don't want these Ugly Stepsiblings sitting on the couch, sleeping in our bed, and eating the food in our fridge, but guess what? These emotions are your companions in grief. They are totally normal and necessary reactions, and they're here to stay—at least until you have worked through them. Trust me, things will only get worse if you try to repress these feelings and kick them out of your psyche. The more you repress them—through avoidance, numbing, overworking, overeating, overdrinking, and overshopping—the more the Ugly Stepsiblings push back, getting meaner and louder until you can't do anything because they have taken your energy, your life force, and your dream for life. The result of this sad state of affairs is that you are now facing full-blown depression. My point? These bitches will take you down unless you make space for them.

The Difference between Feelings and Emotions

Before we understand why we have to feel these emotions and feelings, we need to understand the difference between them. Feelings, emotions, thoughts, and beliefs tend to get all smooshed up together so that we aren't even sure which is which. Very often, when I ask a client how they feel, they will answer with what they are *thinking*. They describe, in a seemingly emotionally disconnected way, something really painful, saying things like, "My mother walked out right in the middle of Thanksgiving dinner," or "My boss had his secretary call to tell me I didn't get the promotion." I can tell that these explanations are disconnected from the feelings the incidents caused. In response, I might say, "I can't tell how you feel about this. What are you feeling?" I often get a blank look and a tirade of additional dispassionate thoughts that don't get us any closer to the feeling that underlies the thought.

· · ·

"We were talking the other evening about the phrases one uses when trying to comfort someone who is in distress. I told him that in English we sometimes say, 'I've been there.' This was unclear to him at first— I've been where? But I explained that deep grief sometimes is almost like a specific location, a coordinate on a map of time. When you are standing in that forest of sorrow, you cannot imagine that you could ever find your way to a better place. But if someone can assure you that they themselves have stood in that same place, and now have moved on, sometimes this will bring hope.

'So sadness is a place?' Giovanni asked.

'Sometimes people live there for years,' I said."

>> **Elizabeth Gilbert, *Eat, Pray, Love***

I know that it's difficult to differentiate emotion and feeling. Even though I am a therapist, I sometimes catch myself smooshing feelings, emotions, and thoughts into the same thing. If my significant other, Keith, asks me how I am, and I am not fine, it is rare that I tell him how I am feeling. I don't, for example, say, "I'm frustrated." I usually start with a soliloquy on the stimuli that led to the thoughts that preceded the feeling. "I couldn't find my keys, and there was horrible traffic, and then I didn't have time to get coffee, and by the time I got to the office, my patient was standing there waiting for me, and it was so embarrassing." What I am telling him is that there was an outside stimuli/event (loss of keys and traffic), and that my body responded to those stressors with emotions of fear (my breathing changed, my muscles tightened, and I got a sick feeling in my stomach), and my subjective experience of that emotion were the feelings of frustration and embarrassment.

First, let's start ferreting out what emotions are. Some are an emergency warning system that tells us we are facing a perceived threat. The emotion alarm often goes off before we have had time to think about the threat. This loud, intense, short-term high-alert warning system gives us a chance to respond, to act. It's physical—fight or flight. Once the emotion alarm goes off, we start to make sense of and react to the emotion. We start to *feel*. It is possible, due to trauma responses or repeated ignoring of emotions, to be unable to feel in response to an emotion, which is decidedly *not* a good thing. Can you ever imagine removing the obnoxious buzzer from your smoke detector? And can you further imagine hearing the alarm and not responding to it (i.e., not feeling)? The results could be catastrophic, just as they can if we don't know our emotions and ignore our feelings. According to Karla McLaren, an author who writes extensively on feelings and emotions, an *emotion* is a physiological experience (or state of awareness) that gives you information about the world, and a *feeling* is your conscious awareness of the emotion itself.[1]

More differences between the two: Emotions tend to be experienced in universal ways (which makes sense, since they're intense and short-acting alarms) while feelings are experienced in a highly personal, subjective, and idiosyncratic way, since we can interpret and act out our emotions in different ways. Fear, the *emotion,* is a racing heart, tense muscles, dilated pupils; the *feeling* may be terror if we're reacting to a threat, as in, *Run! Here comes Godzilla.* This feeling may then produce *thoughts,* such as *I'm installing triple reinforced doors, buying a security system, and getting a pit bull.* Feelings, unlike emotions, can be much more long-lasting, which is swell with love, happiness, and contentment, and a little less delightful when they are worry, depression, and bitterness.

What's the Point of These Emotions and Feelings?

The point is that your body is programmed to respond to a loss in this particular way and that you are normal to have the reactions that you are having. We came fully equipped with a brain and a nervous system that allow us to have emotions and feelings, and it is simply part of being human. Emotions and feelings, both the "good" and "bad," are information. According to evolutionary theory, we need emotions like fear to tell us to feel afraid when we see something dangerous so we know to run from it, and we need emotions like pleasure to give us good feelings like love and happiness to motivate us to procreate and survive and do things that give us a better shot at longevity. Emotions are there to tell us we are facing a threat or a source of enjoyment. Feelings are there to give us a way to respond to that threat or source of enjoyment; these are not things we want to shut off.

And, I can hear you: *I don't have the same need early man had for always being alert to a hungry lion.* No, of course you don't. The loss of a dream isn't a predator, but it is a loss that our body and brain are both reacting to for a reason. Can you imagine the consequences of not being able to detect heat, pain, and other stimuli that could cause your body physical harm? Bad, right? The danger of not being able to access your emotions or feel your feelings is similarly grim—a life without love, passion, bliss, contentment, or gratitude, a life without being able to be angry over injustices, a life without "the thrill of victory and the agony of defeat." Can you, or would you want to, imagine being indifferent to the loss of a loved one? Of course not. You have emotions and feelings, and they are there for a reason. They are always trying to tell you something.

But I Don't Want to Feel

I remember a cheesy Morris Albert song from my youth, "Feelings," in which he sang "Feelings, wo-o-o feelings." I've often thought he could be saying, "Woe, woe, woe, feelings," wishing that he didn't still have feelings of love for the woman who had left him and that he could escape his sadness. I get it. I have heard the following words out of myriad people's mouths: "I just don't want to feel. Feelings suck. I would rather think; thinking doesn't hurt. I want a feelingectomy. Why should I feel? There is no point to feelings." When they are good, emotions and feelings can be very good, but when they are bad, they can be scary, isolating, and overwhelming. And of course, as a therapist, I know that an excess and distortion of emotions can lead to feelings of depression, anxiety, and irrational fears that manifest as phobias, so I take seriously these people's thoughts on feelings. I empathize with the desire not to feel. I don't tell them how miserable they would be without feelings—and they would be. As crappy as feelings like hurt, disappointment, sadness, rage, anger, and envy can be, it is much worse to feel nothing. Feeling nothing feels . . . like *nothing.* Without feelings, we are Pinocchio or Data from *Star Trek.* We are machines, or puppets, and all Pinocchio and Data want is to have real human emotions and the resulting feelings. Yes, I know, they aren't grieving, so it is easy for them to say that. But try to remember that without feelings, we'd have no happiness, contentment, or love, and see if that changes how you feel about feelings.

Not All of Us Know How to Feel

Some of us aren't exactly good at handling our emotions and feelings to begin with. If that is the case with you, it might be especially difficult to deal with the onslaught of emotions and feelings that are overtaking you as you deal with the grief of giving up on your dream. How does someone become bad at responding to their emotions? Patient after patient tells me that anger, sadness, and fear were not welcomed in their childhood homes. They got the message that their parents, family, and friends would not like it, or maybe even *them,* if they were to express anger or sadness. So they were taught that they'd better stuff, hide, repress, bury, and otherwise zip up and tuck away these socially unacceptable emotions and try not to feel them, much less express them.

When a patient apologizes for their emotions and resulting feelings, I will stop and ask them, "What were your family's rules about this emotion?" Every family has rules. Some families are totally okay with anger, and others not so much. My family's rules were that my parents were allowed anger, but I wasn't. Sadness was definitely not allowed. And in some families, you might be surprised to learn, happiness isn't allowed or encouraged either. It wasn't really welcomed in my household. "Wipe that smile off your face" was one way that happiness was discouraged. Another way was the subtle message of, "How nice for you that this good thing happened"—a message that teaches you that it is better to keep your happiness to yourself. If you were too happy, that might create envy in someone else. The emotional range of what is allowed in families can be pretty limited. Is it any surprise that so many of us ignore our emotions and couldn't identify an emotion (and tell someone what we're feeling) if it hit us on the head?

If, like me, you didn't have healthy models for dealing with emotions, or ways to learn how to identify your feelings, or healthy ways of regulating feelings, it makes dealing with grief even more difficult. You are more likely to believe that you can't cope with your grief and that you have to play hot potato with the emotions you have in response to the loss. You may get rid of them, deny them, numb them, or displace them onto someone else. Or you might be so flooded by them that you can't function socially or can't delay expressing the accompanying feelings in healthy and appropriate ways. When therapists talk about one's ability to deal or not deal (sounds like a game show starring Howie Mandel) with our emotions, we talk about our capacity for *affect regulation*. Affect regulation is how we deal with emotions in a way that allows us to feel what we feel in an authentic and spontaneous reaction, and also delay the expressing of feelings in a way that is socially appropriate. If you didn't have models for dealing with emotions when they came, this is something you may need to learn (and this is something that therapy can most definitely help you with).

If I Feel It, Something Bad Will Happen

Some people are afraid of their emotions for the same reason we are told not to make faces as kids: "Don't cross your eyes, or they'll stick like that." We are told, in so many words, that if we allow ourselves to feel emotions like sadness, anger, fear, or envy, they will stick and we will remain in that state forever—or at least have that emotion define us negatively as people. So we become afraid to feel, and we repress and push down our emotions, and they build up and build up, and we ignore them and keep on repressing them until they build up like Mount Vesuvius. One day, it all blows up and makes a mess and can be seriously destructive. Repression of any emotion is more destructive than healthy expression of the same emotion.

And, yes, of course, emotions can become habitual. We can learn to respond to every stressor with one emotion only—anger or fear, for example. That leads to an emotional imbalance. In this case, it can be very helpful to go into therapy to see why you only get access to this single reaction. But just experiencing anger today, just having normal outrage at feeling a sense of injustice or the unfairness of life, is not going to get you stuck in the stage. Repressing that same anger is likely to be more destructive than feeling it. (And note that I am not talking about *acting* on the anger. I am talking about *feeling* it.) Keeping those feelings buried is toxic and causes all manner of negative and destructive things like depression, self-loathing (for feeling there's something the matter with you for feeling what you do), guilt and shame (I shouldn't feel that), projection (I can't feel that, so I am going to project it onto another person, as in "You're the one who's angry, not me!"), and alcohol or other drug misuse (I do feel it and I shouldn't, so I have to numb out this feeling with this substance or behavior).

We do all kinds of stuff to avoid feelings. The basic formula for no feeling goes like this: I experience X emotion. If I feel X, it is intolerable. So I can't feel X. I need to do something to not feel X. I will introduce Y to not feel X. Only X keeps coming back, and I need to do more and more of Y to avoid X. Y can be many things. Y can be avoid, deny, repress, numb, use drugs, displace, work, drink, eat, have sex, self-mutilate, sleep. None of these behaviors make the pain go away for good.

The Costs of Numbness

I can't stand it. I'll die. It will kill me. I have heard it all and, dear one, I have seen it all, and I am here to tell you that emotions can't kill you. It's the decisions we make about them that can kill us. Your mother may have told you to turn that frown upside down, and your dad may have told you to go back into your room until you could come out with a smile on your face, but let me assure you that the emotions they were asking you to cover up are solely threat detective systems. It isn't the alarm that's bad; it is what you do in response to the alarm that can get you into trouble. Anger as an alarm can't do anything; it's how you express anger that has the potential to get you into trouble. Even love can be expressed inappropriately. It's not your emotion or how you feel it that is the problem; it's the way you express that feeling that can cause trouble. No, of course it isn't okay to vent your anger at everyone and throw a hissy fit and break all of your plates (well, it might be okay as long as you aren't hurting yourself and others, and they aren't your great-great-grandmother's antique Limoges dinner plates), but it's also not okay to express your love of humanity by kissing perfect strangers. Judging your feelings is not helpful. "This one is good, this one is bad, this one is stupid" is going to gum up the works and force you to deny and repress feelings that have the "bad" label attached—which will likely lead to numbing. When you numb one emotion, you numb all of them, and you don't want to impact your ability to feel the good stuff, do you?

Hi, Emotions and Feelings, Nice to Meet You

You know how you can buy field guides to birds, plants, and trees in order to know the lay of the land in a given area? Well, this chapter is a sort of field guide to your emotional life as you navigate the terrain of grief. It's a kind of meet and greet of grief feelings. You are definitely feeling something in response to the loss of your dream, and I want to help you get to know what you are feeling and understand that it is normal and make space for it. To repeat: When we don't feel them fully, the feelings actually end up taking more space, and the more we avoid looking at them, the scarier they become. Awareness is a much better path. Matthew Lieberman, PhD, professor at UCLA and the author of *Social: Why Our Brains Are Wired to Connect*, conducted a study published in *Science Magazine* that examined the reactions of people's brains to feelings. When watching people's brains (through MRIs) as they talked about how they felt, he discovered that the simple activity of naming the feeling and talking about it could activate the prefrontal cortex while simultaneously suppressing the part of the brain that makes us feel distressed.[2] What this means is that by simply naming and voicing how we feel, we can change how we feel for the better. Just the action of putting the feelings into words has the potential to change your brain state and change how you feel. So it seems wise to say, "Hello, anger. I am really feeling you." That is, if you can name that feeling.

Name That Feeling

When working with kids, it isn't uncommon to use a feeling chart to help them find a way to talk about their emotional life. You show the child the chart of emoticons and ask them to identify the feelings they have felt in the day. The child will review their day and circle the feeling faces that they identified with. You see, we don't come into this life knowing what emotions are; we have to learn this stuff, and some of us learn the periodic table or the names of all the Kardashian clan more readily than we learn about our emotional life. If we don't have the words for an emotion or never had anyone in our life mirror our experience, we need to learn the language of our feelings. I want to help you learn a bigger vocabulary of feelings. It will help.

According to the Center for Nonviolent Communication, the feelings we have when we are getting what we want include those listed on page 88.[3]

As this is a book that deals with the death of dreams, and we are still in the early chapters, it is likely that you are feeling more of the feelings that come when your needs *aren't* satisfied. Feelings when your needs are not satisfied include those listed on page 89.[4]

FEELINGS WE HAVE WHEN WE ARE GETTING WHAT WE WANT

AFFECTIONATE
compassionate
friendly
loving
open hearted
sympathetic
tender
warm

ENGAGED
absorbed
alert
curious
engrossed
enchanted
entranced
fascinated
interested
intrigued
involved
spellbound
stimulated

HOPEFUL
expectant
encouraged
optimistic

CONFIDENT
empowered
open
proud
safe
secure

EXCITED
amazed
animated
ardent
aroused
astonished
dazzled
eager
energetic
enthusiastic
giddy
invigorated
lively
passionate
surprised
vibrant

GRATEFUL
appreciative
moved
thankful
touched

INSPIRED
amazed
awed
wonder

JOYFUL
amused
delighted
glad
happy
jubilant
pleased
tickled

EXHILARATED
blissful
ecstatic
elated
enthralled
exuberant
radiant
rapturous
thrilled

PEACEFUL
calm
clear headed
comfortable
centered
content
equanimous
fulfilled
mellow
quiet
relaxed
relieved
satisfied
serene
still
tranquil
trusting

REFRESHED
enlivened
rejuvenated
renewed
rested
restored
revived

© 2005 by Center for Nonviolent Communication
Website: www.cnvc.org Email: cnvc@cnvc.org Phone: +1.505.244.4041

FEELINGS WHEN YOUR NEEDS ARE NOT SATISFIED

AFRAID
apprehensive
dread
foreboding
frightened
mistrustful
panicked
petrified
scared
suspicious
terrified
wary
worried

ANNOYED
aggravated
dismayed
disgruntled
displeased
exasperated
frustrated
impatient
irritated
irked

ANGRY
enraged
furious
incensed
indignant
irate
livid
outraged
resentful

AVERSION
animosity
appalled
contempt
disgusted
dislike
hate
horrified
hostile
repulsed

CONFUSED
ambivalent
baffled
bewildered
dazed
hesitant
lost
mystified
perplexed
puzzled
torn

DISCONNECTED
alienated
aloof
apathetic
bored
cold
detached
distant
distracted
indifferent
numb
removed
uninterested
withdrawn

DISQUIET
agitated
alarmed
discombobulated
disconcerted
disturbed
perturbed
rattled
restless
shocked
startled
surprised
troubled
turbulent
turmoil
uncomfortable
uneasy

unnerved
unsettled
upset

EMBARRASSED
ashamed
chagrined
flustered
guilty
mortified
self-conscious

FATIGUE
beat
burnt out
depleted
exhausted
lethargic
listless
sleepy
tired
weary
worn out

PAIN
agony
anguished
bereaved
devastated
grief
heartbroken
hurt
lonely
miserable
regretful
remorseful

SAD
depressed
dejected
despair
despondent
disappointed
discouraged
disheartened

forlorn
gloomy
heavy hearted
hopeless
melancholy
unhappy
wretched

TENSE
anxious
cranky
distressed
distraught
edgy
fidgety
frazzled
irritable
jittery
nervous
overwhelmed
restless
stressed out

VULNERABLE
fragile
guarded
helpless
insecure
leery
reserved
sensitive
shaky

YEARNING
envious
jealous
longing
nostalgic
pining
wistful

Sadness: The Sometimes Accepted Stepsibling

Meet sadness. This probably isn't the first time you've met this "stepsibling." Sadness comes around when we have breakups, disappointments, and deaths. You might feel sadness when you watch sad movies, and maybe you, like me, cry when you see cheesy commercials or when you watch the Olympics, or see something sad on Facebook. Maybe you are okay with that, and maybe you aren't. When you are sad, you cry, hurt, ache, feel loss, and despair. I like to think of sadness as the sometimes accepted stepsibling. There are times we are okay with sadness and times we are less okay. This stepsibling seems to be more acceptable to women than men, especially if there is crying involved. Very often our families were really not okay with this stepsibling. "In my house," says Louise who dealt with the pain of miscarriage, "it was said that you could go somewhere else to get happy. So I grew up replacing sadness with anger. It wasn't until I was pregnant that my hormones overrode that habit, and I began to be more of a crier. I now allow sadness to just be. I understand that it is a natural part of the human existence, and necessary to heal. It's been almost a year since the miscarriage, and I'm still sad. But I've found it's been beneficial in pushing me to be a better mama, to appreciate the happy things."

Even though sadness is sometimes accepted, there is only so long it can stay with us before we are likely telling this emotion that it needs to pack its bags so happiness can take its place in the guest room of our psyche. When sadness wears out its welcome, I hear patients say things like, "But I should be happy. I have so much to be happy about. People are suffering more than me."

Sadness tells us that we cared about our dream—a lot—and that we now feel loss. It allows us time and space to say that this loss is significant to us. If we could let go of our dream and feel nothing, then that would mean that our dream meant nothing to us. When we let go of our dream, sadness is natural, normal, and to be expected.

When we are sad, we don't have energy for things we usually enjoy, and we might feel ennui, tiredness, and lethargy. Yes, sadness impairs our ability to do stuff—no doubt about it. But doesn't that sort of make sense? We poured our heart and soul into this dream, and for now we need to stop business as usual and pause and reflect. When we are sad, we tend to isolate and not want to be around others. This pulling in is twofold: First, when we get hurt physically, our impulse is to pull in and protect the hurt, and that is exactly what we do when we are hurting emotionally: *I hurt. I need to protect myself from further injury.* All of that kind of pulling in is normal and to be expected.

There is, however, a second kind of pulling in that is in response to cultural and family-based rules about sadness. People hate to see us sad, so they tell us to smile. It hurts loved ones to see us hurting, so they tell us to see the positive, only we can't, so we isolate so we don't have to pretend to feel any other way than how we do. We pull in and then feel like we can't come out until we have it all together, and that is no good. The problem with this approach is that isolating can prolong grief. It took me a whole lot of time to get to this point (and hopefully you can benefit from my experience), but it was a major turning point in my grieving when I learned that there were people whom I could be sad around who could let me be sad and didn't need to change how I felt. It was awesome. It was so good that I have made a point to continue to be honest about how I feel around people who can take it, people who can hear, "I'm sad . . . but I still want to meet you for lunch."

Tears: A Symptom of Sadness

What is crying? I know you know what crying looks like. It's when the wet stuff starts coming out of our eyes, and we make ugly faces, and (if you're a woman) we do our best to keep mascara from getting all over our face. There are times when we are okay with our crying and with other people's crying, but there is a limit to what we can take before we decide something is "wrong." My mother had a particularly low tolerance for crying. I remember one time when I was breaking up with a boyfriend, and I couldn't stop crying (in retrospect I am guessing that this endless cry was in fact about an hour in length), and my mother, without any humor, suggested that if I didn't stop crying, she would have to take me to the hospital. Her message to me was: *If you are sad, you are sick, and you'd better stop it now or there are going to be serious consequences.* The sad truth is that her family taught her that she couldn't have emotions or feelings that weren't "okay,"—in other words, those that upset the decorum that her family valued so highly—and she learned that it was preferable—and even a sign of strength—not to express feelings. It's quite a paradox that her daughter spends her days getting people to share their feelings and normalizing their tears.

When people apologize to me for crying—and it happens almost every day in my work as a therapist—I often ask them if they would apologize for sweating in the gym. They usually laugh at the absurdity of that. Can you imagine suggesting to people that they really ought to seal their pores because we are uncomfortable watching them sweat? Well, just as sweating is normal and necessary, so is crying.

The reason my patients apologize for crying is that they got messages in their past that it isn't okay. "If you have to cry, go outside." "Big boys don't cry." "If you are going to cry, I will give you something to cry about." "There's nothing worth crying over." "Don't cry over spilled milk." Sound familiar? The message is simple: Crying is a sign of weakness, and you need to stop or leave.

I wish the following statements were as well known as "Big boys don't cry":

"It is a grave injustice to a child or adult to insist that they stop crying. One can comfort a person who is crying, which enables him to relax and makes further crying unnecessary; but to humiliate a crying child is to increase his pain, and augment his rigidity."
— Alexander Lowen, *The Voice of the Body*

"But a mermaid has no tears, and therefore she suffers so much more."
— Hans Christian Andersen, "The Little Mermaid"

"Heaven knows we need never be ashamed of our tears, for they are rain upon the blinding dust of earth, overlying our hard hearts. I was better after I had cried, than before—more sorry, more aware of my own ingratitude, more gentle."
— Charles Dickens, *Great Expectations*

Many people are afraid of our tears for the same reason they are afraid of our sadness: They fear that we will always feel this way. They are uncomfortable with their own emotional life. They don't know what to say or do for us or how to make it better. They love us, and they don't want us to hurt. I understand this discomfort; I do. So now when someone tells me, "Don't cry," I tell them that crying is good for me, that I am releasing stress hormones, and that I understand that they don't want me to hurt, but the truth of the matter is I do. If you tell them that and they still tell you not to cry, then tell them to call me.

Here are the right things to say to your sadness and tears:

- It is normal for me to feel sadness. Sadness means my dream mattered to me.

- I am not always going to feel this way.

- I understand that you, my sadness, may tell me I need to be alone; that impulse can be self-protective—it can also be untrue.

- Isolating when sad can exacerbate the grief. I don't have to isolate because I am sad. I can feel how I feel *and* be around people.

Anger/Rage

Anger is an Ugly Stepsibling that is not shy. It's hot, heated, fiery, loud, impatient, frustrated, and confrontational. Anger makes vessels dilate, blood pressure rise, and muscles clench. It grunts, growls, snarls, snorts, and bares its teeth. Anger is likely to say things that you don't want to hear. It might lash out and break a plate or pick a fight or use an expletive or two. Unlike sadness, anger has a lot to say and wants to be heard and is not above raising its voice. We *really* don't want anger around. Most people don't like it when we are angry. They're afraid of anger. They want anger to shut up and act nicely and to stuff it. These people say that anger's wrong, dangerous, and destructive, and that it's always bad and never productive. What they're forgetting, and what I want you to remember, is that it's not anger that's bad; it's how it's expressed that can cause the problems that give it its bad reputation.

Anger is a natural response to the loss of a dream. It is a normal reaction to not getting what we wanted most. Our initial anger comes out of a desire to reject the reality of the loss. "This can't be the truth of this. No, no, no!" Anger is a kind of outrage at the truth of where we find ourselves. There may be lots of things we are angry at. We may feel anger at ourselves. We may be mad at others: partners, bosses, parents, and even God. We also can feel anger because this loss is making us reevaluate our worldview, and that leaves us feeling out of control, and out of control is definitely the kind of experience that leaves us humans very pissed off.

> *"Beware of him that is slow to anger; for when it is*
> *long coming, it is the stronger when it comes, and the longer kept.*
> *Abused patience turns to fury."*
> —Francis Quarles

In my work as a therapist, I tend to see two major camps when it comes to anger. The first is the camp that is totally okay with anger and avoids sadness like the plague. (Guess what lies under their anger? That's right. Sadness.) And then there are patients who tell me that they don't do anger. They may consider themselves virtuous, but it is no better to be avoiding anger than it is to *only* do anger. Using anger to cover our sadness, hurt, and fear is no better than not feeling anger at all. Both extremes are a way of not feeling what we feel.

People who are anger averse didn't learn that anger can be healthy and productive. Anger is a stepsister who has had some bad PR. Yes, she can get ugly and destructive, but her righteous indignation and her standing up for what is right has been a powerful force for good. I know, we don't like to give anger the credit for change, but it is anger that makes us fight against what isn't right. Anger, like love, is simply an emotion. The emotion of anger can be profoundly productive, or it can, like all emotions, be expressed in ways that are hurtful to ourselves and others. Even love can be expressed in destructive ways: "I did this because I love you" has motivated all manner of crimes of passion.

Anger gets a bad rap because people do some unspeakably bad things when they are angry, and that is part of what makes us so afraid of it. I am certainly not encouraging you into vengeance, violence, repression, displacement (lashing out at others about something other than what we are really angry about), and/or using and abusing drugs, alcohol, or food as a means of coping with your anger. I want you to have a way to constructively vent your angry feelings. It is okay to yell and scream and have tantrums and be mad at God, fate, or your mother. Just make sure you are in a safe place and only with someone who is able to be there for you in your feelings.

The Upside of Anger

> *"Love implies anger. The man who is angered*
> *by nothing cares about nothing."*
> **—Edward Abbey**

> *"Usually when people are sad, they don't do anything.*
> *They just cry over their condition. But when they*
> *get angry, they bring about a change."*
> **—James Russell Lowell**

Do you remember that movie called *The Upside of Anger*? I love that title. I want you to see that there is a definite upside to the anger you experience in the process of moving on and letting go. Anger wants to help you, to move you, to get you up and out of your pajamas so you can get dressed and say, "No, this is bullshit!" In contrast to the contracting and withdrawing feeling of sadness, anger is physical and energizing. If we make space for our anger, we will see that it allows for movement of our grief. However, if we reject our anger and don't let ourselves feel it or communicate it, then we get stuck in the anger and may become bitter. If we become bitter, we are not getting better; we are no longer responding to the anger at hand, but our entire worldview has been changed in response to the loss. It's better to feel the anger than to have unconscious anger that will impact our ability to move on, let go, and find our next happy. If we get stuck in our anger and don't allow sadness, then we can move into resentment, which is a way of hanging on to our anger. And hanging on to anger is physically destructive. People who experience frequent and high levels of anger experience physical consequences: too much of the stress hormone cortisol, high adrenaline, higher levels of glucose in the blood, more fat in the blood, damage to the artery walls—and all of this can raise your risk of cardiac disease.

I am not ashamed to admit that I had a whole lot of "It ain't fair" temper tantrums. In my anger, I railed against everything that I saw as part of what prevented me from being a mother—my childhood, the traumas that kept me from getting my life together so I could have tried to conceive before I was thirty-five, the lack of medical insurance, the cost of IVF, the doctor who was rude to me, God. *Life's not fair* was the refrain of my anger, and it's true, life *isn't* fair. It helped to vent, to tell my story, to place blame, to be angry at God.

As icky as it felt to feel anger, it moved me out of sadness and was enormously helpful for me in my moving on and letting go and getting to the other side. Feeling anger helped me feel some energy and sense of agency. Getting uptight and outraged helped me feel less down. Even though I wasn't from a family where anger was much allowed, I found that feeling angry felt a whole lot better than feeling sad. Something in the anger allowed me to feel like there was movement, and I wasn't stuck in the wet and lonely sadness anymore. It wasn't good to feel the prickly heat of anger, but it was different, and different meant that I was moving toward acceptance.

Here are the right things to say to your anger:

- You are an important and normal step in my grief.
- I will listen to you and not make you wrong.
- I will express you, because if I don't, you will become stuck in me.
- I will not allow you to take over and be the only emotion I have.
- I will express you in productive and constructive ways.
- If you take over, I will get help (therapy, support group, etc.) to work through you.
- I will see how you are helping me move through this. I will see the upside of my anger.

- I know that it can be easier to be mad at the traffic than at the loss of my dream, but I will look at the real source of the anger and name it and give it space.
- If I misuse alcohol or other drugs, including nicotine, or overeat to not feel the anger, I will seek help, as these coping strategies will do nothing constructive in dealing with the anger.

Fear

This stepsibling has its amygdala (the brain's emotional center) in overdrive: racing heart, pumping lungs, sense organs in high alert, and adrenaline flooding. Fear tells us there is a danger, a threat. Fear might make us freeze, get small, and try to be invisible, or it might have you running the mile faster than the canine action hero Bolt. Either way, fear is telling you that you are at risk and that you have to do something about it and fast—only that ain't necessarily so. Fear is an emotion that needs to be tended to, but some fears are valid and deserving of our attention, and others are not. Fears that come up when we are grieving our dream can be a tricky business. We need to approach this stepsibling and really listen to what the fear is saying: Is this fear real and valid? Fear likes to tell us that it is looking out for our best interest and protecting us from harm, danger, and monsters that go bump in the night. But very often in grief, our fears are a kind of masochism in which we tell ourselves the most monstrous and self-destructive stories. Fear acts as if it is concerned for us as it tells us dreadful stories that involve worst-case scenarios. But is it really? It kind of reminds me of a bratty older sibling who tells us scary stories just before bedtime. As we're struggling with the loss of our dream, this kind of fear can have us asking questions like *What if I am never happy? What if people stop loving me? What if? What if?*

If those "what ifs" aren't addressed, they can leave us feeling hopeless. Okay, so is it really likely that I will never find another job, love, house, passion? Really? Each person I spoke to when writing this book had the "what if I am never happy again?" moment, and every single person has found some unexpected happiness—every one. Yes, I know, this fear wants to tell you that you are especially unlucky and you will be the one exception to the rule. It isn't true. You will be happy again. Challenge the fear, comfort it, hold it in your arms like you would a crying child. "Yes, I know you are afraid that you won't . . . but you will. You will be happy again." Look at each fear and shine a light on it, the way you would for a small child who is sure there is a monster in the closet. To not look at the fear is to let the monster live there, even if the monster is only a figment of our active imagination.

According to *Merriam-Webster* online dictionary, the origin of the noun *fear* is "Middle English *fer,* from Old English *fǣr* sudden danger; akin to Old High German *fāra* ambush and perhaps to Latin *periculum* attempt, peril, Greek *peiran* to attempt. First Known Use: 12th century."[5]

So, inherent in fear is danger but also attempting, trying, and risking. It is important not to let fear stay stuck on the danger side and prevent us from trying again. After a loss, we are more likely afraid to take risks. We are afraid that we are going to be hurt or be disappointed again. Fear tells us not to move, not to risk, that something bad will happen to us if we do.

One of my favorite books by James Hollis, *Finding Meaning in the Second Half of Life: How to Finally, Really Grow Up,* explains that, at the intersection of the unknown, it is normal for fear to pop up its ugly yet self-protective head. Hollis tells us to expect the fear:

> Each morning the twin gremlins of fear and lethargy sit at the foot of our bed and smirk. Fear of further departure, fear of the unknown, fear of the challenge of largeness intimidates us back into our conventional rituals, conventional thinking, and familiar surroundings. To be recurrently intimidated by the task of life is a form of spiritual annihilation. On the other front, lethargy seduces us with sibilant whispers: kick back, chill out, numb out, take it easy for a while . . . sometimes for a long while, sometimes for a lifetime, sometimes a spiritual oblivion. . . . Yet the way forward threatens death—at the very least, the death of what has been familiar, the death of whomever we have been.[6]

When fear is stopping us from acting, he advises us:

> In every decisive moment of personal life, faced with such choices, choose anxiety and ambiguity, for they are developmental, always,

while depression is regressive. Anxiety is an elixir, and depression is a sedative. The former keeps us on edge of our life, and the latter in the sleep of childhood.[7]

As tempting as it is to surrender to the fear of nonaction, we need to expect this stepsister and tell her we understand her warnings and that we are going to act anyway, even though she fears it might all go terribly wrong. We will get that flashlight out for her and face the fear and see that the monsters and predictions she makes for us don't exist.

How to Approach Fear That Comes with Loss of a Dream

- Shine a light on it, bring its "what if?" out of the darkness, and see what the fear is really saying to you.

- Listen to it, ask if it is rational or not.

- Don't let it stop with "what if?" Look and see if the "what if?" is just a way to make yourself more scared and immobilized.

- Burn your "Fearless" bumper sticker. Fear is there and is important.

- Accept that the fear is going to be part of your letting go and moving on—and just living.

- Befriend fear. I used to try to avoid it, and now I welcome it as an expected friend in my journey of risking and moving on. Now, if I am not a little afraid, I know I am not risking and growing.

- Is this fear reasonable and likely? Am I trying to scare myself or prepare myself?

- If the fear is legitimate, then take it seriously and come up with a plan. Any action step is likely to lower the anxiety by a smidgeon. Don't let fear get all Henny Penny on you. If it tells you the sky is falling, then buy an umbrella. The fear will keep nagging at you until you address it. So address it!

- See the fear. Jack Black gave an interview in which he addressed his relationship with fear. He said, "Fear, that's the rocket sauce, that's what pushes you to . . . go to new places."[8] See fear as your friend, as your copilot, and not what keeps you under the covers.

Margaret writes: "I guess the fear is that that was my one opportunity, and it is now gone. Am I too old for success or a career? Did I somehow ruin my one chance?"

Alex says: "I was afraid that since I failed at bringing my big idea to life, I would fail at everything else, too. I was terrified of dating, of looking for a job. It got so bad that I was even afraid to go on a road trip to visit friends. All I could imagine was what would go wrong."

The Unwelcomed Three: Envy, Guilt, Shame

As much as we don't like sadness, anger, and fear, I am about to introduce you to the most despised and unwelcome feelings that come when you are grieving the loss of a dream. I like to think of them as the triumvirate of terror. They are the triple threat of toxicity that we often face when we are grieving the loss of our dream: envy, guilt, and shame. These are emotions that make us feel like crap and ones that we *really* aren't comfortable sharing with others. We would prefer to share our bank balances, talk about our sex life, and tell people how much we weigh before we talk about our envy, guilt, and shame. These three make us feel like we are, as George Thorogood sings, "Bad to the bone." Yet they are a normal part of the grief we feel when we are letting go of a dream and having to function in a world where other people may have exactly the thing that we want. No, you might not want to tell your mother that every time you see your sister gloating over what you have most wanted that you want to kick her in the shins. But these are totally normal feelings, and looking at the reality of what others have (and not idealizing it) will help you move through your envy, guilt, and shame.

Let's meet envy first. Envy is green-eyed and green-faced. She shows up when we are around someone who has what we dreamed of. We might even feel some anger or outrage and sadness when we see that they have it. This is an emotion that we are super-duper not okay with. And if it wasn't bad enough to have envy, it often brings up other unwelcomed emotions: guilt and shame. Guilt arrives on the scene because we feel wrong for feeling envy. Guilt is an icky-sticky feeling that, once in place, can be hard to shake off. Guilt tells us we have done something that we shouldn't have, that it is wrong to feel envy, anger, rage, and outrage and have less-than-lovely thoughts about others who have what we most wanted. Enter shame, stage right. According to author and researcher Brené Brown, shame "is the intensely painful feeling or experience of believing that we are flawed and therefore unworthy of love and belonging."[9] When we feel shame, we want to hide and withdraw. Guilt is the feeling that comes from believing that we did something bad. Shame is the feeling that tells us we *are* bad.

One Final Word on Feeling Feelings . . .
Okay, Maybe a Whole Paragraph

As a therapist, there are some stories I tell more than others, and if you were a client of mine, I promise you I would bring out the "feelings are like weather" story a lot. If you don't remember anything else that I am saying, I want you to take this message from this book and hold on to it. "I feel" may mean to you some kind of truth, so that "I feel fear" means "I will always feel fear." It simply isn't true. Feelings pass like the weather. Today may be storming, but spring is coming, sunshine is coming. Rain and sleet and hail? They all will come, and they will eventually pass, too. Your feelings will also pass. You will not always feel as you do today. Feeling what you feel is what counts, because by feeling it you can move on.

The Inside Story

The Inside Story this time is mine. I really and truly wanted to interview someone to talk to you in gritty and grimy detail about the shame, guilt, and envy that came up when dealing with the loss of a dream. I searched and scoured and put the word out on Facebook and LinkedIn, and I emailed everyone I know and emailed them again and sometimes three times, asking, "Would you help me normalize these feelings by sharing your story?" There weren't many takers. People wrote me back and said things like, "I would prefer to tell you my weight, my Social Security number, and how many people I have slept with."

People were particularly not keen on talking about envy. A rector of an Episcopalian church wrote me a note and told me, "Sure, I know people who are dealing with envy in regards to a loss. Individuals come to mind who have had issues along these lines, but it would be kind of weird for me to point that out to them: 'Hey, you're the envious type.' 'Hey, remember that time you got screwed over and lost out?'"

The few people willing to talk about their envy—and the shame and guilt that went hand in hand with it—told me anecdotes about how hard it was to see others who had what they wanted most. Diego, for example, told me this:

> There was this one guy I competed with who didn't suffer any of the problems I did. He was made for martial arts. He was beautiful to watch. He and I had been on a similar trajectory, but once I quit, he seemed to go the opposite direction. Everything he did was gold. He was invited to prestigious tournaments, landed a big sponsor. The nail in the coffin was when he got tapped to be in a Gatorade ad. I was like, "Seriously? National TV?" I threw my laptop on the floor when I first saw that ad. I had to take it to get the screen repaired, and I was so ashamed of what I had done that I lied to the guys at the shop. I told them it had accidentally fallen off the table.

I asked Diego if he would speak further with me about envy, and then, like all the rest of them, he said yes but then days later emailed to back out. At the end of the day, the only person willing to talk at length about envy was . . . me.

I am mildly terrified to admit my envy and may be sitting under a table as I write this, because I am pretty sure by the end of it you are going to think I am a bad person for what I felt (see how easily the shame kicks in?), but here goes: In the early stages of my grief, when I would manage to pull myself together and get up and get dressed and go to the market or out to brunch, I would inevitably see pregnant women and newborn babies. They are, you may have noticed, a natural part of the world. But to me, they were a personal affront. Every time I saw one, I would get slammed by an envy attack: *Why not me and why them?* I had other meaner and uglier thoughts about why God, or whoever it was who was handing out baby dust or fertility juice, would choose *that* person, who was obviously not as good a parent as I would have been. Seeing a pregnant woman having a bag of Skittles and a Diet Coke as her lunch would throw me into a tizzy tirade in which I would have an internal tantrum that involved lots of four-letter words. Then I would think, *Ooh, it's really not okay to think that about that stranger that way* (guilt). Next I would have a wave of *You are not okay for having this feeling. You are bad-bad-bad. You, Tracey, are a bad person. Oh and speaking of you as bad, clearly there is something wrong with you for not getting what you wanted most* (shame).

It was, I can tell you, awful to have this triumvirate of feelings every time I saw a pregnant person. Once, an acquaintance who had nine children, and who knew I was doing everything in my power to have just one, admitted to me that she regretted having kids and that she took the job she did in order to be away from them. Can you imagine what kind of thoughts that might trigger in someone who has spent more than $100,000 and endured countless painful procedures to have a child?

There were times when I would isolate just so I didn't have to experience this trio of unwelcome feelings. However, in time, I learned to expect the three to come with me. I knew they would likely show up, and for me they showed up much more with strangers than with friends. With friends, I could eventually be genuinely happy for them, and I had some friends who helped me make space for my feelings of envy when I did feel it. Once, when having lunch at a fancy-pants Georgetown eatery, the maître d' put my two friends and me next to a gaggle of new mothers and their beautiful babies dressed in Janie and Jack, an expensive, classic style of clothes for children. I took one look at the table and was hit hard by an envy attack. My friend's mother took one look at the table filled with the mommies-who-lunch set, turned to the maître d', and said, "Can we have a table far away from these little shits?" I, for the first time ever, was able to laugh out loud at my envy.

My friend's mother, of course, didn't really think the babies were little shits, but she understood why I couldn't be near them, for now. And us being able to laugh at it helped me immeasurably. I was no longer alone in my envy, and so my guilt and shame melted away. Brené Brown says that empathy is the antidote to shame. It "cannot survive being spoken and being met with empathy."[10] As soon as I was able to call babies a name, to make my envy okay and even laughable and have it witnessed with empathy by my friend's mother, it made me feel like my envy was understandable and not something that threw me into guilt and shame and isolation.

I certainly wouldn't say that I am in active baby grief any longer. I am, for the most part, happy about how it all turned out, but some baby envy still hits me from time to time. Just last night, Keith and I went out to dinner, and at the table across from us was a lovely family and their two beautiful children. Their two-year-old toddler started making goo-goo eyes at my boyfriend and me, and I, of course, fell in love with the little girl. As I delighted in her delicious toddler goodness, I started to have the "but you will *never, ever, ever* have that" thought that took me away from her, and from my dinner, and brought up that old unspeakable sadness. Then the envy hit me in the head like a ton of bricks. I started to judge the woman just a bit, I suppose to make myself feel better, and tried to evaluate why she was more deserving than me to have so easily (I imagined) gotten what I had wanted so much and never would have. I had trouble going back to my pan-seared Chilean sea bass and instead was consumed by the envy stew that sat in front of me. It sucked. I hated it, and I wanted to be happy with what *is,* but I was feeling sorry for myself. I let myself cry on the way home; I didn't hide it. The sadness was up, and I made space for it. I even asked my boyfriend to stop at the market for some Cherry Garcia ice cream. The sadness and the envy didn't last as long as they used to. Actually, by the time I bought the Cherry Garcia, I didn't even need it anymore. Just saying, "I am sad, I am envious, and I need to acknowledge that in some way" (by buying the ice cream) was all it took to get me to the other side of the feeling.

The truth is that we all, whether we admit it or not, don't get everything we want, and it doesn't mean that there is anything wrong with us. Not getting what you want can induce a shame attack, but there is nothing shameful about it. Cassandra, who didn't get her dream house, says this:

> The hardest part about dealing with others had to do with the shame. The few people who knew what I felt let me know, in a way, that they thought that I was being ridiculous. No one, except for my husband—which was tricky—really mirrored my feelings. I don't think that those who knew believed that not getting the house was a "loss" issue. I think that my nuclear family has been through so much loss that what I felt did not really matter. There is the sense that if something is not life-threatening, it is not worthy of grief.

What hurts more than not getting what we most wanted? Seeing someone else get what we wanted and have it come to them super-duper easy, and then seeing them not appreciate or treasure the fulfillment of that dream. *Amadeus* is a film about the composer Mozart that epitomizes the envy of seeing another who has what we want most.[11] The movie is narrated by Mozart's rival Antonio Salieri, a classical composer whose dream had been to create beautiful music to honor God:

> While my father prayed earnestly to God to protect commerce, I would offer up secretly the proudest prayer a boy could think of: Lord, make me a great composer. Let me celebrate Your glory through music and be celebrated myself. Make me famous through the world, dear God. Make me immortal. After I die, let people speak my name forever with love for what I wrote. In return, I will give You my chastity, my industry, my deepest humility, every hour of my life. Amen.

Salieri had some success, but he was definitely no Mozart. At a key scene in the movie, Salieri asks a priest, Father Vogler, "Can you remember no melody of mine? I was the most famous composer in Europe. I wrote forty operas alone. No, of course you can't." After playing several selections of his music for the priest, who is not familiar with any of them, Salieri smiles and plays the opening measure of "Eine Kleine Nachtmusik," one of Mozart's most famous works. Vogler recognizes it and begins to hum along.

Father Vogler: [smiling] Yes, I know that! Oh, that's charming! I'm sorry, I didn't know you wrote that.

Salieri: I didn't. That was Mozart. Wolfgang Amadeus Mozart.

Salieri works diligently and struggles to write beautiful music, but he falls short. Mozart, meanwhile, excels. His work "showed no corrections of any kind. Not one. He had simply written down music already finished in his head. Page after page of it, as if he were just taking dictation. And music, finished as no music is ever finished. Displace one note and there would be diminishment. Displace one phrase and the structure would fall." It comes easily for Mozart. It doesn't for Salieri. He struggles watching Mozart flitter away his talents and generally act like a fool, yet still have success come so easily. "Wolfie" churns out more hits than the Beatles as he drinks, debauches, and entirely disrespects his talents. Watching this drives Salieri so mad that he could easily do a cameo in *One Flew Over the Cuckoo's Nest.*

Seething with envy, he plots revenge and even murder. "If I can't have the dream, then I don't want anyone else to," Salieri says in less direct language. He, like all of us, faces understandable envy when he sees other people living his dream. His holding on to a dream that cannot be, instead of deciding to move on, let go, and discover some unexpected happiness, is his undoing. Watch his story and see what happens when we aren't able to let go and move on. Also, I think there is another lesson to learn, which is this: Just because someone has what we most wanted doesn't mean that they are guaranteed a life of happiness.

SELF-HELP SUGGESTIONS

☐ Do you know what you are feeling at any given time? Don't feel bad if you don't. My educated guess is that most of us don't know. We don't even ask ourselves. Do you ask yourself? This might be a good time for you to work on getting to know your emotional self. Perhaps if you aren't so familiar with your emotions, you could check in morning, noon, and night (if not more often) to chart the course of your feelings. This morning I felt _____. Midday I felt _____. This evening I felt _____. It might surprise you that you can't always answer those questions. Over time, you will expand your emotional self-awareness, which will likely lead to less numbing, avoiding, repressing, and acting out. Knowing what you feel and naming it changes it.

☐ What are you afraid will happen if you feel what you feel? That you'll die? Explode? What? You have a story about it . . . tell it. Make the story conscious. Which emotions are you okay with? Which emotions aren't you okay with? Are there a few emotions that are your "default" emotions? What are they? What is the worst-case scenario for you? Is there a history of getting stuck in a certain feeling? It might be interesting to do a biography of each emotion: What is my history with sadness, anger, fear, envy, guilt, and shame?

☐ What did you learn about feelings when you were a kid? What were your mom's feelings about feelings? Your dad's? What were the rules about feelings in your family? How did you learn those rules? What were the consequences of breaking those rules? How have those rules changed? Are you compliant with your family's rules about feelings? Can you see how your family's rules about feelings impact you now? Can you see the consequences for your family of keeping to those rules? If your family required you not to feel, this might be a really good time to rebel.

☐ If you are having trouble connecting (or making space or conscious awareness) with your sadness/anger/fear, it can be helpful to write some prompts and see what surfaces: I am sad about_____; I am angry about_____; I am afraid of_____; I am envious of_____; I feel guilty about_____; I am ashamed of_____.

☐ Notice where the emotion is in your body. Feel it. Get to know it. How big is it? What color is it? What's its shape? Notice it. Don't try to change it. Simply notice it. Breathe into it. Notice how breathing into it impacts the feeling. See what emerges by giving the feeling the space to be known. Just to know "I am angry" is better than being unconscious of it and acting angry all over the place. The sneaky-snake part of this, and what might not make sense, is that by feeling it and knowing the feeling, it changes, but by avoiding, numbing, denying, repressing, and projecting it, the feeling is likely to get bigger.

☐ Create a self-care plan for your sadness. Be good to yourself as you feel sad. I am a big believer in massages. If you are as well, make sure you have a massage therapist you feel comfortable crying in front of, because a good massage—just the intimacy of human touch—can unleash our sadness. Take a hot bath with lavender oil, some Epsom salts. Hug a dog or a cat (if they'll let you), or if you go for the inanimate, hold a stuffed animal when you need a fuzzy friend who isn't going to tell you to feel any way other than you do. Yes, I still have my floppy bunny from childhood, and she is the perfect container for tears when there is no one around to hug me as I cry. I have a soothing playlist on my iPod of Enya, Loreena McKennitt, and Jewel singing me lullabies. I also have a few friends whom I know I can call on when sadness takes hold.

☐ Create a self-care plan for your anger. I tend to like to make noise when I am angry—I literally growl. Okay, not so much of a growl, but more like "grrrrrr" sounds. For some reason, it helps me to get the anger out. I also like to vocalize in the bathtub, even underwater, and letting the sounds of anger up and out—letting out the "No!" or "It's not fair!"—in a safe and contained place allows me to get the anger out of me and moving, which helps anger not get stuck inside. For me, moving my body helps move the anger, too: running, fast walking, dancing, kick boxing, hitting tennis balls against a wall, swimming, even doing yoga can help me access anger and get it moving.

☐ Get to know your envy. How does envy happen for you? When do you turn into Salieri? What are your envy triggers? Where do they happen? When? How? What ugly thoughts won't you allow yourself to think? How do you "should" yourself ("I should be stronger, better, nicer," etc.), shame yourself, and tell yourself that you are wrong? How do you tell yourself that you shouldn't be feeling what you feel?

☐ This one may seem obvious: If you are feeling envious and struggling with the resulting sadness, anger, guilt, and shame, you might want to stay away from Facebook. Facebook is something I hear a whole lot about from patients when they are struggling with grief and loss. It can be hard to see everyone else *looking* (emphasis on that last word) so darn happy. When you're grieving, it might not be the best place to go.

☐ I am about to suggest an antidote to envy that you might not like. I want you to get out of idealizing what it would have been like if your dream had come true. Wait for it . . . it's called reality. Yeah, you see, when we see people who have what they want, we tend to imagine that they are totally and blissfully happy, that their world is all good and perfect, and that that is what would have happened for us, too. Only it wouldn't have. Nothing is all good and perfect. The baby, the job, the degree, the house, the relationship, being an award-winning actress, or winning on *American Idol*—whatever it was, it had a dark side. Looking at that reality can help with the envy. Taking a clear-eyed look at that side of things and seeing the reality of the dream can help with your envy. Seeing that mothers were stressed, tired, overwhelmed, and unable to wear an outfit that wasn't accessorized with baby barf sometimes helped me a little bit. Yes, that sounds shallow, but sometimes we need to let ourselves see the downside of having what we wanted. There is even a downside to being George Clooney or Oprah, if that is what you wanted to be. Trust me, they would tell you that it isn't all sunshine, unicorns, models, and cashmere jogging suits. Everything has a downside—everything. Salieri could have benefited from seeing the dark side of Mozart's life. He didn't see the price Mozart paid for his genius. It wasn't all Viennese pastries, chocolates, and tea parties.

☐ And what about your need for people in your life? How have your social needs changed? Are you isolating? If so, why? I definitely isolated in my grief. Everyone I talked to in this book admitted to isolating, but the truth is that no matter how introverted you are, you still need people—Barbra Streisand sang a song about it. What do you need from others that you aren't getting? People are not great at mind reading, so you are going to have to ask for what you need. We'll talk about this at length in chapter 6.

☐ What are people saying to you that is making you cuckoo for Cocoa Puffs? Perhaps it is a good time to create a list of things *not* to say to someone going through the loss of a dream, as I did (see page 113). You may want to share the list with people in your life so they know what is helping and what isn't.

Everybody Needs Somebody to Lean On

"Anything that's human is mentionable, and anything that is mentionable can be more manageable. When we can talk about our feelings, they become less overwhelming, less upsetting, and less scary. The people we trust with that important talk can help us know that we are not alone."

>> Fred Rogers

There is a famous story about the Buddha and a grieving mother. The inconsolable woman came to the Buddha seeking help (what she really wanted was the Buddha to bring her son back to life). The Buddha instead gave this women the following piece of advice: Go out into the community and get a mustard seed from each home that has not known loss and then bring them back to me, and we will go from there. She did. She went door to door looking for a single seed that she could bring back to the Buddha. Guess how many mustard seeds the mother got? None, zilch, nada, not even enough for a jar of Grey Poupon, but she did come home with a new sense of understanding, she felt less alone, and she had expanded her community of support. Buddha knew that understanding the universality of suffering can actually make you feel less alone. Creating a circle of support and knowing whom in your life you can be totally honest with about your feelings and, just as critically, whom you can't, is an important self-care strategy. But when we are grieving, we are often not able to reach out, even though this simple action of sharing our pain goes a long way in making it more bearable. Not all of us like to ask for help, especially when we are at our most vulnerable, but when you're dealing with the death of a dream, you're going to need some help—so you're going to have to learn how to ask for it.

Asking for Help from Friends and Family

Since you are an adult and have roamed the earth for at least eighteen years, you have probably had the experience of being disappointed by other human beings. (If not, then you need to write a book explaining how you managed it.) Well, I need to prep you for the fact that you are going to have that happen again when you share how you are feeling. This is why social isolation in grief is so common. People mean well; they do. Most of the people in your life do care about you and they don't want you to hurt, yet they often feel helpless. They will turn to platitudes because they don't know what else to do (see the next chapter on the attitude of platitudes). They will tell you to stop crying, to stop being sad, that you are better off without the dream. They will make suggestions about what didn't work and why it is your fault that it didn't work. They will tell you to think positively and to get over it, and they won't be able to listen to your pain. They will say things that will make you batty, and maybe even make you want to take a bat to *them* (best not to).

. . .

"People think they know you. They think they know how you're handling a situation. But the truth is no one knows. No one knows what happens after you leave them, when you're lying in bed or sitting over your breakfast alone and all you want to do is cry or scream. They don't know what's going on inside your head—the mind-numbing cocktail of anger and sadness and guilt. This isn't their fault. They just don't know. And so they pretend and they say you're doing great when you're really not. And this makes everyone feel better. Everybody but you."

>> **William H. Woodwell Jr.**

I collected a list of all of the horrible things people said to me during my active grieving days and wrote a piece inspired by these incredibly insensitive suggestions called "Infertility: 16 Things You Should Never Say to a Woman Who Is Childless but Not by Choice."[1] It was published on the *Huffington Post* website. These are some of the things that well-meaning people told me:

> "You must not *really* have wanted to have a child or you would have one."

> "If you would just change your beliefs about all of this, you would get pregnant."

> "God has another plan for you. God doesn't want you to be pregnant."

> "Well, you get to sleep late and go on vacations and have nice shoes and that's better than having kids."

> "If you would adopt, you would get pregnant."

And my personal nonfavorite:

> "God wants you to be in service, and if you had a child, you couldn't do God's will."

And perhaps the worst of all:

> "Maybe God knew you wouldn't have made a good parent."
> (Ouch. That hurt.)

Why would people say such things? At the end of the day, I believe that people want you to snap out of it as quickly as possible because they are scared. Seeing your grief scares them. They are bebopping along in their own life and doing their own thing, and they just don't want to imagine that *their* dream might not come true, that *they* could lose their house, their job, their husband, and that maybe _____ (fill in the blank) might not happen for them, either. It is too scary to consider. So if they can get you to stop being sad, snap out of it, and see the bright side already, then there is hope for them. Only it doesn't really work that way. Your snapping out of it and being happy will not protect them from the grief and loss and disappointment that is part of life. You can't protect them from their grief, just as their platitudes can't protect you from yours. Harold Kushner, author of *Living a Life That Matters,* said:

> At some of the darkest moments of my life, some people I thought of as friends deserted me—some because they cared about me and it hurt them to see me in pain; others because I reminded them of their own vulnerability, and that was more than they could handle. But real friends overcame their discomfort and came to sit with me. If they had no words to make me feel better, they sat in silence (much better than saying, "You'll get over it," or "It's not so bad; others have it worse") and I loved them for it.[2]

My friend in infertility, Stephanie Baffone, is a gifted colleague. She has dealt with her own share of grief and has worked extensively with patients dealing with grief. She writes:

> It is the lucky few who have that one person who REALLY gets the idea of being present to our pain. Who can sit with our powerlessness, hopelessness, etc., and just be. When I was grieving the loss of my mom and working for hospice, my gifted co-worker taught me so much. He said, "Most people won't get you. They will think you are grieving too long, not 'right,' will wonder if you'll ever be the 'same again.'" Sadly he said, and boy is this true, the burden of educating those around us on how they can best help us, lies with us. What insult to injury but often more the rule than the exception. I wish I knew this upfront. I was so hurt by so many until I later realized this harsh reality. I tell my clients, be as specific as you can. We often make a list or I have them write an open letter of sorts to family and friends, outlining what kind of help they could actually use.

You may be saying to yourself, "If I wanted to be an educator, I would have gotten a master's in education." But with or without that master's, you are going to have to school some people on grief. You may feel that you barely have the emotional bandwidth to deal with your own stuff, let alone go about telling people about how you feel when they tell you how you should be feeling. It may feel too scary to set limits with them and tell them that it hurts when they tell you not to cry. It may feel easier to pull away and isolate, but the truth is that grief is worsened through isolation. This grief experience might be the first time we have had to be direct and tell people our unvarnished truth, which may include telling them in the nicest way possible to shut up. They may let us down when we do and, yes, good God, how that sucks. But if we don't take that risk and we pull away from social relationships that were once meaningful to us, we are creating more pain by losing those relationships.

And, no, of course not everyone is a person to share your pain with. If your mailman asks you how you are, it's probably best not to go into a forty-five-minute diatribe about the state of your grief—but people in your inner circle who really care? Yes, absolutely let them know how you are doing. Tell them; spill your guts if they are your safe people. Not everyone is safe; you know this. Aunt Ethel may not be on the list, even though she loves you dearly. You likely know who in your life is safe to tell what to, and who isn't. It is up to you to make these judgments. Listen to your instincts. Honor them. And if someone in your inner circle of trust is all of a sudden telling you to stop crying and that you should feel something other than what you feel, then tell your friend/family member that Tracey said to say, "My anger/sadness/fear/pain/tears are okay and will end, and it will only exacerbate the grief and lengthen it if you make me repress it. So I am not going to stop feeling this now, but someday I won't feel this way anymore." Feel free to stamp your foot for dramatic flair and to demonstrate defiant obstinacy to their suggestion that you stuff it. Temper tantrums can, on occasion, be effective (if done in a mature and self-regulated manner; I suppose that a mature temper tantrum is something of an oxymoron—however, that doesn't mean it can't be done).

Sharing where you are at can't cure the pain, but it does help. My grandma used to say that a trouble shared is a trouble halved. Now, I am not sure if she got the measurements right, but telling my story to someone who can *really* hear me and empathize with my pain makes me feel less alone in that pain, and comforted. That's what the Buddha knew when he sent that sad woman out searching for mustard seeds. When I was in the height of my grief, there were a few people in my life who could hear me without needing to fix me, and

I will be forever grateful to them. But even those dear, sweet people had limits. It is hard to see someone you love hurting for a long time and not be able to fix things for them. Even as a trained therapist, there are times when I hear my patients' pain and I want to move it, change it, transform it, make meaning of it, and make it better lickety-split, when the truth is that sometimes what they really need most is to be heard and have someone really empathize with them, exactly where they are today. I can fix some things in therapy, but I can't fix grief. I can't bring a dead and destructive dream back to life. I am a therapist and not a magician, and as a therapist, I know that the reason they are coming to me is to be heard and to have a safe place for their pain, a place where they don't have to worry about taking care of other people and their feelings.

I can tell you for sure that when I was complaining to friends about my plight, I was never looking for suggestions on how to make the pain stop or guidance on what else I could do to try to conceive. *Never.* Let me repeat that, I was *never* looking for advice. Trust me, I am a pretty clever gal when it comes to getting my needs met; if I wanted you to tell me how to fix it, I would ask. I just simply wanted to be listened to. And when I was listened to, I felt validated, relieved, and as if I wasn't batty for feeling like I did. When I was really listened to, it felt like my pain was okay, that I was okay, and that I was going to be okay. When people couldn't take the pain and rushed in and told me, "You are going to be okay," it felt worse. I know it sounds paradoxical, but if you are in pain, you know what I mean. When you are in pain, you just want somebody, anybody, to say, "I get it." Saying everything will be okay is not the same thing.

Tangible Help Ain't Bad, Either

When people hear how much you are hurting, the people who love you, the good ones (not the snap-out-of-it and move-on-already ones) are likely to say, "I wish there was something I could do to help you." You, dear one, need to let them help you if they can. Of course, they can't take your grief away, but maybe they can help you in other ways. One morning during my grieving, my dear friend Karen Cohen, knowing there was absolutely nothing she could say to make me feel better, came to my house with casseroles and fuzzy pajamas so I would have food that involved four food groups (a diet of Milano cookies has never been proven to be an effective treatment for grief) and something soft and snuggly to grieve in instead of the hopsack, ashes, and hair shirt I had been symbolically donning. It helped—the cheesy hot dish, the soft fabric, and the tangible acknowledging of my pain—all of it helped more than any advice she could give me. Pamela Dixon, a good friend from grad school, knew of my love of a certain tomato basil soup from a favorite local eatery and dropped a quart of it at my door with a loaf of French bread and a kind note about how sorry she was that I was hurting so much. Both of those acts of kindness helped me more than all the "look at the bright side of things" lectures I got from well-meaning friends who were trying to cheer me up. These tangible acts of kindness made me feel loved and less alone in my grief. I learned to let people help me in ways that *really* would help me. Even if it didn't make the grief any less, it made me less likely to isolate and feel all alone in my grief.

If you don't have a Karen or a Pamela in your life to bring you soup or pajamas, there are other ways to get some help that may make a difference: getting a massage, hiring a housekeeper for the day, getting fresh organic food delivered to your door. Let yourself be helped in ways that make you feel just a tiny bit better. A tiny bit better may sound inconsequential to you, but a bit better is a bit better than a bit worse. Right? And having the experience of being helped by others is healing, and it gets you out of the sense of isolation that grief can activate.

Joining a Support Group

In my practice as a therapist, I have recommended support groups to a whole lot of people. And, let me tell you that almost never is how often I hear from the suggestee, upon hearing my suggestion, "Oh, great, yes, absolutely, I can't wait to go sit in a room and hear others share about their pain, and I will share mine with them, and it will be awesome." No, it practically never goes like that. No, it's usually, "Yeah, groups, no, I don't think so; maybe later." But if it seems like a group would really help them, I gently encourage on: "Maybe, just maybe you could just go sit in on a group and try it and see how it feels and then decide if you are even interested. Just go try and see; don't decide if groups are for you before you go." Then, when they go, more often than not, they come back and tell me that people in the group get it, and that it wasn't what they imagined it to be (usually the imagined scene is straight out of *One Flew Over the Cuckoo's Nest*) and when they stay in the groups, they come back and tell me how much the group has helped them and how much less alone they feel. That is because sharing your pain in a support group can be enormously healing. And I get that groups might not be suited for everyone—for example, for someone who is an introvert—but they can be just the thing for more social beings, even social beings in grief.

Irvin Yalom, the acclaimed author and authority on group therapy, talked about universality as one of the "curative" benefits of group process (remember the Buddha and the mustard seed). Group therapy can be a kind of mustard-seed-seeking session. By being in a group, hearing other people's pain, we feel less alone and less wrong for our reactions when we hear that our reactions are universal.

Erica, who attended a support group for help with grief, explained her experience of being in a group:

> There was instant response, sympathy, feedback, and give and take. We got hugs all around at the end of the meetings. We are still in touch with many of the friends we made there. Group support is not for everyone. It can be very difficult to sit there for two hours and listen to everyone else's stories of pain. We emphasized at the start of each session that we were not professional counselors, just volunteers and peers who didn't have any answers but were willing to listen and share our own experiences. Some people also went to individual counseling (and some people probably should have—there were a few whose grief was such that I was really worried about them and how they were coping, and felt that what we were able to offer was totally inadequate). Some came once, and we'd never hear from them again. Maybe we scared them off, but sometimes one meeting was all they needed. We listened to them, we validated that their feelings and reactions were "normal" for what they had been through, and that made them feel better.

In a good grief group, you will experience the following:

- a nonjudgmental environment in which you are given permission to feel what you feel
- the opportunity to meet others who are grieving and who have also experienced a loss
- a place to share your story and benefit from hearing others' experiences
- a feeling of not being alone
- a place to develop and practice coping skills to deal with the grief when it gets to be too much
- a sense of community, a diminished sense of isolation

It might not be easy to find a group that is specific to your exact loss. While there are groups for death of a marriage, job loss, infertility, and empty nests, there may not be ones for "death of the dream of being a vice president" or "death of the dream of being an award-winning scientist." But grief is grief, and if you find a grief group in your community, it is certainly worth seeing if all kinds of grief are welcome, including death of a dream. If not, the Internet was made for this kind of support. Reach out through Facebook or Twitter or simply search on Google to see if you can find other people whose loss is similar to yours.

Asking for Help from a Professional

There may come a day when you need more support than friends and family can give you. Leona explains what made her choose therapy:

> I needed something they couldn't manage, not because they didn't love me, but often because they did. I had to seek more support outside of my circle of trust. When, at my mother's suggestion, [because] she saw that I was starting to withdraw from her and others because I no longer felt comfortable talking about my grief, I went into therapy, it was an immediate relief. Now I had a place where I could spill it all—my anger, envy, shame, bitterness, magical thinking, resentment, sadness, and seemingly endless tears. In the first session, my therapist asked me simply, "Why are you here?" I

told her the story of my failed business. I sobbed as I told my sad story. She never tried to fix it or make a single suggestion about how I could continue to try to make that business work or tell me what I did wrong, and it was awesome. She listened, she cared, and she said these magic words: "I think I can help you with this." You just don't know what those words did for me. They gave me hope that my pain would end, and at the same time she didn't tell me I was sick, wrong, or that I should be any way other than how I was. It was awesome.

Here's what other people have said about their experience with therapy in dealing with their grief:

"Therapy gave me a listening ear without judgment. It allowed me to say the dark things that I couldn't to anyone else. It also helped my husband and me to make it through the worst of the journey and subsequent hard times. It also helped me to frame my thoughts in a more positive manner, gave me permission to set boundaries where they needed to be set with friends and most especially with my mom. Therapy is freeing."

—Lucy, who gave up the dream of having a child

"Therapy was probably the only place that I allowed myself to not drown in shame."

—Ed, who had to let go of his hopes of being a film maker

"I really just find that the act of sharing with an objective person is so helpful. The release of it."

—Rosemary, who grieved the loss of her dream of having her own business

"I remember the first time I went to the group, the therapist asked me to introduce myself. I started to tell her and the group about my mom, and I couldn't get the words out before starting to cry. When I finally said the words, the therapist said, 'Okay, breathe.' I hadn't realized I'd been holding my breath. This has caused me to be more mindful of things like breathing."

—Ruby, mourning the loss of her mother

How to Know If You Need a Therapist

Yes, I am a therapist, so I know I am biased. But I don't think therapy is just for people who have problems, who are in crisis, or who are mentally ill. Yes, it goes without saying that therapy is great for those people. I believe that therapy—good therapy—helps us and allows us to be more ourselves, be more authentic, be more creative, and have greater satisfaction in love, life, and relationships. So, pretty much if you are breathing, I believe that you could probably benefit from some therapy, and you shouldn't be surprised that I am going to suggest therapy for those dealing with the loss of a dream. And no, this doesn't mean you are sick or that there is anything wrong with you. Grief isn't an illness; it is a crisis moment, and you are in that crisis, and if you need help, I want you to get it. You don't have to "qualify" for therapy—anyone who feels they need some help, or a place to talk, or a place to grieve can get help. Here are some signs that you might benefit from some professional help. (If you don't see yourself in these signs, you can still come to therapy if you feel like it might be helpful to you.)

- You are feeling that you are grieving the wrong way, shouldn't be grieving, or should be "over it by now."

- You are beating yourself up over the loss of your dream so significantly that your self-esteem and self-concept are being hurt by these self-attacks.

- You don't feel able to share your feelings about the loss of your dreams with those you love and need a safe place to process your emotions.

- You are consistently editing your feelings, thoughts, and grief experience when you speak to people, so as not to overwhelm them.

- Your grief is leading to an increase in isolation.

- You need assistance developing tools and strategies to cope with the feelings of grief and in learning to manage how you're showing those feelings.

- You feel you are stuck in a loop with the same recurring thoughts, questions, and ruminations.

- You are wanting to find a way to make this grief experience meaningful and are struggling to do so.

- You don't feel that you are coping and/or your functioning is impaired so that you are not able to work, pay bills, or take care of yourself as well as you'd like to.

- You are feeling hopeless and aren't able to imagine getting to the other side of this.

If you feel like you want to get into therapy but aren't sure how to start, hold on to your hat; I will explain in the Therapy Couch section how to find the right therapist for you.

www.makethepainallbetter.com

On the day that I decided that I was D-O-N-E with trying to conceive, one of the first things I did was call a friend—a friend who loved me, a friend who didn't want me to hurt anymore. When she heard that I was done, my friend ceased being a friend and transformed into a human platitude machine. I love her, I adore her, but at the time I could have strangled her. I needed nothing more from her than to hear me cry and to shut up and listen to me. She simply couldn't do it. The more we talked, the more enraged I got. When we hung up, and when I was done grumbling about her, I googled the following phrase: "How+to+live+childless+not+by+choice." The search brought back little in the way of results that offered any comfort, so I went to my own blog and started to write. Up until that day, my blog had been a place for me to discuss my love of all things French. However, that day, I didn't give a single ooh-la-la about anything Parisian. Hopped up on progesterone and overtaken by grief, I didn't have the usual internal inhibitors or executive functions to stop me from sharing very personal materials on a place for the entire world to see. I wrote the following (much of which I've already shared with you, so bear with me):

> I am a very sad weasel [my blog was called La Belette Rouge, which is French for "the red weasel"]. The last few posts have been tough for me. All the things that usually inspire interest have lost their luster, even Paris and red shoes and you know that is serious when

there is no libido for Louboutins. I have for the last four years tried to become pregnant—and yesterday we learned that our last ditch heroic efforts led to naught. Not only is my hair red—my eyes are too. We have endured 4 full IVF cycles and probably 20 IUI's (16 without meds and 4 with). I made the call this a.m. and told my infertility doctor that we are done and that we are not going to try any longer. We have spent nearly $100,000.00 in an attempt to be fruitful and multiply. We have nothing to show for it but a pile of receipts, pictures of embryos that didn't make it and some left over needles, bottles of progesterone—and broken hearts. I have cried every time we haven't gotten pregnant. I have cried in between, too—thanks to the massive amounts of hormones I have endured. I have cried over things I would have never have imagined were tear worthy such as dropping a napkin, forgetting to get milk at the store, and I have cried every time I see pregnant women or a mother at the mall pushing a stroller or heard a mother complaining about the challenges of her children. Now that is over, I can't seem to stop crying. I find myself wondering if I will ever stop crying. Maybe, I will be like that woman who had the hiccups for over a year. Medical science will marvel and the media will pursue me—the woman who can't stop crying. Ann Curry will empathetically ask me what impact has all the crying had on my life. Less sensitive reporters will focus on more objective issues such as the danger of dehydration and what doctors have done to try to stop my tears.

I thought of Elizabeth Gilbert, in the first chapter of *Eat, Pray, Love,* when she is in her bathroom crying and praying and she hears an answer from God guiding her to go back to sleep, when I was lying on my bathroom floor this a.m. I decided to try to pray, like Gilbert had, so between animal-like cries I would shout out an expletive to the silent creator who has not heard our prayers. No voice met my queries. No voice gave me guidance—not even a practical suggestion like, "blow your nose" or "get off the floor." Instead, there was nothing.

I pressed *publish* on the above post and sat in silence on my couch feeling something like terror. What had I done? Had I lost my mind? By the time I started to rethink the post and consider taking it down before anyone could see it, the comments started rolling in. Comments from people I had never met, comments that comforted me, consoled me, and made me feel less alone. These faceless strangers brought me palpable comfort, so much so that I kept blogging and I developed a community of bloggers, a following, and a group of real and true friends, some of whom I have met and some of whom I haven't. I made friends and built a forum that I could turn to anytime night or day, a place and a community to which I could tell my truth when everyone else was tired of hearing it.

Writing a blog allowed me the freedom to share exactly how I felt, in a similar way that therapy did. I can't begin to imagine how much longer my journey would have been without therapy or my blog, and I can tell you for sure that I started to feel some kind of redemption when people started to tell me that my blog was helping them with their pain. I never imagined that sharing my experience could provide any comfort to others, but it did.

Rita explains the value of online support for her experience with the grief of infidelity:

> [It helped] maybe more so than my therapist. I felt so alone and odd for my thoughts and feelings. I had talked to my friends, but unless they had been through what I had been through, they just didn't get it. They wanted me to be over it. Infidelity is such a taboo subject. I had to learn that when they asked how I was doing, they really didn't want to know. My blog friends listened and validated my emotions. They had had every one of the feelings and emotions I had/have. It's weird because you really don't know these folks, but you come to care about them. You can express all your thoughts without any recourse or not much of one. You put it all out there anonymously or with an alias. The main point is you get it out with a sympathetic, empathic group of people.
>
> I think I like and trust my cyber friends more than physical friends. I think I would recognize you, but maybe not. I just knew

in my time of deepest, darkest grief and despair, no one who hadn't been through what I had been through was of much comfort. I learned to keep my mouth shut with family and friends and have become totally reliant on cyber friends.

Pamela Mahoney Tsigdinos, who blogs at Silentsorority.com and is the author of *Silent Sorority: A Barren Woman Gets Busy, Angry, Lost and Found,* explains:

> The collective sharing within a safe and empathetic community encouraged me to process and reflect on my experience. It was sanity preserving to have a safe place to retreat with my wounded soul. . . . Connecting with women who could empathize and validate my emotions provided an important and significant boost in my ability to process disenfranchised grief. Furthermore, it was hugely helpful to hear your articulate, honest, courageous stories. I felt tremendous comfort being in the company of such smart, strong women.[3]

Now, let me tell you, not everyone on the Internet is going to be nice. I got my share of snotty comments, unsolicited advice, and downright meanness. It is, of course, wise to be careful about what you share online and to protect your identity in a way that makes you comfortable. That said, for me and for many of my blogging friends, the good has definitely outweighed the bad. But please, use common sense when developing friendships online.

The Inside Story

Kayla had one dream that motivated her every action: She was going to be the next Oprah. She had spent seven years trying to make the dream a reality, following Oprah's biography like a recipe book. Step 1: journalist degree. Step 2: a handful of impressive internships at WGN-TV, MTV, and VH1. Step 3: an audition at Oprah's "Next New Talk Show Host." The more Kayla worked at her career, however, and the more strongly she held to the recipe for success, the more narrow-minded she became. She refused to add part-time jobs that might take her away from her dream of having a talk show. She refused to listen to friends and family who suggested she try another path. When the grand plan didn't work, she gave up on her dream and decided to attend grad school in order to have a job that guaranteed income and security—but she never talked about how hard it was to let go of what she imagined to be her "calling." She was utterly ashamed and imagined with horror having to admit to friends and family that she had given up and gotten a real job. "I wanted to isolate," she says, "yet I also wanted to be seen. It was important to me that I honored what a big deal this was for me. Yes, there were times when I said, 'You know, I'd rather not speak about it right now,' yet given the opportunity to share about it, I did."

It wasn't until she attended "family week" at her brother's rehab program that she started to see that there were issues she needed to deal with: Her narcissistic father needed to have a star daughter in order to feel good about himself, and without her dream, she believed that she was just ordinary. Kayla joined Al-Anon and a support group for artists, "but even there I felt isolated. I would talk in meetings, but I would leave before the Serenity Prayer. I wouldn't hold hands with anyone." If she really let herself be present in the group, she would have had to admit the reality of the situation—and that was just too hard.

Even though Kayla struggled with Al-Anon, she explains the benefit of the group: "Al-Anon and other Twelve Step groups were great because they have such good boundaries around listening. I could share whatever I needed to share, and I would be heard, and no one could give me feedback. It was a sacred space, like verbally writing a journal entry." In time, Kayla got a sponsor and then began therapy.

By the time she walked away from her once firmly held dream, Kayla had developed a support system that she could rely on without any hesitation. "This included my three siblings, about two close friends, and my counselor," she explains. "These were people who I could call at any time during the night to just cry and be heard. And I would. With others outside this support circle, I would be cautious. I didn't want encouragement to keep trying, and I didn't want to hear that maybe it just wasn't for me. All I wanted was to have a few people around me to hold the space while I grieved each intimate detail of that beautiful dream."

Kayla describes what she did to get support: "I would ask my older brothers to tell me again and again their personal stories about jobs they'd lost, relationships that ended, life changes that didn't go the way they had wanted. I wanted to hear how it turned out for them in the end. And in the end, despite the sometimes-brutal pain of it all, it always worked out for the best. Each job led to another. Each relationship led to the next. Hearing their stories gave me the courage to experience my pain, while also trusting that it would all work out exactly as it was meant to. And that one day I would see the gift in it all."

Kayla shares the words that most helped:

- "I understand."
- "I went through that, too."
- "Tell me more."
- "Your feelings are normal."

Kayla shares the words that most hurt:

- "That wasn't what you wanted anyway, was it?"
- "Maybe you aren't trying hard enough."
- "Did you try this . . . ?"
- "It's okay."

In therapy, Kayla found a place where she could process all of the pain that came from giving up on her dream, without fear of judgment. She began to understand why she actually wanted to be a talk show host so much and what the dream symbolized. "Now, I get to find out if I can be loved without the promise of being the next Oprah, without my own magazine and my own $40 million fortune. And it feels good, and still sometimes a little scary, to find out that I am loved without it."

When she let go of her dream, a new dream emerged for Kayla. She has become a counselor. "The second dream wouldn't exist without the first," she says, having come to a place where she has accepted her grief.

There is a certain kind of irony that we are in the Therapy Couch section of this chapter, talking about finding a good therapist. If you don't have one, and have decided you need one, it is something that you could likely use a little help with, as most of us spend more time researching a toaster than we do a therapist. We often don't bother thinking about what we want in a therapist because we wouldn't necessarily know how to go about finding one even if we did know what we most wanted. When searching for a therapist, most people feel like they can't really make an informed decision, that it is up to luck or chance or synchronicity to find someone who can help—but it's not. In the midst of grieving, you might not be at your most resourceful, and you might not have the energy or inclination to put on your researcher's hat (I am trying to imagine a researcher's hat, and for some reason, all I can imagine is Dick Tracy's hat; however, feel free to wear any kind of hat you like as you read on). When looking online, or asking friends, family, physicians, clergy, chiropractors, or massage therapists for a referral, here are some of the things you might want to consider.

Gender

When deciding on a therapist, gender is a good place to start, as there are only two choices. I think that when choosing a therapist, most people have an instinctive sense of which gender they would prefer to work with. You likely already know your preference, now that I have mentioned it. You may not know *why* you would prefer one to the other, but you likely know your preference. For me, my default therapist of choice has always been male, which, in fact, comes out of my relationship with my parents. When I worked on my grief over not being a mother, however, a woman therapist initially seemed right to me. The point is that there is no right or wrong answer when it comes to choosing the gender of a therapist. Trust your instincts, and perhaps tell your therapist about why you made your choice. There's a chance it might help in their understanding of what you are going through.

Age

This is another area where you might know what you want, whether you are conscious of it or not. When I was in my twenties, I had therapists in their twenties. I can't, now that I am in my forties, imagine seeing someone twenty years younger than I am. In my thirties, I had a therapist in her mid-eighties, and it was an absolutely incredible experience. As a therapist in my forties, I have patients in every stage of life, and I do often ask if my age was a part of their decision-making process when choosing a therapist, especially when I turn out to be the exact same age as their mother. If I am much younger or much older than the patient, I do, if appropriate, check in on how that impacts our work together—sometimes it does and sometimes it doesn't. As with gender, let your therapist know why you made your choice in case it might help.

Cultural Background

Once you know the sex and age range of your therapist, it is time to look at cultural background. Is it important that you and your therapist share cultural backgrounds? Is your therapist's religion, gender, ethnicity, socio-economic status, class background, and sexual orientation important to you? Michael Blumenfield, MD, writes:

> If it were true that in order to receive effective psychotherapy, the patient and the therapist must be of the same gender, it would follow that that they should be in the same age group, socioeconomic group, religion, race, occupation type, work ethic, sibling configuration, health status, life expectancy, marital status and political party and have the same experience with drugs and alcohol, military service, parenting, etc. This is an impossible task, and there is no established validity to the assumption that there must be some type of mirror image between the patient and the therapist. There is no one simple experience of growing up as a man or woman (or growing up as a Catholic or Jew, or being a grandfather, or facing death, etc.) that must be shared by patient and therapist in order for the therapy to work. For the patient to assume that the therapist can only understand his or her experience if they somehow share some

similarities (or for the therapist to assume the same thing) is a recipe for misunderstandings.[4]

That said, for you there may be similarities that are a must for you. Maybe you want your therapist to share the same religious beliefs as you. Perhaps you would prefer to do therapy in your native tongue. Again, there are no wrong answers here.

Qualities

When therapist shopping, there are some basic nonnegotiable and essential qualities that must be a part of the deal. Therapists should be great listeners, nonjudgmental, trustworthy, accepting, empathic, ethical, and make you feel safe to feel whatever you are feeling. However, there may be other qualities that *you* require that wouldn't matter to someone else. And some people require certain qualities that another person would find completely off-putting or even unacceptable. Again, like I mentioned, there is not one answer here. There are as many answers as there are clients and therapists. For example, I need a therapist to be likable (not everyone needs this; there are plenty of therapists who actually try to activate negative transference, i.e., get their clients to get angry at them, and this can be helpful with some people). I need to feel like the therapist is a bit of an intellectual and has a sense of humor. You might not care whether they know Greek philosophy or have the ability to laugh easily, but for me these are nonnegotiable. You might want warm, fuzzy, and nurturing, while someone else might be looking for academic, cool, calm, and introverted. There's no right answer; it's just important for you to know what you want.

Theoretical Orientation

When you start looking for a therapist, either online or through a referral, you will likely see some language in which the therapist describes their "theoretical orientation," and unless you majored in psychology, that might not mean anything to you. There are many theoretical orientations: cognitive-behavioral, psychoanalytic (Freudian, Jungian, or a number of variations on their approaches), narrative, object relations, gestalt, transactional analysis, humanistic, existential, interpersonal, and on and on, and I couldn't possibly describe them all to you here without turning this into another book. And while theoretical orientations are interesting and important and tell you a whole lot about how the person works and conceptualizes your work together, studies show that theoretical orientation isn't eventually what matters for the client in terms of outcomes. Theoretical orientation simply isn't the change agent in therapy. The studies show that it is the relationship with the therapist that is the source of healing and *not* the theoretical orientation. So even though I work psychodynamically with a dash of Jungian/Freudian and a good bit of existential thrown in for good measure, I would not begin to tell you that this is the only kind of therapist to see. Here is what I would recommend: Call some people whom you have found—either through a direct referral from friends, family, or your physician or on *Psychology Today's* "Find a Therapist" page (http://therapists.psychologytoday.com) or Theravive.com—and ask if they work with grief. Talk to them. Tell them what's up with you. If the connection feels good and you feel comfortable with them, ask them to explain how they would work with your grief. You will know if it feels right or if it doesn't.

What to Do in Therapy
(and Stuff I Do in Therapy to Help People Going through This)

Okay, now that you have a therapist, what next? Well, it is pretty straightforward: You go in, you sit on the couch or chair, you start talking about how you're feeling, and ideally the therapist will get it and make you feel heard, listened to, and understood. Now that you know what to do, you might want to know what the therapist might do. If I had a patient come in mourning the loss of a dream, here's what they might expect:

- First and foremost, I want them to have a space where they can feel/think/say anything they need to feel/think/say. I am normalizing their experience.

- I do *not* pathologize their grief or tell them they are wrong for feeling what they do.

- I absolutely do not tell them to take their mind off it, or to just change their thinking.

- I help them explore more deeply why they wanted the dream so much, who they imagined they would have been had the dream become reality, and who they imagine they will be without it.

- I explore what it is like to be in the now without the dream to give their life purpose and meaning.

- I explore how past griefs might be impacting this grief.

- Gently, slowly, and not immediately, I work to help find a meaning of this loss and the (yikes, dare I say it) kind of good stuff that may have emerged because of it (see more in the next chapter on meaning making).

Movie Rx

If you were to ask him, my boyfriend would happily tell you that I don't like to see movies without therapists in them. I didn't realize that about myself until he started to point out that every movie that I loved had a therapist in it—*Lars and the Real Girl, Best in Show, The King's Speech, Grosse Pointe Blank*. It's better still if there is a French therapist involved, but sadly there are fewer of those films. It's true; I do love films in which the character is seeking meaning, to better understand themselves and/or to make significant changes in their life. (Why wouldn't I? I *am* a therapist, after all!) And if a screenwriter wants to demonstrate such a quality in a character, what better way to demonstrate that than to send your character to therapy?

Ordinary People,[5] the movie I am prescribing to you in this chapter, is the movie that made me first decide that I wanted to be a therapist—well, either that or *The Bob Newhart Show;* I am not sure which came first, but I do know that Bob and Judd had an impact on me.

Ordinary People is a story in which the Jarrett family grieves the loss of an idealized son, Buck, who died in a sailing accident with his younger brother, Conrad. The surviving family experiences the impact of not allowing for grief. Beth, the mother, is a real piece of work. She is played by Mary Tyler Moore in a way that will make you forget she was darling-sweet Mary from *The Mary Tyler Moore Show.* This Mary is more Medea than Madonna. She refuses to speak of her grief; she buries and suppresses her pain. She believes that feeling pain is a sign of weakness, and she hates her son Conrad for surviving the accident. Conrad is racked with guilt and overwhelmed by depression. He has no place in his family to deal with his feelings, and he attempts suicide. The film begins after Conrad is released from the hospital—another experience that his mother doesn't want to talk about. Conrad, who is still far from okay, withdraws from his friendships, quits the swim team, and becomes seriously isolated. His father, Calvin, concerned for his son's well-being, encourages Conrad to find support for his grief and his feelings in therapy (thank God Conrad had his father!). Conrad is initially resistant to seeking support—good gravy, why wouldn't he be? Everything in his family model tells him it isn't okay to talk about it, or feel it, or even to be. But Conrad does go; something in him knows he needs a place for the pain.

Dr. Berger, the therapist, played brilliantly by Judd Hirsch, gives him that place. Dr. Berger is a warm, available, and accessible guy, everything Conrad's family is not. Dr. Berger wants to know how Conrad feels; he invites his feelings. Conrad protests.

Conrad "Con" Jarrett: When I let myself feel, all I feel is lousy.
Dr. Berger: Oh well excuse me, I never promised you a rose garden.

Conrad "Con" Jarrett: Oh fuck you Berger.
Dr. Berger: What?

Conrad "Con" Jarrett: FUCK YOU!
Dr. Berger: Hey, that's it!

You may not see it in the interchange, but Dr. Berger is saying, "Yes, you get to be angry here. It is okay. I can take it. Let it out. Make a mess. Feel!" Conrad starts to feel, but it's hard and scary. Dr. Berger normalizes this experience for him.

Dr. Berger: Feelings are scary. And sometimes they're painful. And if you can't feel pain . . . you won't feel anything else either. You know what I'm saying?
Conrad "Con" Jarrett: I think so.

Dr. Berger: You're here. You're alive. Don't say you don't feel that.
Conrad "Con" Jarrett: It doesn't feel good.

Dr. Berger: It is good. Believe me.
Conrad "Con" Jarrett: How do you know?

Dr. Berger: Because I'm your friend.

When Conrad starts to feel, absolves himself of his "guilt," and stops blaming himself for his brother's death, he starts to move on and finds a way to start enjoying life again. Dr. Berger gives Conrad permission to start living again. Conrad returns to life when he gets the hots for his choir mate, Jeanine Pratt. At McDonald's with Jeanine, she does what no one in his life, save his doctor, ever did: asks about his pain. Conrad is sort of surprised and yet, because of the therapy with Dr. Berger, he can do what his mother couldn't do, which is talk about the pain, let it go, move on, and return to life.

This movie can reduce the most stable and griefless person to a puddle of tears, so be prepared to be hit hard by it. But be open to its healing energy as well, and its message that messy feelings are important, and that it is important to find tangible support for those feelings, and that when you do there is life, love, and joy to be had on the other side of it. This kind of path is open to you, too.

SELF-HELP SUGGESTIONS

- ☐ Is there a part of you, like the woman in the Buddha story, that is still hoping for a miracle? Are you isolating so you can stay in hope? Is there some way, in not telling your story or sharing your pain, that you're not fully accepting the reality of where you are?

- ☐ With whom have you shared the news that your dream is done? Who haven't you told? Who knows of your grief? Do you find that you want to tell no one or everyone, or something in between? What has it been like to share your grief with others?

☐ How have people reacted to the news that the dream is dead? Have people been supportive? What have they said? Have people disappointed you? Hurt you? Let you down? Has their reaction impacted how you feel? Do you find the need to edit your grief for others?

☐ If you saw the movie *Meet the Fockers,* you may remember Robert De Niro's character, the father, and his "Circle of Trust." Well, it is time to create your circle of trust. Who is in your circle? Are there people with whom you can share all your feelings? Whom should you be more careful with? It might be good to create a list of all the people in your life and actually write it down.

☐ Create a self-care plan that involves asking others for help. What kind of support do you need from friends and family? If you were to have your perfect support team, what would that look like? What is it you need from other people?

☐ What tangible support can you enlist while you are grieving? Who is asking to help you? Who keeps wishing there was something they could do for you? How can you let them? What might help just a little bit? Can they give you a hug, make you soup, or pick up your kids at school for you? Let yourself be helped. There are people who love you and want to be there for you—let them. What do you need? Ask for it!

☐ If you were to write a manifesto of the things that aren't helpful to say, what would it include? What advice can you simply not hear one more time? Right a letter or a list and share it with the people in your circle of trust. They don't know that what they are saying is hurting you unless you tell them.

☐ What are your feelings about seeking support outside of your family? Do messages from childhood make you feel like it isn't okay to seek therapy or attend a group?

☐ Which feels more right for you, group or individual therapy? Why?

☐ In *Ordinary People,* Beth refuses to ask for help because if she does she has to admit that there is something wrong. What are you afraid of admitting?

☐ If looking for a therapist, you might want to check out *Psychology Today*'s "Find a Therapist" page (http://therapists.psychologytoday.com/rms/). The Internet is most often how people find me. When looking for a therapist, you might want to ask yourself the following questions:

- What gender would I prefer to work with? Why?

- How do I feel like therapy would be different with a man than a woman, and vice versa? Are there reasons that I trust one gender over the other? Are there gender biases I have that might impact my choice?

- Do I want a therapist to be older, younger, or the same age as me? Why is that important? What age range would I feel most comfortable with? What age would I absolutely not consider? What qualities do I believe the therapist of my chosen age range has that someone older or younger wouldn't have?

- Do I need my therapist to have the same background and cultural history as I do?

- Do I need them to share my sexual orientation?

- Would I prefer that my therapist fluently spoke another language?

- Are there parts of me that are essential that I share with my therapist? Why does this feel essential?

- What qualities are nonnegotiable? What qualities would make me run out the door?

☐ Find a blog or message board that deals with the loss of your dream. If one doesn't exist, you might want to create your own. Google until you find something, and if you don't find what you need, make what you need.

☐ If you were to write a blog on your experience, what would you call it? What would you write about? Who would you want your audience to be? What would you hope to get out of it? If you'd rather not blog, you can use journaling to get your feelings in writing.

☐ Check out Hellogrief.com, Grief.com, and The Grief Toolbox (thegrieftoolbox.com).

chapter 7

Man's Search for Meaning

*I have always believed, and I still believe, that whatever
good or bad fortune may come our way we can always give it
meaning and transform it into something of value.*

>> **Hermann Hesse,** *Siddhartha*

Please, dear reader, if you're using a highlighter, put it down, as I promise you will not need to highlight the following sentences. Rest your hand for a moment, as you already know this stuff inside out. You have undoubtedly heard these platitudes a million times:

- All's well that ends well.
- Every rainstorm has a rainbow. And each cloud has a silver lining.
- Things could be worse.
- You are better off without him.
- There are other fish in the sea.
- This is a gift in disguise.

This crap ain't news you can use. These trite little sound bites of pseudo-sympathy are an attitude of platitude that don't help you move on, get over the loss of your dream, and get to the other side of this. What they do try to do is stop you from talking about your pain; after all, you've just been told to "turn your frown upside down." Somebody just took your pain and put a bow on it, and while a bow sounds nice, it ties you up and tells you to shut up and just be happy about the way things are. The psychiatrist and writer Robert Jay Lifton calls these kinds of unhelpful platitudes "thought-terminating clichés," which is a name I deeply love. Here is how he explains it: "The most far-reaching and complex of human problems are compressed into brief, highly reductive, definitive-sounding phrases, easily memorized and easily expressed."[1]

It's the "easily memorized and easily expressed" that's going to make you crazy, because when you tell people your dream didn't pan out, they're going to spout off with these clichés:

- You will be okay.
- You'll get over it.
- God doesn't give us more than we can bear.
- You need to focus on the positives.
- Some people have it worse.
- This too shall pass.

Yes, I know the pain will pass eventually, but while I'm in the middle of it, it's pretty freaking miserable. As I said earlier, I believe that most people say these simple clichés because it makes *them* feel better. (Remember that the next time you are consoling someone. Silence is the best response, or a simple "I'm sorry you're going through this.") But back to how the simple platitudes make *me* feel when I'm in the midst of pain: invalidated, infuriated, misunderstood, judged, as if I'm so dumb that the obvious has escaped me, and, depending on the particular nugget of wisdom, offended. (God doesn't give us more than we can bear? My spirituality tells me that my God doesn't give anyone problems, so it is presumptive of people to give me a sanctimonious lecture about *their* beliefs.) *Grrrr.* The bottom line is that these clichés make us feel dismissed, like our pain or grief or struggle isn't even worth "dwelling" on. And that is patently untrue.

Rethinking the Big 3 Platitudes

Here are what I call the Big 3 Platitudes, the ones you're most likely to hear and which are probably the most insidious because they sound so wise at first.

1. Everything happens for a reason.

2. What doesn't kill you makes you stronger.

3. Time heals all wounds.

Let's look more closely beneath their apparent profundity and explore why they probably aren't what you need to hear when you're in the throes of struggling with the loss of your dream.

Everything Happens for a Reason

Perhaps you are hip to my not-so-subtle bias that I am not at all sure that this is true. In that philosophy, I hear an implication that we can't know that reason or, more specifically, that the reason we didn't get what we wanted is yet to be discovered—as if there is a plan that we are not yet privy to, but just hold on, tiger, and all will be revealed. This use of the phrase implies a future in which it all will make sense, and we will say, "Oh, *this* is why that happened! I get it now!" And in that scenario, of course, it is implied that whatever happened was, in fact, for the best.

In my humble opinion, it's not that there is some big cosmic conspiracy theory or that God intervenes and stops you from getting what you most want in order to teach you stuff. I simply can't believe that. My version of God, while sketchy and not formed enough to be articulated into an elaborate cosmological or theological discourse, is for sure not the kind of God that would tell you, "I am putting you through intense pain in order to teach you a lesson." It just doesn't sound like the modus operandi of a loving God. I don't for a second believe that you didn't get X because some divine or cosmic force meant for you to get Y. That is not to say that meaning can't be made from what happened to you. Let me explain.

I am not sure if Marilyn Monroe ever actually said this, but this quote is credited to her:

> I believe that everything happens for a reason. People change so that you can learn to let go, things go wrong so that you appreciate them when they're right, you believe lies so you eventually learn to trust no one but yourself, and sometimes good things fall apart so better things can fall together.

This philosophy is more complicated than "everything happens for a reason." But it still implies that there is a purpose to the pain and maybe even some kind of intelligence that is intervening that sees that you need to learn this lesson. I am arguing that that meaning may not be inherent, but that doesn't mean that meaning can't be made. We can take the pain, disappointment, loss, and despair that comes with not getting what we most wanted and make it meaningful.

I would like to change this sentence from "everything happens for a *reason*" to "everything happens from a *cause*." This, to my mind, is a vital distinction and an important one that allows us not to feel quite so crappy, cursed, victimized, or prone to turn our pain into something more than it is. Let's take a minute and look at the difference between *cause* and *reason;* the two may seem synonymous, but to my mind they are most definitely not one and the same. If we break it down, it goes like this: Your dream ending didn't happen for a reason, but it did happen from a cause. The causes of dreams not fulfilled are varied, wide, and complex, but there is always a cause, which is something that can be explained.

My cause goes like this: I didn't conceive because I was very late in trying to conceive (after thirty-five), and my then-husband and I had physiological and biological issues that made conception much more unlikely. We utilized the best medical minds at our disposal, and they gave us the statistics. We knew full well that the odds were stacked against us, we tried anyway, and we failed to conceive. Our doctors, who were skilled and professional, were not baffled by the results. They knew our odds were slim.

Okay, that is the cause. That is the truth of why I didn't get pregnant. When I was in my grief, however, I did not look at the cause—not even for a second. I tried to come up with a heuristic (a rule that I could use to explain my unhappiness): I was unlucky, I was cursed, and I never, ever, ever get anything I want. Yes, I know that last line was histrionic and dramatic and highly tantrummy, but at that time, I couldn't see anything else as the cause. I didn't look at the real facts, uncolored by emotion. And in my attempt to protect myself by turning the loss into evidence that I would always lose, I made myself especially unreceptive to other people giving me "it will all work out for the best" reasons. Those kinds of assertions brought me 0.0 percent comfort.

We can each come up with the cause that crushed our dream. It is important, I think, to know this cause so we can finally say that this didn't happen because of X, with X = all the emotionally charged reasons I've come up with. Naming that and knowing it allows us to take some of the magical thinking out of our "reasoning." I didn't conceive because I was over thirty-five and there were physical factors that made it unlikely that I would conceive. That is not some bizarre anomaly, and it certainly does not indicate that I am unlucky or cursed or that God wants me to have some other path, be a mother to the world, or teach me some valuable spiritual lesson. It's just a fact. The spiritual teacher Jiddu Krishnamurti said, "Understanding comes through being aware of what-is. To know exactly what-is, the real, the actual, without interpreting it, without condemning or justifying it, is surely the beginning of wisdom. It is only when we begin to interpret, to translate according to our conditioning, according to our prejudice, that we miss the truth."[2] This philosophy can be found in many belief systems, including those of modern-day online marketing gurus.

Just the day after writing the above section on how platitudes make me cranky, I saw this quote from Danielle LaPorte, the Internet marketing star and author:

> But contrary to a lot of new age lit theory, gratitude is not always the best immediate response to what life throws at you.
>
> As enlightened as it may sound, "finding the gift in the pain" isn't the first priority when you're actually in pain. Our suffering does NOT want to be denied or avoided, or glossed over with thankfulness. It wants our attention. **When we paint over pain with premature or unexamined gratitude, we're actually delaying our healing.** We're denying a critical part of our experience—the actual suffering, in which there is incredible power and agency.
>
> Are you grateful that you got ripped off? Or that s/he cheated on you? That you missed your flight, were utterly disrespected and/or neglected, got humiliated, had your bike stolen, grew a tumor, lost the love, were harmed, failed the test?
>
> *Wait, don't answer that yet. 1-800-New-Age-Justified-Feedback called and they said that some affirmations of gratitude will make it*

alllll better. That everything happens for a reason, that anger is a toxic emotion, that all is well in the universe. (All these things are true, by the way, but they're only part of the truth.)

When all is NOT well in your part of the universe, THERE—where the wound happened. Don't make the pain pretty with the **theory** of gratitude; be hurt, be pissed, be furious, be weak. Be where it's ugly and uncomfortable—without adding sweetener to it. Spare yourself the karmic explanations, the family of origin connections, the "it's all good" bullshit.[3]

This gal knows of what she speaks, and I can bet that she herself has been in all kinds of pain in her life. She speaks with the wisdom of someone who has felt it.

While on the topic of New Age thought, I want to digress from our platitude revising for a second talk about New Age guilt—no, guilt isn't just for Judeo-Christians anymore. I got my fair share of this kind of guilt when I was in my grief. I had a teacher at a seminar tell me in front of a good-size crowd of people as she sat clad in Chico's hippie-chic on a futon with candles burning and incense flowing, pointing her mudra finger at me, "If you really wanted to be pregnant, you would be. It is your lack of clarity of intention that is keeping you from conceiving."

I can proudly report that after I picked up my jaw from the floor, I immediately hightailed it out of her stupid-worthless-caca-poopoo workshop and did not pass Go or collect $200 (well, I did later write a letter in which I told her how harmful that kind of assertion was, and I requested a full refund and got one). I cried all the way home, because I really wanted a baby—on that I was clear. You really wanted whatever it is that you wanted. We wanted it enough, you and I, and we tried our sweet little tushies off to get it. You visualized it, I am sure. You knew what it would be like. You imagined the details of it. You focused time, energy, money, and resources on having it. You made sacrifices and paid costs to try to make this dream a reality. Don't take that New Age guilt on. It is *not* your fault. Yes, there may be causes that you have responsibility for—I am all for taking responsibility—but it isn't because you lacked clarity, intention, or the vibrational energy to make it happen, or that you had a weird-colored aura. That is not the reason, nor is it the cause. Don't do that to yourself. The truth is that bad things happen to good people, and everyone alive has had the experience of having something they wanted not happen for them, regardless of the state of their aura, the quality of their intention, or the beauty of their visualization board.

What Doesn't Kill You Makes You Stronger

Kelly Clarkson has made a mint singing about a phrase hijacked from the much-quoted German philosopher Friedrich Nietzsche: "What does not kill you makes you stronger." (Oh, how I would love to see Nietzsche sing a duet with Kelly on *American Idol.* Go on, Simon Cowell, I dare you to give crap to the author of *Thus Spoke Zarathustra.* "Freddy, I think you were a little pitchy. And you're a little old to be a pop star.") But back to the platitude at hand: It ain't necessarily so that our pain will make us stronger. It can make us weaker (just as Nietzsche's syphilis didn't kill him, and it didn't make him stronger, either, but caused him to have a mental breakdown). And it is, in fact, possible to become totally defeated by loss and sink into hopelessness and despair and never try again. People do it. It's a thing. You've seen it. You have to know somebody who has had a loss and now refuses to ever take another risk because they can't bear to be hurt again. When you ask them why they don't date again, apply for another job, or look for another house, they drag out their tale of woe, and, even though the woe is really true and valid, they turn their loss into evidence that they always lose.

Noam Shpancer, PhD, in his article "What Doesn't Kill You Makes You Weaker: A History of Hardship Is Not a Life Asset," explains that "the bulk of psychological research on the topic shows that, as a rule, if you are stronger after hardship, it is probably *despite,* not because of the hardship. The school of hard knocks does little more than knock you down, hard. Nietzschian—and country song—wisdom notwithstanding, we are not stronger in the broken places. What doesn't kill us in fact makes us weaker."[4]

Dr. Shpancer explains why we hold on to this belief:

Now it is true that, in an evolutionary sense, those who survive a calamity are by definition the fittest. But it is not the calamity that made them so. For our minds, however, the leap is short between seeing the strong emerge from a calamity and concluding that they are strong because of the calamity. Our brain is a meaning-making machine, designed to sort vast and varied sensory information into coherent, orderly perception, organized primarily in the form of narrative: *this happened, which led to that, which ended up so.* When two things happen together, we assume they are meaningfully linked, and then we rush to bind them in a quite unholy cause-and-effect matrimony.[5]

So, yes, while physiologically we get stronger in a muscular sense by training, working out, and enduring some heavy lifting, psychologically and physiologically our bodies and spirits are *not* strengthened by enduring hardship, pain, and suffering. The opposite can sometimes be true. Dr. Shpancer cites studies that have looked at the effect on the brain of those who endured difficult and traumatic events that hypothetically had the potential to make them "stronger." The science shows that those who endured such events were *not* stronger for enduring them. Being exposed to traumas and tragedies can lead to mental health issues later in life. Such events can have an impact on the amygdala and the hippocampus; changes to these two regions of the brain may make an individual more susceptible to depression. A study on earthquake survivors, for example, observed both amygdala-hippocampal resting state functional connectivity and hippocampal volume to be reduced within twenty-five days post-trauma in survivors. In a study by Ganzel, Kim, Glover, and Temple, "Resilience after 9/11: Multimodal Neuroimaging Evidence for Stress-Related Change in the Healthy Adult Brain," it was discovered that the September 11, 2001, survivors who were closest to the disaster had "lower gray matter volume in amygdala, hippocampus, insula, anterior cingulate, and medial prefrontal cortex, with control for age, gender, and total gray matter volume."[6]

What doesn't kill you, in other words, can be really damaging. I don't think this is the kind of "what doesn't kill you makes you stronger" that Kelly and Uber-Master-Puff-Freddie-Daddy-N (Nietzsche, that is) are talking about. If the pain and loss aren't at a level that is traumatic and brain changing, they can motivate us to learn from them and to have a certain kind of emotional strength, but this isn't something that just happens. If something good is going to emerge from this, it is because you are active, not passive. Pulling the meaning out of an experience doesn't happen by lying on your couch. You can choose not to find meaning in what has happened to you—it is an option. No one is going to make you do it; it takes work and emotional strength to do so. But if you were my patient, on my couch, I would take your pain seriously, *and* it is likely that I would also do everything in my power to get you to see what strengths, qualities, and insights emerged out of it—I would help you turn the crisis into an opportunity. It is up to you whether you hear me or not. You could always put your fingers in your ears and sing "La-di-da-di-da" until you got me to shut up; that said, I am tenacious, so you'd better get ready to sing for a while.

We can't just sit back and be passive and hope that everything will all work out for the best. There is work that has to be done. It takes work, I believe, to turn scar tissue into emotional strength, and it is easier not to let that happen. But that work is what I am trying to help you to achieve in this chapter. I want to reiterate, I believe this is an active process and not one that just happens. It isn't the surviving that makes you stronger, or just enduring. If you are stronger, it is because you are doing something with the pain, not letting it incapacitate you and leave you weakened.

If I could revise this platitude, I would rewrite it like this: *What doesn't kill you makes you stronger as long as the trauma isn't so severe that it changes your brain functioning; and, if it isn't that severe, that you don't collapse and give up and refuse to do the work that is required in order to make this suffering meaningful to you.* Sure, it is harder to turn into a bumper sticker or a best-selling song, but it is more accurate.

Time Heals All Wounds

This is another platitude that tries to argue the idea that good stuff will automatically come your way if you simply endure your suffering. You know intellectually that this isn't true. You know that if you have a cut, there are things you have to do to optimize the likelihood of healing: wash it, keep it clean, apply antibiotics. There is stuff to do in order for healing to happen. However, there are wounds, both physical and emotional, that won't ever get all the way better, for which there's no complete cure. And, yes, let's take a minute to differentiate between *cure* and *heal*—even timeworn bromide doesn't promise that it will *cure* all wounds. Why? Because it just doesn't; yet, we infer in this context that *cure* and *heal* mean the same thing. They don't and it won't.

Again, this pity party of passive pontification inspires zero action, digging, meaning making, or processing. It urges you to just sit back and wait for the healing to happen through the sands of an hourglass, which, dear you, is not the way healing works.

The truth is something more like this: *Time won't necessarily heal this wound, but it won't always hurt like it does now, and it doesn't mean you won't ever be happy again—and above all, since you have time, why not use it wisely to move through your pain in an active and conscious way?* That said, this wound is part of you, it is part of your story, and it is unlikely that it will totally heal (you won't be cured). There are things you can do to make the wound less likely to get metaphorically or psychologically infected, but totally gone? Not likely (we'll get more into the myth of closure in the final chapter—and I promise it is not as bleak as it sounds).

Shit Happens, but Good Stuff Happens, Too

As you can tell, I am really not a huge fan of platitudes, but if I had to pick one that I would use for myself, one that would acknowledge that life is complex (both good and bad) it would be "shit happens." But then, I would expand it to include the phrase "but good stuff happens, too." I like to add in that second part to remind myself that just because I didn't get what I wanted most doesn't mean good stuff doesn't happen to me. It's sometimes easy to lose sight of that. For a while, I just told my story through the lens of feeling cursed, but even as I was committed to the cursed narrative, good things were happening.

To illustrate my point, I am turning to one of my favorite Taoist parables from 500 BCE. It's the story of a farmer who has good stuff happen and some fair amount of shit happen, too:

So there's this farmer, and he has lots of farmer type stuff to be done. And his horse bails on him. Horse is gone, and no theft prevention software or tracking device is on hand. His friends and family hear the news and sympathetically say, "Wow, that's some bad luck." The farmer, being wise, replies, "Good luck/bad luck." Some time later, the runaway horse returns and brings with him some wild horses. The farmer's friends and family get all excited: "Wow, that's great luck you've got." The farmer replies, "Good luck/bad luck." The farmer's son takes one of the wild horses for a spin and is thrown from the horse and has severe injuries. The friends and family share their usual refrain, "Wow, that's some bad luck there." The farmer answers, "Good luck/bad luck." When the son is in bed, lying around and recovering, the military recruitment officer arrives to enlist all the young men in the village into mandatory service. Guess what? The son is spared because he can't get up and out of bed. His friends and family say, "Wow, that's some good luck." The wise farmer, remaining true to his Taoist outlook on life, replies, "Good luck/bad luck."

You get me? Good things happen, bad things happen. It's too early to decide how everything in your life is going to turn out. Your life isn't over yet. None of us knows for sure what is going to happen next.

The Things We Might Learn

In the vein of making meaning of your pain, I want you to keep in mind that you are likely learning stuff about you, the world you live in, and your strengths that you might not have learned any other way. Even before I gave up on trying to conceive, when I was still in "make it happen" mode, I could see that there were benefits to what was happening beyond what was intended. I was learning to tolerate ambiguity, for example, which did help a bit. You see, prior to infertility treatment, I was not a person who did well with the following phrases: "Let's play it by ear," or "We'll see what happens." Yuck! Just saying those words can take me back to the person I was pre-infertility. I needed to *know*. I needed to have things be clear and certain and tied up in a big red bow with absolutely no strings hanging around. But infertility treatment taught me to tolerate ambiguity like nothing before had ever been able to. Much of life is ambiguous, so this was a very valuable lesson. Not knowing exactly how things are going to turn out or not having the perfect solution to a problem no longer gives me hives. Another benefit to my experience came in the professional realm. My own experiences with infertility have been enormously helpful in my work with patients. I am more empathic and feel like I better understand other people's pain about life not turning out the way they wanted it to. Of course, I could have learned these lessons in other ways, but learning them the way I did gave me the awesome benefit of now getting to help others find a way to move on and let go and find their happy ending—and that is, as the Baskin-Robbins slogan goes, "31 flavors" of awesome.

I learned other stuff, too. There is nothing like enduring double-digit rounds of IUI and four rounds of IVF to teach you that you *are* tenacious and have the stick-to-itiveness of an angry badger. I didn't know that about myself before. I had mistakenly seen myself as a quitter and a flibbertigibbet—a girl who innocently decides that she really doesn't want to play the guitar, and the next thing she knows, she has been labeled a quitter. That I possessed tenacity is only one of many things that going through infertility treatment taught me. I learned that feelings, as big and bad and overwhelming as they were, do change and end. I didn't, as I told you before, really know that. These may not seem like big lessons to you, but these insights about myself have allowed me to perceive myself differently, which has allowed me to act differently and ultimately has led to a birth of a different me and a different kind of life than I had prior to the loss of a my dream. As we consciously take inventory of what we gained in this loss (just asking that question is a strength in itself), we will come to see what good qualities and strengths might have come out of the experience. Even though these strengths were hard won, they are strengths nonetheless, and they help us feel like we got something out of all this, even if it isn't the something we wanted most.

Here are some things other people have learned about themselves through adversity:

> Cassandra, who dreamed of a dream house that she never got: "I thought that I was actually a lot more fragile than I am. I think that I also developed a deeper sense of gratitude for what I did have. In fact, focusing on what was right in front of me saved me."

Kim, who lost her dream of a certain kind of life: "It ends up that I am more than I thought I was. That's not saying that I am particularly special, but that I am not as much the quiet, forgettable nerd I supposed, and had been brought up to believe I was. I think I am a much broader person, and qualities I had but were unrealized are perhaps coming out more. Who knew? I think I learned to take parts of myself that others criticized and recognize that they are in fact strengths, and that also has made me a more compassionate person. But I had to learn to be compassionate toward myself first."

Aamir writes: "The most important things I learned were that (a) the world doesn't stop for me, and (b) even I don't stop for me. It sounds trivial, but at seventeen, in India, getting to study engineering at the Indian Institute of Technology was very important to me. It is like getting into MIT with way more competition. I didn't. But I also steadfastly refused to sit the exam again—I didn't want to waste the prime time of my life. I am now bracing to embrace another huge loss around the corner. I know I will get over anything eventually."

Flores, who had to give up her dream of a career in diplomacy: "I learned that I am creative and multidimensional. I always saw myself as only one thing: a nerd. I thought that defined me. Now I know not one thing does."

The Inside Story

When Simon was a little boy, all of his friends dreamed of careers as athletes and firemen, but when he was twelve years old, his uncle took him on a trip to see the stirring sights around Normandy, France, the site of the D-Day invasion in World War II, and that trip changed everything for him. Simon heard the stories of the courageous men who stormed the beaches and parachuted from the sky in the name of securing freedom, and from that moment on, he dreamed of being an officer in the Army. He worked with single-minded devotion through junior high and high school, and in his senior year, he received admission into the exceptionally elite United States Military Academy at West Point.

He arrived at the hallowed campus along with his other new classmates, as proud as could be, but within the first week, Simon was told that he had a condition that would prevent him from continuing in the academy program: He was color blind. He packed his bags and went home, completely distraught. The young man who had studied with such passion now couldn't find the energy to get out of bed each morning. The physical challenges that used to bring him such pleasure—running, lifting weights—no longer held any appeal. He found himself losing weight and failing to get enough sleep. No matter how hard he tried to shake himself out of it, he couldn't. He had fallen into full-blown depression. At the urging of his parents, he ended up seeking treatment from a psychiatrist, who did, in fact, have effective tools to help.

He struggled to find meaning from the path he found himself on. "What good could come of this?" he asked the doctor. They worked on that question, and Simon eventually decided that if he couldn't be an officer in the Army, he would become a scholar of war. He picked up classes at his local community college, transferred to a four-year college after a year, graduated, applied to a PhD program at Duke University, and graduated not only with top honors, but with a Fulbright fellowship. He has spent the last forty years teaching military history. "Yes, I would have loved to have been an officer in the Army," he says, "but if I couldn't be an officer, I was determined to help those who could be." Simon could have easily given up because he felt cursed. He could have blamed God or West Point and used this as a reason to collapse and feel that there is no way out. Instead, he took action, took a look at his deepest needs, found a way to make it work, and ended up with a good and happy life.

The Therapy Couch

Meet Vic. His life was turned upside down, from no fault of his own. Vic was separated from his wife, lost his home, lost his professional life, lost his entire family, and ultimately discovered that he had lost his wife for good.

His dreams were destroyed. As a dream crusher, this was massive. As bad as you think this is, it's worse than that. Yet Vic decided in the midst of this horrible situation to figure out why those who suffered devastating losses and traumas were able to survive—what did they have that others didn't have? Vic felt sure there was something in common with people who survived loss and those who didn't. Vic is Viktor Frankl (I used the nickname for dramatic effect—pretty clever, huh?), and he is the Viennese psychiatrist and neurologist and the author of *Man's Search for Meaning* who lost his entire family in Nazi concentration camps. When Frankl was working in the camp hospitals, he interviewed hundreds of inmates. He discovered something interesting: Those who managed to survive the horrors of the camps had a deeper meaning or purpose in their lives.

Frankl himself had a deeper meaning that motivated him: He was determined to survive in order to reunite with his wife. "He who has a *why* to live for," he said, quoting Nietzsche, "can bear with almost any *how.*" He wrote, "In some ways suffering ceases to be suffering at the moment it finds a meaning, such as the meaning of a sacrifice."[7] So let's find you a meaning, even if you aren't really sure that it is the real meaning. What I'm saying is, create a meaning if you must. You need a *why*, and you can find it if you try. Frankl warns, "Woe to him who saw no more sense in his life, no aim, no purpose, and therefore no point in carrying on."[8] I don't want anyone to say about you "Woe to him" or "Woe to her." So just humor me . . . come on, find one thing about this experience that is meaningful—just one.

Humor as a Survival Strategy

You really wouldn't expect a book about someone who endured the unspeakable horrors of Nazi concentration camps to tell you to laugh it up. Humor and the concentration camps are not things that you'd immediately connect. I mean, I still wonder how *Hogan's Heroes* ever got made. But Frankl claims that a sense of humor about things was hugely important in helping people to survive their situation:

> It is well known that humor, more than anything else in the human make-up, can afford an aloofness and an ability to rise above any situation, even if only for a few seconds. . . . The attempt to develop

a sense of humor and to see things in a humorous light is some kind of a trick learned while mastering the art of living. Yet it is possible to practice the art of living even in a concentration camp, although suffering is omnipresent.[9]

And yes, it is hard to imagine being able to laugh while death hangs in the air, but Frankl and others managed to. "I would never have made it if I could not have laughed. Laughing lifted me momentarily . . . out of this horrible situation, just enough to make it livable . . . survivable."[10]

Remember how my calling babies "little shits" allowed me to laugh and acknowledge my pain in a way that made it possible for me to tolerate seeing what I most wanted? Being able to laugh really helped me. To this day, I remain ever grateful to Ann McBride Norton for helping me to find a way to laugh at my pain. You know what else helped, and gave me permission to laugh at my pain? You aren't going to believe this, but the video game Angry Birds helped me. I know, it's silly, but it's true. You see, in my narrative of Angry Birds, it is the pigs that stopped me from having a child, and I want to blast the pigs and make them pay. I laughed as I blasted the pigs and maybe even said out loud lines like, "Go on pigs, make my day," or "Take that, you stupid pig." Mature, no? But it helped me to be able to laugh again, and laughing, as you know, is a huge relief when you have been crying like a weepy waterfall.

Another thing I want to say about laughing at your pain is that most everyone I spoke to about laughing at their pain reports feeling some sense of shame about it. "I know it's wrong," they say, or "You'll think it was sick that we could laugh at this," or "It sounds twisted, but this made me laugh." It is not wrong, and I don't think it's sick or twisted, and here's a secret: We all do it. If you can find something to laugh about, more power to you!

_____ *Movie Rx*

Harry Potter and the Sorcerer's Stone.[11] I will admit to you that it is an utter and total delight to recommend a movie to you that might not dissolve you into a hot, sobbing mess. And, yes, while this film begins after a tragedy, it is still a relief to watch wizards in robes and mystical magical make-believe after the all-too-real suffering in *Ordinary People*. Yes, Harry Potter's first film begins in a dark place, no doubt: Harry's parents are killed by "He-who-shall-not-be named," and that is a devastating loss for him—the loss of the dream of a normal childhood. Harry is orphaned, and he is both literally and symbolically scarred by the experience. A lightning bolt scar on Harry's forehead is a constant reminder of what he has lost and how that loss impacts him and what it has required him to face.

It is interesting to note that in the first meeting with Ron, his first and best friend at the school of witchcraft and wizardry, Hogwarts, Ron misreads the scar as a badge of honor and not as a reminder of pain.

> *Ron: I'm Ron, by the way, Ron Weasley.*
> *Harry: I'm Harry. Harry Potter.*
> *Ron: So . . . so it's true! I mean, do you really have the . . . the . . .*
> *Harry: The what?*
> *Ron: [in a hushed tone] The scar?*
> *Harry: Oh.*
> *[shows him the scar on his forehead]*
> *Harry: Yeah.*
> *Ron: Wicked!*

Yeah, not so wicked for Harry. It is a sign of a loss, a trauma, and a great deal of emotional pain (since in his case, it led to living with family members who housed him in a cupboard underneath the stairs and deprived him of emotional and physical nurturing). But people do this. They misread our scars, and they do what Ron did and try to transform it into something "awesome." "Oh," they say to me. "You are so lucky not to have kids. You get to spoil yourself." I, like Harry, have to muffle the scream and stop myself from saying, "Yeah, it's awesome to lose what you wanted most, totally wicked."

Harry's scar connects him to his past. He is changed by the experience that gave him that scar, and his identity is not what it would have been had it never happened. Just in case you might miss this fact, author J. K. Rowling made it so that Harry can't hide this wound; it is on his forehead, for goodness sake, and people are constantly reminding him of it. So what's the point for you and me, who don't boast lightning bolt scars on our foreheads? Out of his loss, Harry loses his identity, and he is on a journey to find himself, to discover who he is and what purpose will make his loss meaningful for him. That's our gig, too.

If Harry hadn't known this loss, he would not have had the motivation to confront his fears. If his parents had lived, he would have been an ordinary wizard, but instead he becomes one of the greatest wizards of all time. Okay, let's take a moment and tell the truth . . . if we were to ask Harry, he would likely tell us that as awesome as it was to be a famous wizard, at the end of the day he would have preferred that his mom and dad had lived, and he would have picked a life that was a tad bit more ordinary. Yes, the terrible loss does allow Harry the opportunity to transform into his truest self, but there may have been other ways for him to achieve this.

Now let's take a look at what Harry did to become his truest self. He did not simply make wizardy lemonade out of lemons, which is, after all, just adding sugar to something sour and unsavory. Nor did he just cast a spell to make his loss meaningful and say insincerely: "Hocus-pocus-phony-opus, I am so happy to be an orphan. I am just tickled to bits to have a scar that marks me as a target for He-who-shall-not-be-named. And I am super-delighted to live with these miserable Muggles and to have to go on adventure after adventure in which I risk life and limb." Harry instead accepted his reality, saw the cause of his life situation, and set about to make it meaningful. We need to do the same. Like young Mr. Potter, we need to face the scar and see our strengths, our resources, our tenacity, and other unexpected qualities that emerge out of this experience, help others if we can (like Frankl advised), and have a laugh or two. What we need to do is more psychologically satisfying and sophisticated than mere lemonade making or the fancy spinning of pain into an instant positive. It is, methinks, more like making a delicious lemon liqueur, as I said in the introduction to this book. You accept the situation: I have lemons. You sit with your lemons. You cry a bit. You taste the bitterness of the fruit. You slice into them and see what they are made of, and you start making an effort to do something with what is before you. With a little effort something transformative truly emerges that can be enjoyed. This isn't just (to mix a metaphor) putting lipstick on a pig; it takes real work.

Harry Potter shows us that we can discover strengths through facing the death of our dream that we might not have otherwise recognized or that might not have emerged.

Grief serves as a transformative experience for Harry, as it can for us. He finds his strength and resiliency and is able to confront and overcome what he fears most. He doesn't collapse and refuse to take action and stay living in the cupboard of his aunt and uncle's house. He becomes stronger in the broken places; he takes risks. He chooses not to let the loss stop him from living. Confronting and ultimately killing "He-who-shall-not-be-named" does not give him what he wants most (for his parents to be alive, to be a part of a loving family), but it does allow him to become a stronger person and to use his own grief (and the strength that emerged from that grief) to help others. Yes, it might be easier to transform your pain more quickly if you had a wand, a cape, and a PhD in the Dark Arts, but watching Harry, Ron, and their friend Hermione overcome their enemies reminds us that we can find strength and a new identity in the most dire circumstances. Phoenixes never rise out of grassy meadows; they rise from ashes. Those ashes, the manure, the chaos and confusion, are the birthplaces of new possibilities—even if it feels like there are eight movies between you and that happy ending.

SELF-HELP SUGGESTIONS

- [ ] What platitudes have you heard from others? How do they make you feel? How might you respond to these platitudes? How can you gently and lovingly explain that it doesn't feel good to have a bow put on your pain?

- [ ] What is the cause (not the reason) of your dream not coming true? Look at the reality of it. Look at the unemotional truth of it. Seek the statistics. Does this loss happen to other people? Are there others who know this pain and disappointment?

☐ Have you created a malignant or self-destructive "reason" for not getting your dream? Are you telling yourself a horrible story in which you are being punished, that you are cursed? If so, what other narrative can you create in its place?

☐ We talked in the last chapter about how healing your wound can be a help to others who are going through the same thing you are. How might you help others who have endured what you have? If you don't feel that you are in a place where you could be a help to anyone, consider trying it with just one person. You'd be surprised to know how many others might benefit from your sharing exactly where you are.

☐ Ask others to tell you the strengths and qualities they see in you in how you went after your dream and how you are coping now. Be prepared to write down what they say, as you will have a hard time actually believing they are talking about you. Later, you can take out the list and let it soak in.

☐ Have you come up with faulty rules/beliefs/heuristics based on this one loss? What are they? What are you generalizing into your now and into your future based on this loss?

☐ How has your philosophy of life changed? What was it before? What is it now?

☐ What was your maxim/motto before the loss of the dream? What is it now?

☐ How has this experience changed who you are? How has your identity changed? Can you see how this scar can serve you? How it might be purposeful in some way? You might not be able to see this now, but maybe you will in time. Where might you be stronger than you were before? What qualities might have been revealed through this experience?

☐ What meaning can you find in your experience? What could you possibly say, if you had to, about yourself through the loss of your dream? Come on, there is something.

☐ What *why* can you use to motivate you? Why do you need to carry on? Move on? Find a happy ending? What motivates you to get to the other side of this?

☐ Could you be ignoring all the good things in your life? Are there good things in your life that this pain has made you edit out in some way? Do you believe that if you see that good, it means you are no longer taking that loss seriously? (It doesn't—I promise.)

☐ Dumbledore's advice to Harry is gold: "It does not do to dwell on dreams, Harry, and forget to live." How can you benefit from this advice? Are you forgetting to live? Is there some area of your life that you are forgetting that serves you and that you actually enjoy with or without the dream being a part of your life?

☐ Read Viktor Frankl's classic book *Man's Search for Meaning*—it is truly a must-read. If people can find meaning in a concentration camp, it is possible to find meaning anywhere.

☐ While I am in book-suggesting mode, also check out Harold S. Kushner's *When Bad Things Happen to Good People* and *How We Grieve: Relearning the World* by Thomas Attig.

☐ Can you find something, anything, to laugh about here? What in this situation is funny? Even gallows humor is okay. If you don't find it today, maybe you will soon. It is said that comedy is tragedy plus time. So, it might take some time to see the humor. Viktor Frankl's peers challenged themselves to come up with a joke a day. Can you do the same?

chapter 8

The Symbolic Meaning of Your Dream

"Nothing I know matters more than what never happened."

>> **John Burnside, Hearsay**

*"The only thing worse than not getting what you want
is getting what you want."*

>> **Oscar Wilde**

*"Ultimately, it is the desire, not the desired, that we love."
[Or, paradoxically, desire is not the means, but the end—
so there's no way it could ever be fulfilled.]*

>> **Friedrich Nietzsche**

One of my favorite shows is *Girls* on HBO. The main character, Hannah, had a *big* dream. She longs to publish a book of essays and imagines that when she does, it will come with instant happiness, social cachet, and a life in which everything is well. She moves to New York to follow her dream, but instead becomes a financially dependent coffee shop worker. That doesn't stop her from identifying as a writer and dreaming her dream. Hannah finally gets an offer of publication; her ship has come in! She finally has the reality that she's dreamed of—only she does not actually get what she imagined. No one reacts the way she imagined they would. No one cares. No one sees her differently. She is still Hannah; she feels alone, insecure, and disappointed, and she even has a mental breakdown. Why? She didn't just want the achievement of publication; she wanted a whole host of things that she thought would come with publication. And she, my friends, is a mirror we can hold up to ourselves because we are very likely doing a very similar thing with our dreams.

Looking at Only the Bright Side of Life

In our fantasy version of things, we don't have any of the stressors, headaches, or impingements from the dream. The fantasy version is mostly good and free of frustrations and almost all awesome—and this makes sense. Because, goodness gracious, why would we go fantasizing about the bad part of our dreams? Well, there might be a reason. According to Adam Phillips, the British psychoanalyst and author of *Missing Out: In Praise of the Unlived Life*, if there are no frustrations, then there is no reality.[1] When someone thinks about playing in the big leagues, for example, they imagine the cheering crowds, the newspaper headlines, standing on the field during the playoffs, the camaraderie of being on a winning team. They tend not to think about the booing crowds, the shoulder surgeries, the scathing commentary after a poor performance, the lonely nights in strange hotels. When we think about the dream, we tend to idealize how it would be; the harsh truths of reality are rarely part of it. Deconstructing the dream and seeing how unreal many aspects of it likely are can help us to see how our desires create fantasies that we end up striving for in place of what's actually possible—what's real. We want a dream world where there are no frustrations. But a life without the realities of life is not possible, *ever.* All dreams, when realized, have realities that are frustrating. No matter the dream (getting the guy, becoming a congressman, having the successful business, winning an Olympic gold medal), it is the dream without the consequences that we desire and the dream without the consequences that we are likely to mourn. These realities are never the pure, perfect, and ideal versions of what we imagined them to be.

St. Teresa of Ávila wrote the famous line "More tears are shed over answered prayers than unanswered ones." Now, I don't know if Teresa is actually right, but I can tell you that I have seen people who tried to heal past pains through relationships, achievements, fame, and success, and it is a rare person who comes bounding into my office, saying, "You know what? Now that I have achieved X, I totally feel released and satisfied, and everyone and everything is entirely as I imagined it to be." I tell you this not out of sour grapes; I tell you this so you can understand the simple truth that as wonderful as accomplishments, degrees, TV shows, marriages, being on the cover of *Fortune,* or being on the best-seller list might be, these things don't heal old wounds and don't all of a sudden protect you from pain, loss, loneliness, or despair. You are wise, so I know you know this. But sometimes, often usually, we believe that a dream come true will cure some of that stuff, and as long as the dream is in its *potential* state, it is not burdened by any of these realities—the disappointments, losses, failures, and everything else that make up the dark side of getting what we want. And, yes, every single dream come true comes with a dark side.

Ask people who have "made it," and you will hear them speak of this dark side. They use words like *letdown, anticlimactic, lonely at the top.* It's a cliché to say that it's the journey, not the destination, but when it comes to dreams, it also happens to often be true.

Analyzing Your Dream

If I had a dollar for every time a patient told me that they had a "crazy dream last night," I would be writing this book from the Four Seasons in Bora Bora, lounging in my waterfront hut and drinking a $35 mai tai. And as I find myself wanting to laugh at the dreamer's disclaimer, I do get what they are saying—dreaming of ice skating with Martha Washington and the kid from *The Wonder Years* and the next thing you know you are on a TV show where you are taking your SAT exams with your pants off? Yeah, it can seem a bit on the wackadoodle side. However, the kinds of dreams we dream when asleep are only crazy and confusing because we don't understand what they *really* mean—we don't know their language. These dreams are coded in a symbolic language that isn't always easily accessible but is most definitely decipherable. However, this is not a code that you can ask someone else to crack; we don't find the answers to what our nighttime dreams mean by turning to a dream dictionary or even to a therapist who works with dreams (though we *are* pretty good at teaching you how to crack your code). No, each dream is as different as the dreamer who is having the dream and can only be fully understood by you investing the time and energy required to understand it. You and I could have the exact same dream, but it would mean something totally unique and idiosyncratic to each of us; that is to say, it is the dreamer who determines the meaning of the dream. As your dreams were custom built especially for the contents of your psyche, it is you who has the secret decoder ring to figure out why you are figure skating with the wife of "I can't tell a lie" Washington.

In therapy, I help patients understand the meaning of their nighttime dreams by unpacking each image and exploring their memories, associations, thoughts, recollections, and feelings about "ice skating" and "Martha Washington" and when your "Wonder Years" were and how you feel naked and exposed in a testing environment. When you start to work at making sense of your nighttime dreams, you will see that you have very personal associations to each image, and that your reactions to ice skating and George's better half are as unique and idiosyncratic as you are. Take the time to look at your personal meaning and association to the imagery, and all of a sudden you are aware that you are really afraid of falling, failing, and losing support from your mother if you don't get the job you have been interviewing for. What was crazy suddenly becomes meaningful, by just taking some time and energy to unpack what the dream *really* meant.

According to the grand pooh-bah of nighttime dreams, Sigmund Freud, our dreams are expressing our unconscious desires, or are wish fulfillments. And according to Cleantis (that's me), our daytime dream, or life goals, can give us a whole lot of insight into what we want psychologically, in other words, our not-so-conscious desires. Our dreams to be something or somebody have a certain hidden and obfuscated meaning, the same as nighttime dreams do, and it is very likely we don't know that meaning. Sound crazy? I know, I know, I know (another $1 just went into my mai tai slush fund)! We get so locked into the manifest content of our dreams and desires—*I want this man, this job, this career, this life, this goal*—that we stop there and we don't ask how this desire speaks to a more unconscious psychological desire. But, trust me, there can be more to it than we just want what we want; we are, I believe, more complicated creatures than that. What I am saying, and I kind of hope that this makes me the grand pooh-bina (that is the feminine version of grand pooh-bah of analyzing daytime dreams) is that there can be latent content to our daytime dreams just the way there is to our nighttime dreams. What that means in fancy-pants psychoanalytic-speak is that there's more to why we want the things that we want other than just "we want them."

The Unlived Life Must Be Examined

Socrates, when he wasn't donning a toga, getting into some serious "what's the meaning of life?" chats with perfect strangers, or downing unwanted hemlock, was famous for saying that the unexamined life wasn't worth living. Adam Phillips, whom I mentioned earlier, goes a step further and argues for the importance of examining the *unlived* life. The unlived life—or who we failed to be—can, according to Phillips, become the story of our lives, and it is, therefore, a story worth examining. Our unlived life, our dream that never was, gives us clues into the essence of what we *really* hoped life would give us. Phillips says that our unrealized dream makes us who we are. "And what was not possible," he writes, "all too easily becomes the story of our lives."[2] Phillips asserts that we need to find a way to "learn to live somewhere between the lives we have and the lives we would like."[3]

It's Take-Your-Dream-to-Therapy Day

If you press deep into your daytime dream, you will likely find some emotional and psychological reason that you want it so badly. Go on, dig deep. How? Simple enough. Here's what I am asking you to do: I want you to take that dead dream out and put it on the psychoanalytic couch for a moment. Once it stops squirming and gets comfortable, I want you to ask it some questions. I want you to ask it some stuff to get to the deeper psychological significance of why you wanted this dream so much. When you start asking these questions, it is likely it will say, "I don't know," or "Nothing." Or it will just stare quietly at you and ask you where exactly you did your training to be a therapist and that it would like to invoke its Fifth Amendment privilege on the grounds that it might incriminate itself. Or it might try to change the subject by reminding you how sad you are that you don't have the dream— but don't let its laconic grunts, condemnatory tones, or distractions stop you from your inquiry. Keep on asking, "Who was I going to be with the dream, and who do I think I am without it?" Don't race through that question. Take a minute . . . take a breath. Let yourself answer that question. Let yourself see what answers come, what ideas, images, and associations might be hiding there. And keep asking questions like

What did I imagine this dream coming true would give me?

How did I imagine that would change things for me?

Would it right a wrong?

Would it heal an injury, hurt, wound, insecurity from the past?

Did I think I would finally be lovable if I got that dream?
Who would love or approve of me if I got that dream, who I am not sure does now?

Would it give me the one thing that would make me invulnerable to hurt, poverty, loneliness, illness, aloneness, insecurity, and criticism?

Would having that dream compensate for some imagined deficit from the past?

When I was singularly focused on my dream to have a baby, there was no one telling me that there was any symbolic reason that I wanted a baby so damn much. I just wanted what I wanted, damn it! And initially, if you asked me why I wanted it, I could have told you loads of reasons, but I couldn't tell you the psychological meaning of why I wanted it so much. Of course there was meaning—I likely knew it then—I just didn't want to know why I wanted it. There was something in me that just wanted the literal interpretation and was a bit afraid of the *why* that motivated this kind of singular devotion. I wasn't willing to look at the *why* of it until after I was done trying to conceive. One day, my therapist wouldn't let me get away with "I just wanted it!" any longer. She kept pushing and helped me to get to the heart of what I *really* wanted in wanting a baby.

So many people I spoke to as I did interviews for this book admitted that they believed if they got X, then Y would happen, meaning they thought their dream would come with added benefits that they hadn't explicitly made known to themselves. A brilliant writer friend admitted, somewhat embarrassed, "The truth of why I wanted a best-selling book (and I didn't know this at the time) was that I dreamed of having a reason to go to fancy stores to buy the kind of outfit you'd wear on TV or when giving a speech—the dress, the purse, the shoes, everything. I imagined that I would then walk into a room and, just by my fabulous clothes, people would know that I had made it. I wasn't just one of the legion of desperate wannabe writers. I was legitimate. That was what I really wanted—a visible mark of achievement." I am happy to report that even though she hasn't had a book go to the best-seller list yet, this friend has an incredible career that is very rewarding for her. She has found her way to a deeper, more personal sense of her own legitimacy—and she hasn't let the lack of a best seller stop her from getting a "best-seller outfit" or two.

We rarely just want the "best-seller." We want the stuff that we imagine will come with it.

If I got the house, then I would have had the ability to socialize without effort, and I would have friends and family, and I would love to cook.

If he loved me, then I would never be alone again, and I would feel confident and secure and safe all the time.

If we had made that business a success, then I would finally belong and be one of the cool kids; I'd fit in and everyone would know it.

If I got that job, it would prove once and for all that I am a success.

If I had made my dream a reality, then my father would finally love me.

If I did this kind of work, it would mean my life is meaningful.

If I were an astronaut, it would mean I was doing something important with my life.

If I had a child, I would have a family and wouldn't feel like an outsider anymore; I would belong to a family.

Dream Fulfillment = "Happily Ever After" Ending

As you start to see the answers come to the surface, you might see that underneath the dream is a belief that when the dream comes true, we will be bulletproof, and "happily ever after" will actually exist for us. Sadly, even if you get the dream, it doesn't have the power to give you happily ever after.

One of the big benefits of understanding why we wanted the dream is that it helps us look at the reality rather than the fantasy. We can evaluate whether the dream would have given us the secondary psychological benefits we desire. Sometimes the dream come true does indeed give us what we really want, but many times it doesn't. There are plenty of people who get the man, the job, the house, the Academy Award, and a seat on a space shuttle and who still don't feel loved, secure, valued, and healed from past hurts.

Seeing What We Wanted from the Dream Can Sometimes Give Us Another Chance at It

Looking at the dream symbolically also allows us to disengage from the idea that our happiness is dependent on realizing the dream. Understanding the *why* of the dream and discovering the essence of what we really wanted from it allows us a way to have satisfaction that we had not imagined possible. If we were after love, healing, meaning, value, purpose, self-worth, belonging, or some other quality, there are other ways of getting those things than through writing the great American novel, owning a clothing store, or being the next Steve Wynn or Steve Jobs.

When I got to the core of why, psychologically speaking, I wanted a baby so very badly, it turned out that it was because I wanted to give my inner child a different kind of childhood than I had. I wanted to right the wrongs of my childhood by giving someone the kind of childhood that I wished I'd had. I wanted redemption. Beyond having a child, I wanted to have the experience of a great child-focused childhood. I even planned out a sweet Pottery Barn bedroom for my not-yet-born little girl. Yeah . . . that girl was me. I was, God help that child, determined to give it all that I hadn't had. And this is where Jung's wise words of warning pop into my head like a proverbial weasel: "The greatest burden a child must bear is the unlived life of the parents." Hopefully, if I had actually had a child, I would have caught on to the fact that

I was trying to heal my own issues through parenting, and I would have found a way to proceed so that I wasn't parenting out of a response to my own pain, but instead was parenting the real tangible kiddo in front of me and taking care of him or her and not my own needs.

Once I understood what I really wanted from the dream psychologically, I could see how I could begin to be a better parent to myself, nurture myself, and heal the wounds of childhood in other ways than having a literal child. Even as I mourned that I couldn't give a child what I wanted, I started to see that dealing directly with the psychological desire underlying my baby dreams was a more direct route to healing that desire than actually having a child. Understanding why I wanted a child did not completely cure me of the pain of not having a child, not by a long shot, but it did allow me to explore other ways I could meet that need, and that did take some, not all, of the sting out.

The Danger of a Dream Giving You Self-Worth, Happiness, and Love

When we imagine that there is only one way we can be loved, valued, prized, safe, secure, or have meaning in our lives, we are not seeing things so clearly. There are a lot of issues that need to be dealt with if part of your dream fulfillment was to gain worth, approval, validation, and love through an accomplishment. First, how great would it feel to know that you get to feel good about yourself only if you achieve X? And what if people in your life agreed? What if they said things like, "Well, Rita, the truth is I only like you because you are a doctor," or "Bob, because you have managed to buy a Maserati dealership, you are lovable and valuable," or "Jessica, I want you to know that because you didn't make that dream a reality, I have to cut you loose. You are simply unlovable without realizing this dream." Can you imagine? Well, the truth is that we do this to ourselves and believe others will join in on this unfortunate shaming reindeer game.

No achievement, be it job, personal, or relational, can be the golden ticket to feeling loved, appreciated, valued, and awesome about yourself. If it were, then the rates of depression, suicide, and addiction would be less for those who are rich, successful, and famous, but in fact the opposite is true. Suicide rates are much higher among the famous than those who are living ordinary lives.[4] People who are the most successful don't report feeling more loved or valued than others who are less successful. A whole lot of fame, success, and accomplishment can actually make you feel more insecure, because suddenly you are not always seen for who you really are, but are instead seen for what you achieved. There are some dreams that you might not imagine have this kind of impact—the dream of a relationship, for example, or to parent or to own a home—but even those kinds of dreams may have at their core the belief that they prove our worthiness, value, and belonging and might guarantee some sense of safety or worth.

Richard M. Ryan and Tim Kasser conducted a study in 1996 at the University of Rochester in which they asked 100 adults about what they aspired to, what their motivations were.[5] Ryan and Kasser concluded that those whose goals were related to how they were perceived by others had higher levels of distress than those whose goals were more about self-acceptance. What that means is that you are more likely to be bummed out, even if you get the dream, if what you are after through your dream is admiration, love, and acceptance from others.

The Inside Story

Sally's dream was for a committed relationship with one specific man. "I had always harbored a strong attraction to a man I had known as a friend for over ten years. I sensed he had a similar attraction toward me, yet we were both married and did not explore anything more. After my divorce, this man told me his wife was gay, and while they had made a conscious decision to remain in family, both openly had other relationships. We became lovers, and the connection was intense for me, like no relationship before. I was very much in love with him, and he loved me, too, but he consistently said he was not looking for a relationship and might never be in a committed relationship again. My dream was that he [Elliot] would eventually claim me and give me the commitment I longed for, and we would be a couple."

Sally was looking for a happily ever after, but Elliot couldn't be tied down. Even as she acknowledged how commitment-phobic Elliot was and suffered due to his intermittent availability, Sally worked hard at winning Elliot over, making herself available on a moment's notice, creating romantic dinners, and being all that any man could want. She ignored his explicit warnings that he wasn't available, wouldn't commit, and never would. "When we were together, it was so incredible that I continued to believe he would eventually choose me, but I was continually wounded when he didn't. It took a very long time for me to accept that I was not going to achieve my dream with this guy. I not only loved him very deeply, [but] we were best friends, and I felt he was the kind of person I had always wanted to be with—a poet, savvy in matters of depth, a student and devotee of many of the same mentors I admired. It was easy for me to attribute his reticence to the fact that he was still married and not truly available. Letting go meant hard-core grief and fear that I might never love someone that much again—maybe even that at root I was simply unlovable. It was easier to stay in the relationship than it was to accept that."

And so she didn't let go. She pursued the dream for three more years. Her epiphany came during a poetry salon when he recited a poem he had written about extreme passion for a lover's kiss. "The truth landed on me with authority: I would never be that lover—the one and only Beloved incarnate—for this man. A few weeks later we walked under a super-moon, and I told him I could not continue our relationship because I needed more, and I needed to respect my need and act on it. I grieved hard and completely. I was just beginning to heal when (less than three months later), he informed me via email that he was 'in love and in a relationship.' It was a what-the-fuck moment and a further blow to the fragile sense of worthiness I was nurturing."

When Sally got into therapy, she started to look at why she wanted him so much. She believed Elliot to be her "soul mate" because he represented things that she wanted: He was an artist, poet, and drummer and was loaded with mythopoeic goodness, and Sally had grown up in a family that didn't allow her to access that side of herself, so she made practical choices instead. She loved that Elliot was more likely to read a poem in the morning than the *Wall Street Journal*. In wanting Elliot, Sally wanted to be with that part of herself that she didn't feel like she could access on her own. "[Through therapy] I realized I was attempting to heal an ancient wound of feeling unworthy of love. I found my commitment and connection to myself increased exponentially, and I knew I could create a fulfilling life even if I never found a loving, committed partner. I attained a solid position from which my lovability and worthiness were not in question."

In retrospect, Sally came to understand that it wasn't Elliot that she wanted so much, it was something more. "My dream might be more accurately stated that I wanted to be claimed. I wanted to be with someone who was proud to be with me and wanted to shout it from the rooftops. I wanted to be somebody's person/partner." Sally wanted to have the experience of being chosen:

> Before I gave up on realizing that dream with Elliot, I felt a lot of hope alternating with shame and unworthiness. I figured if what we had and what I had to offer was not enough to make him want a "relationship" with me, there must be something wrong with me. It was particularly baffling because he would tell me how fantastic he thought I was, praise my good qualities, gifts, depth, intellect, compassion, beauty, etc., and tell me that he loved me, yet none of that was enough to make him want me for his person/partner. I kept believing that one day he would "see the light," and there were times when he was more attentive that kept me stringing along. During phase one of giving up that dream, I accepted his version of things, that he just was not cut out for a relationship and probably never would be. I had reached a point in my process where I knew I had to step away and accept that my dream was not forthcoming with him and that that wasn't about me.

Sally also realized that in all of her romantic relationships, she was looking for a partner to provide some kind of spiritual salvation.

> This was a big aha for me! I can remember very specific examples from each major relationship. And I also connected this (very easily) to my background in the Mormon church; for example, in the temple ceremony, men covenant to follow and obey God, while women covenant to follow and obey their husbands. There is this whole thing about "line of authority" in which men stand between women and God, and a woman is only held accountable for following her husband. If he makes a "bad call" and she believed that call, well, that

is not really her fault, right? Because she's just an inferior woman. In short, women cannot be "saved" without a righteous man, yet men are to have a direct relationship with God. Women get to try to find salvation in a mortal man.

So, not only was Sally looking for love, to be chosen, but also for salvation. It was a tall order, to be sure.

Everyone has a reason they wanted their dream so much—a wrong they wanted to right, a hurt they wanted to heal. They might want love, approval, safety, validation, immortality, or belonging. Here are some of the things the people we have met in this book wanted:

- Margaret, when she really thought about it, wanted a graduate degree in art so she could be taken seriously by her family.
- Kayla wanted to be Oprah because, like Oprah, she was drawn toward turning her personal pain into a platform—and because she thought it would give her love and approval from her father.
- Betty wanted a big success so she could finally be a part of the in-crowd. Betty wanted salvation.

Looking at their motivations can show you how these folks might be able to address these needs in other ways, and how maybe their dreams might not actually have given them what they hoped for. That's my goal for you, too—to have the kind of perspective that allows you to see that there is not only one path to happiness.

The Therapy Couch

If we can only be happy once we get some one *thing,* then it isn't likely that the thing would actually have given us permanent and lasting happiness. If we would have gotten the thing, it might have given us some short-term happiness, but no matter how extraordinary the dream, once we acclimated to having it, we would have likely tried to come up with yet another dream that would promise us a perfect happiness that would have never ended. You see, we pretty quickly get used to good stuff. According to the hedonic treadmill theory by Brickman and Campbell,[6] impactful events, successes, and the achievement of goals doesn't, as we imagine it would, make us much happier than we were before the accomplishment. The bad/sad events don't negatively impact our set point of happiness much, either. Brickman looked at the happiness levels of both lottery winners and paraplegics, and found that both groups returned to their pre-win or pre-trauma level of happiness within a few years of either event.

Many studies show that it isn't the things we think will make us happy that actually do. When crunching the numbers, it turns out only 10 percent of our happiness comes from life circumstances, according to psychologist Sonja Lyubomirsky, author of *The How of Happiness: A Scientific Approach to Getting the Life You Want.*[7] The rest of happiness is set by our genes (50 percent) and by our actions (40 percent). So, if all your happiness was on hold until you got that dream, then it is time to look at creating a life that includes the things the researchers say really are likely to make you happy: having good friends, finding ways to give back, being involved in a spiritual community, getting exercise, and enjoying the small pleasures of life. None of these actions require you to have the dream come true. Happiness, dear you, can happen even without the dream.

Movie Rx

It may not be December when you are reading this book, so you might not take this Movie Rx to heart. But trust me, this movie is just as powerful in the blazing sun of August or the cool rain of spring as it is at Christmas. It is very likely that you have seen this movie before and may not have noticed how it was not really a movie about Christmas, but rather a movie about how to live a meaningful life without reaching your dreams. I am talking, of course, about *It's a Wonderful Life.*[8] This Christmas classic is an iconic example of how meaningful your life can be even without fulfilling your dream.

George Bailey was not always an overworked and overtaxed banker; he was once a man filled with dreams. Before he became a hero of Bedford Falls, George had a serious case of little town blues. He wanted a bigger life than was available in his little hometown, and he dreamed of traveling to distant and exotic places and then coming back to build something grand. He was, in other words, sort of a handsome, charming, and ethical version of Donald Trump.

George explains his dream better than I can:

> I know what I'm going to do tomorrow and the next day and the next year and the year after that. I'm shaking the dust of this crummy little town off my feet and I'm going to see the world. Italy, Greece, the Parthenon, the Coliseum. Then I'm coming back here and go to college and see what they know . . . and then I'm going to build things. I'm gonna build air fields. I'm gonna build skyscrapers a hundred stories high. I'm gonna build bridges a mile long.

That's not, of course, how things turn out. Over and over, George's dream of travel and college are thwarted. First, his father has a stroke. Three months later, his planned trip to Europe and his dreams of attending college are sacrificed so his brother can have tuition money. When his brother returns from college, four years later, again George's dream of leaving Bedford Falls is dashed. This time it is because his brother is accepting a job that will prohibit him from returning to work at the savings and loan, so George is again stuck out of a sense of responsibility.

"Now, you listen to me!" George tells his future wife, ". . . I don't want to get married—ever—to anyone! You understand that? I want to do what I want to do." Shortly after this diatribe of desire, George marries Mary. It looks like he is finally going to travel on his honeymoon, but ultimately they have to cancel their trip to the big city and to a tropical paradise when there is a run on the banks and they have to use the honeymoon money to save the business. With each loss, George's dreams become more and more distant, he becomes firmly rooted in Bedford Falls, and he never manages to achieve a single aspect of his detailed dream.

When George fails to make his reality a success, and he is pushed to the brink by a snafu at the savings and loan, he considers giving up on himself and his life. Enter Clarence. Clarence is an angel who has failed to fulfill *his* dream of getting his wings. He is determined to help George to see the good that has come out of his dream not coming true, and how his life is valuable anyway.

While I am no angel, and I am not in the market to get wings, and I do think Clarence does a fine job helping George see that his life is worthwhile, I think that George might benefit from reading this book and figuring out what he really and truly wanted from his dream. I would like George to analyze that unlived life and imagine what travel and building skyscrapers would give him and what he thought he would feel by doing those things. I believe that in doing so, he would have likely seen that he wanted to have a bigger world, to build something and leave the world a changed place. Even without his dream fulfilled, I believe George likely achieved the essence of his dream, if not the specifics.

What about you?

SELF-HELP SUGGESTIONS

☐ How is the unlived life impacting your present life? Your choices? The narrative of your whole life?

☐ What is the psychological significance of why you wanted your dream as much as you did?

☐ What did you want that you haven't allowed yourself to cop to? What side benefits did you imagine you would get when you got the dream?

☐ Is it possible to get the essence of what you wanted in another way? Let's not stop there; how about ten or twenty other ways?

☐ Was there some hope of being more lovable, likable, wanted, or secure that came with the dream fulfillment?

☐ Who did you think would love you more if you had your dream? Who would finally approve of you? Who would be the first person you would have called and told that your dream came true?

☐ How did you think you would change if you had the dream?

☐ How are you editing out frustrations? What was the perfect version of your dream that you told yourself? How would your dream look differently if you included frustrations and realities?

☐ What was the shadow side of this dream? What costs would you have had to pay? How could it have hurt you to get what you wanted?

☐ Now that you know what you thought your dream would give you (security, love, meaning, fulfillment, acceptance, validation), can you find other ways to get those things?

☐ What are the fantasies about your unlived life trying to tell you?

☐ If you had an angel like Clarence, what would he want you to see about yourself that you haven't been seeing? What would your loved ones say about you, with or without the dream?

☐ What is the good about your life even without the dream? How is it important?

☐ How have you, with or without your dreams coming true, made a difference?

☐ What is it that you really want underneath the desired dream? What is the essence of it? What quality did you believe having this dream would give you?

☐ How can you symbolically make this dream a reality?

☐ Is there another way to attain the qualities you are seeking other than the way you imagined?

chapter 9

The Next Happy

"Do not be afraid; our fate cannot be taken from us; it is a gift."
>> **Dante Alighieri, *Inferno***

*"What if we never 'get over' certain deaths, or our childhoods?
What if the idea that we should have by now, or will, is a great palace lie?
What if we're not supposed to? What if it takes a lifetime . . . ?"*
>> **Anne Lamott**

*"You must let go of the life you planned, so as to accept the one
that is waiting for you."*
>> **Joseph Campbell**

As this book draws to a close, you might expect me to talk about closure. Well I'm not going to. Okay, so I am going to, but not in the way you might expect. When it comes to dreams that have died, I don't really believe in closure. When we're in the midst of a dream, people want us to never, never give up, but when the dream has died, they suddenly change their minds (ironic, isn't it?) and want us to get over it *fast* and then also quickly act as though it is the best thing ever that we didn't get what we wanted. I'm not jumping on that bandwagon. You had to give up on your dream, or your dream was taken from you, and although closure may indeed happen, it also might not. It just might not.

The Myth of Closure

People love to talk about how one day you will be totally over this—done, complete, and totally devoid of pain around the topic. They tell us that putting this all behind us as soon as possible is the best way. And, as we explored in chapter 7, they further believe that "everything happens for a reason," so we should find that reason ASAP and get on with things. I am fairly mild mannered, and as I mentioned before, I only occasionally want to turn people into toads, but this kind of thinking has me wanting to go into some major amphibian production.

Oh, how I hate to tell you this, but the grief of a major loss of a dream is not the kind of thing that is just going to go away. This is a loss, a wound, and a hole in your heart. It will heal and you will not always feel as crappy as you do now, but it has changed you and it is part of you, and it is important.

Acceptance Happens—and It Is Different Than Closure

Closure is a concept that is simply too final for our purposes. There will come a time when you will be able to talk about this grief as if it were something from the past, and you will be able to talk about how you are glad that it all turned out as it did, and you won't cry, and you might think you are over it—but here's the catch: It probably won't last the way "closure" promises. All of a sudden you will see a film, or run into a friend who wants to know all of the details of your life, or see someone else who has what you wanted most, and you will be flooded by the loss, and the grief will return. It might, on occasion, take you straight back into the anger and the sadness. Every Mother's Day, for example, I revisit my grief. On occasion, grief comes when I see baby pictures on Facebook. It also comes sometimes out of the blue. Recently, when Keith and I were shopping for a home, a realtor asked us if we were empty nesters. I was taken over by a kind of pain that I hadn't known for years, and I sat in the car and cried loud and hard. The good news is that when grief returns, it doesn't usually stay as long as it did the first time.

Maybe you can find another book or another therapist who will promise you closure, and also promise that someday this loss will never again hurt you, ever, but I am not that therapist. I also believe that if it were possible to wipe the pain of this loss from my mind, I wouldn't choose to do it. There are some days when I want to feel that pain, days where I intentionally walk into the American Girl store or Baby Gap, and I pick up a dress and I open the door to that wanting. There are days when I look at mothers with their children and tell myself, "You will never know what that is like, ever." In these actions, I am inviting grief back into my heart. It may sound like masochism, but it isn't. It is honoring something I deeply wanted; it is honoring all that I did and tried and endured. This wound is a part of me and it will live in me, always. I don't want to forget that dream any more than I want to forget the people I loved who have died: my grandmother, my father, and even my cats, my Inkey and Sparkey. I remember them, and that is not masochism; it is love. I miss them. And I miss that dream that I could have a child of my own, and I honor it the same way I do any death.

Remember back when I talked about Kübler-Ross's stages of grief? Well, acceptance is the stage in which we really and truly accept the reality that we are not going to have the dream. Secret hope is no longer present. We are living with the reality that we will never have the dream, and we are making modifications to our life that accommodate for the dream's absence. We may revisit anger, sadness, and fear from time to time, but we have arrived somewhere peaceful. Acceptance, not closure.

Recently I spoke at the 2014 Fertility Planit in Los Angeles, a full year after my first appearance there. In 2013, I was flooded with pain, loss, and a sharp awareness that I represented these couples' biggest fear—ending up childless. My grief revisited me in a big way, and I cried and cried. However, this year when I spoke, I saw the women and couples desperate to conceive. I saw women sitting in my panel crying as they imagined ending up like me. But you know what? This time it didn't hurt at all. The wound wasn't as open; more healing had occurred. I wasn't just in acceptance, I was in, to borrow a term from Nietzsche, *amor fati,* which means that I am loving how it all worked out, even though it still hurts not to be a mother. That is what acceptance looks like.

I still have dreams, only now they are "little d" dreams. My "little d" dreams are that I hope that I will write another book, that Keith and I will live happily ever after, and that someday I will be able to spend summers in France. None of them are so big that I believe they are the only thing that will make me happy—which is a good lesson to learn. I also know that not every dream comes true and that I will be okay no matter what happens. Good gracious, are those big lessons! How nice to know these things and not to have to spend the rest of my life possessed by the idea that happiness can only come through one way.

Acceptance and happy endings are entirely possible; however, they can be miles, and even years, apart. It takes time to get to happy, and everyone is different. How and when you get here will be as unique as you are. It will happen if you work through the stages of grief, use all the tools at your disposal, keep yourself open to the possibility of the next happy, and let time do its work. I can offer you no set timetable for this process (my crystal ball is in the shop), but what I can give you is example after example of how happy endings snuck into people's lives when they were not expected. It happened to me, and it happened to every person I talked to for this book. Trust me, none of us believed it would.

What's Next? How Getting to the Next Happy Works

When in the stage of acceptance, you might start to wonder "what's next?" You might start to feel ready. You might not know the answer, and I am a big believer in letting it come organically. Forcing it can lead to trouble. When I let go of the dream of having a biological child, people wanted to hurry and come up with a solution for my pain. They wanted to force the next thing. "Adopt," they would say, because it was such an easy "fix" for my problem. And I might have adopted. I moved in that direction, but a near adoption left me more despondent than all my attempts at trying to conceive, and I knew I couldn't do it. I knew I had to stop, and to grieve. I am so grateful to have had that insight and further grateful that I honored it, even though at the time it might have felt better (less painful) to get myself involved in another dream that was going to be the "answer" to the pain caused by the loss.

I have seen many people on my clinical couch who tried to fast-forward the pain of grief by quickly filling the empty space. It is a way of not dealing with their grief, and I don't believe this kind of sublimation ever works. Yes, of course, you can find some happiness and certainly some pain relief from filling the emptiness with a new project, a new relationship, or some busy-making activity. I have certainly met many people who didn't fully grieve before they jumped with both feet into a new dream without grieving the old one, and I tend to hear a lot about regret and how the new dream (even if fulfilled) was impacted by the last dream not fully being mourned. Imagine this if you will: You lost a loved one, and instead of grieving, you just replaced the person. Does that even seem possible? Can't you see all the possibilities for disaster that such a solution would suggest? Bad idea. And, yes, it may not seem as disastrous to jump fully into another dream . . . but it can be. I have seen it destroy a number of lives.

I once had a client, Lila, who tried for years to land a coveted spot on a Broadway show. She had all the chops—a degree in musical theater (yes, there is such a thing); the so-called triple threat of being able to sing, dance, and act; and all kinds of experience and credentials everywhere except Broadway. She spent five years living in tiny New York apartments with a revolving cast of hopefuls, waitressing and auditioning, over and over again. Many times, she got very close—final callbacks, huge praise from big directors, last girl dropped. She did some off-Broadway work and community theater. She continued to do master classes and take lessons, which took all her money.

Then one day on the subway on the way home from yet another audition, she realized she had to stop. She was almost thirty years old and had never had health insurance, a savings account, or a permanent address. "I was just suddenly, irrevocably done," she said. But instead of mourning her loss, giving herself time to process it, and giving herself time to heal, she quickly launched into a new quest—to become an orthopedic surgeon. She knew plenty about bones and the body from her life in dance, and she had loved science classes in school. It seemed a perfect idea to bring stability and seriousness into her life—after all, what surgeon doesn't have a permanent address and health insurance? Within two weeks, she was enrolled in a program that crammed all the pre-med coursework into a year of intensive study, but she never finished the program. She kept getting sick—the flu, bronchitis, mono—and had to walk away from the new dream, which meant she now had *two* dreams to mourn and a narrative of failure that would take her many, many years to unwind.

It is, I believe, much better to fully mourn your dream, to make meaning out of it, to understand why you wanted it so much and to let the land lie fallow for a minute (you know how farmers let the land that they harvest rest before replanting). Wait and see what is next. Something will emerge, if you stay open and engaged.

As I said above, I don't believe that forcing it will work. If you are thinking to yourself, "This is what I should do to make the pain go away," then you may be filling the hole where the grief lives. That kind of action is very cognitive, up in your head: "I should do something. I should act. I should do X, Y, or Z, and when I do, I won't hurt anymore." Usually, those kinds of actions are not about interest but rather about some cognitive reaction that relates to the loss of the dream. What I have seen, over and over, is that the cognitive action or choice is never as surprising or as delightful or as happiness inducing as the unexpected. Yes, you have to wait for the real unexpected interest to emerge, but the wait is worth it. Forcing things may sound better (just make the pain go away), but since it doesn't really work, it is best to wait for the organic interest to come.

Perhaps the new interest will be as simple as deciding to write a blog, acting on a whim to join Match.com, reading everything ever written about mountain climbers, taking a yoga class, growing a vegetable garden, or taking a trip. It might not feel like a "big D" Dream or even a "little d" dream, and that is okay . . . it is better than okay. It is a sprout of an interest, and it is important not to tear up that little sprout and say, "That isn't consequential enough. It isn't going to get me anything, and by the way, I never get what I want, so there is no point to taking any action anyway." Hold on, tiger, take a breath, perhaps take a chill pill, and hold your horses. I am not asking you to commit your life to this interest, and there certainly are no guarantees that this interest, action, or energy is going to take you anywhere. But the truth is that life is better when you have things you are interested in.

For me, a little bit of libido for life, and some interest, started to sneak in when I was at the end stage of my grieving and moving into acceptance. Even as I remained flattened by the pain and the reality of my child-free life, I slowly started to find things I was a little bit interested in, which led to little bits of action in which I said to myself, "Yes, of course. I can't be happy in any big kind of way—nothing will ever make up for the fact that I didn't get what I wanted—but I am sort of interested in this, and wouldn't it be nice to have my own practice and, perhaps, I might like to hire interns, and wouldn't it be nice to maybe write a book?" None of these things were dreams in the way having a child was. This time around it was more like preferences. Everything felt lighter and easier, with less attachment and less "my life depends on it" thinking. I think that lightness is actually a gift that comes from enduring this kind of loss. I started to take one step and then another step, and things started to take shape and form, and then much to my surprise, these actions were leading to fulfillment, meaning, and surprisingly—most surprisingly—happiness.

I am, in fact, giddy. My life is a dream—no, not the dream I had, but it is a dream nonetheless. I am a therapist with a great practice that I love. I have the pleasure and privilege of mentoring and supervising interns, helping them develop professionally, and watching them bloom, grow, and succeed (for some reason the song "Edelweiss" from *The Sound of Music* just came to mind). I am in a relationship that gives me more joy than I could have ever imagined. My life is rich and full and ridiculously happy. If you were to meet me, you wouldn't need to ask if I am happy, because I think that I beam with happiness. If anything, I can get a little self-conscious about how happy I am. I am almost a zealot in terms of wanting to share this possibility of a real happy ending with everyone I meet. Good stuff emerges from bad stuff (if you work at it), and I really want people to know that and help them get from the pain to the next happiness.

I don't have any idea what the next happy will be for you, obviously, but I can tell you that it will likely be something totally unexpected. It might be another job, another marriage, an adoption, a new hobby or interest, or simply getting to the place where you are just happy with what is, and wow, that would really be something. That is not to say that there won't be times when you feel the grief (as I said, you will feel it) or times when you will get triggered and regress for a minute (you will regress) or that there won't be stupid people who say, "See, it was all worth it to get here" (there will be). The point is that happiness happens. You have suffered, and you have the wounds to show for it, but you can still be happy.

How Not Getting the Dream You Wanted
Impacts Your Next Happy
(Weird Stuff That Can Happen When We Get into Acceptance)

When you have had the experience of not getting what you wanted most and then you start to have some happiness sneak in, and you find you are somewhat (or a whole lot of) happy even without that dream, it *can* bring up some feelings. You might not feel like you should be happy; you might feel some guilt or fear or even some magical thinking—in other words, that if you are happy now it will all get ruined and you will lose it. Fear not. That is just some post-traumatic dream trauma. Okay, don't go googling that—I just made it up. That said, just because you can't find it in the *DSM-5* doesn't mean it doesn't happen; it does.

Yeah, I know, it seems weird, wrong, and counterintuitive to be unhappy, afraid, and guilty about having a new interest emerge, and it seems downright bizarre to say we might stop ourselves from taking action that could increase our happiness, but we do this all in the name of not getting hurt again. When we have suffered loss, we can, in an attempt to defend ourselves from more loss, not allow ourselves to enjoy anything good. We may have created a heuristic, which is a rule about the world: "I don't get what I want, so it is better for me not to want." If we have done that, it can be scary to dream again, or even to enjoy the fulfillment of an unexpected happiness. However, setting new reasonable and achievable goals is an important step in healing from the death of a dream, proving wrong that heuristic and seeing that you can have good stuff in your life even if you can't have that dream.

As I mentioned before, true happiness is not found in the big achievements in life, or through money or accomplishments (remember the hedonic treadmill). In her book *The How of Happiness,* Sonja Lyubomirsky suggests that happiness is created by spending time with people you love; being grateful; letting go of grudges; developing gratitude, mindfulness, and kindness; and getting enough sleep and physical exercise.[1] I would add that having work that I find to be meaningful and having a dog are big things that impact my happiness. Almost daily I find myself verbalizing my gratitude for the happiness my work brings me and for my West Highland white terrier, Lily.

Regrets Even as Happiness Happens

As happy as I am, I sometimes find myself feeling a little sad and wish that I had met Keith earlier and that maybe we could have had a child together. I suppose it is a natural feeling that when you are in love with someone, you might imagine a child coming out of the relationship. Sometimes I will turn to Keith and say something that may as well be straight out of Haruki Murakami's novel *1Q84*:[2]

> I've been lonely for so long. And I've been hurt so deeply. If only I could have met you again a long time ago, then I wouldn't have had to take all these detours to get here.

Then Keith says something very much like this:

> This way is just fine. This is exactly the right time. For both of us. . . . We needed that much time . . . to understand how lonely we really were.

I know Keith and Murakami are right, and yet there is the natural desire to wish it had always been as it is now. And truly, when I am able to be honest with myself, part of what makes my life so sweet and satisfying and delightful now is that it was so entirely unexpected and came out of a whole lot of unhappiness and a mess of unfulfilled dreams. My greatest fear was that I would never be happy without children. As I look back now, I see that if I had had children, I would have never known the happiness I am enjoying so fully today, and I wouldn't trade that for anything, not even children.

Yes, your newfound happiness may very well trigger regret. *Why didn't I find this sooner? Why did I waste my time on that old dream? Why didn't I know that this would make me so much happier?* These kinds of "could-haves, would-haves, and should-haves" are the mental equivalent of raining on your parade. As you know, there is nothing you can do about this, and to focus on it is a masochistic attempt to destroy your happy. Instead, ask yourself, "Self, would you prefer that your happiness be in your past or in your present?" That question usually gets me to snap out of it and enjoy where I am.

Stupid Stuff That People Say as Your Next Happy Emerges

You might have people respond to your new interest and budding happiness with a question, either direct or implied: How can you be happy without what you wanted if you actually wanted it at all? Maybe, they say, you didn't actually want the dream as much as you said you did if you can just move on and let go and find happiness elsewhere. Yes, people have actually said this to me. I am here to tell you that they are dead wrong. And you have my full permission to tell them that. You did want it, and it didn't work out, and it is not a betrayal of what you wanted most to move on and to find something that actually works for you. It is okay to be happy. Really, it is. You do not need to prove you really wanted it by refusing to live on and choose things that make your life meaningful and satisfying.

The Therapy Couch

You've heard of Nietzsche. I mentioned him briefly back in chapter 7. He was the German philosopher that twenty-something philosophy-loving guys tend to love. Yeah, I know, I didn't expect him to show up so frequently in a self-help book either, but one day I woke up and there he was. He was sitting at my desk and telling me in his best *Thus Spoke Zarathustra* highfalutin intellectual tones that he had something to say that might be helpful to those letting go of a dream. I was a little nervous about introducing you to him, because Nietzsche isn't exactly warm and fuzzy, and he rarely hangs out in the self-help section, but it turns out that he does have something to say that I think can be helpful. You see, Nietzsche came up with a concept he called *amor fati,* meaning "the love of your fate," which I mentioned earlier. Let me have another wise man explain why this is so important. Joseph Campbell, the acclaimed mythologist, explains:

> At a certain moment in his life, the idea came to him [Nietzsche] of what he called "the love of your fate." Whatever your fate is, whatever the hell happens, you say, "This is what I need." It may look like a wreck, but go at it as though it were an opportunity, a challenge. If you bring love to that moment—not discouragement—you

will find the strength is there. Any disaster you can survive is an improvement in your character, your stature, and your life. What a privilege! This is when the spontaneity of your own nature will have a chance to flow.

Then, when looking back at your life, you will see that the moments which seemed to be great failures followed by wreckage were the incidents that shaped the life you have now. You'll see that this is really true. Nothing can happen to you that is not positive. Even though it looks and feels at the moment like a negative crisis, it is not. The crisis throws you back, and when you are required to exhibit strength, it comes.[3]

This, I think, is what Nietzsche and Kelly Clarkson were talking about when they said, "What doesn't kill you makes you stronger." And, again, I do want to reiterate that it isn't necessarily true (see the chapter 7), that there are some pains, sufferings, and experiences that can be just pure pain that can lead to nothing. But, can you find some way to accept what is and own it and say, as Campbell does, "This is what I need. It may look like a wreck, but go at it as though it were an opportunity, a challenge"?

I know that when you are grieving your dream, it is unrealistic to expect you to say, "Yes, awesome! I *love* that I didn't get what I want. This is the best! And I am so privileged to not get what I want." That would be ridiculous. Loving your fate isn't easy; at certain points it can feel impossible. It may be easier to love your annoying, meddling, and halitosis-ridden mother-in-law who always makes sure to let you know you are doing everything wrong. To "love your fate" is a profoundly difficult psychological activity for someone to ask of you, but I am asking you to consider it nonetheless. This is emotional heavy lifting here, I know. If this were luggage, you'd be tipping the guy at the curb to avoid the overweight fees. But, hey, if you bought this book and read this far and haven't given up completely (or thrown this book across the room), you are no lightweight. I say this not to flatter you; I say it because I know it is true. I want you to see the opportunity in this crisis. And I also really want you to know that maybe, just maybe, someday you will be really and truly happy, maybe even giddy, about it not working out. It is possible.

And even if at first it is just an exercise, a make-believe, and you are going to pretend like you are loving your great thing and that it can teach you stuff and that something good is on the horizon, well that kind of lie isn't the worst thing to do to yourself. It can, I think, open you up to start creating meaning out of this even if you don't believe there is any, and that is, according to me and the experts, important in your moving on and finding your next happy.

The Inside Story

Flores had a detailed, strategic, and well-constructed plan to get a job in diplomacy. At the age of twelve, she read a book about a little girl who would save the world by bringing different cultures together. A trip to Europe in adolescence cemented the dream. She spent the next thirty years with a single-minded devotion to the fulfillment of the dream. The most ordinary pleasures were sacrificed—no parties or extracurricular activities would take her away from the plan that would get her what she wanted. All she would do was whatever it would take to make her dream come true; only, no matter how hard she worked, it never seemed to happen.

Each and every time that she interviewed, she was told that she didn't know the right people, didn't have the right credentials, hadn't gone to the right Ivy League schools that seemed to be a prerequisite for the job. She simply couldn't get her foot in the door—but she wouldn't give up. She wouldn't believe it wasn't going to happen, even as family and friends began to say, "Flores, you'll never get the job." After the umpteenth interview in which she heard the same thing, Flores got it. She had to give up on her dream. It was never going to happen. That may sound like it was simple and easy for her to come to, but it wasn't. This acceptance was agonizing and left Flores feel unmoored, not herself, and unsure of who she was without the pursuit of this goal. Not only did she lose the dream, but she lost her purpose, her hopes for the future, and a sense of herself as able to make whatever she wanted happen. "I had such an existential crisis that I didn't know who I was, let alone what I wanted. . . . I wanted to dream new dreams, but when going through the crazy pain I felt empty. . . . When I regained this capability to *want*, it felt like heaven."

When breastfeeding her baby in the middle of the night, Flores needed something to help keep her awake. Reading put her right to sleep, so she started to look at blogs that had images of beautifully designed objects on them, something she would have never done when in hot pursuit of her dream. It was an activity that was pure pleasure with no purpose, so it wouldn't have been on her detailed plan of how to get from here to there. However, devoid of a dream, and in need of a stimulus that kept her awake, she turned to blogs that featured design, crafts, handmade objects, and any objects and spaces that were beautiful. Slowly she started to discover how much joy beauty brought her. And she started to comment on the blogs and started to make relationships with people who didn't know her as a failed diplomat. She got to be seen differently. People online just knew her as herself; they met her where she was at that moment, and Flores was comforted by that.

In time, Flores started to become a crafter. She started a blog on cake decorating and party planning and has even launched a cookbook. This may seem like a ridiculous comedown for someone who had spent her life in pursuit of diplomatic work, and yet, Flores started to find real joy and satisfaction in making things.

> I feel reborn into the person I was meant to be. This wouldn't have happened if I had got what I wanted. My life as a diplomat would have taken me away from my home and my children and, yes, there would have been satisfaction that came through that work, but I see now how much of that desire to be a diplomat was, at the root of it, an attempt to negotiate my early family issues. But now, in crafting, cooking, baking, and creating, I am in the now and I find so much pleasure in doing things that I can complete and finish, and when I am done with them, there is beauty and a sense of accomplishment. I couldn't have imagined ever feeling this way.

Is she happy? "I don't know if *happy* is the word," she says. "I am proud of myself for working things out and making it victorious to the other side. I am proud of myself for having stayed positive through it all, and for my resilience. I am happy to have learned that there never is a single path and that we can always dream new dreams, and I am proud of myself for my openness to learning that lesson." Flores reports that people in her life are not supportive of her next happy: "They are rather negative, actually. They either think I never wanted the dream bad enough, or that I am deluding myself in thinking I'm over it. But I have stopped caring about what others think. I don't give a f*ck about a ton of things anymore," she admits laughingly. "I'm not in the business of convincing anyone about my truth. Not getting my dream has made me stronger, more resilient, and more secure. Now I know that, whatever happens, I can always find a Plan C, D, E, Z. And I'm not so attached to dreams; now I'm just attached to myself and my well-being. I accept my fate and vow to enjoy the journey. I am happy with how things have turned out, yes."

After our interview, Flores sent me exciting news: "I was just invited to join Martha Stewart's circle of bloggers," she said. "One of my new dreams was to be in the pages of *Martha Stewart Living,* and now this!" She also said to be sure to tell you this: "You will get past this. You will dream again, and you will be stronger because of this. Hang in there; there is always light at the end of the tunnel."

The Inside Story

Additional Inside Stories—a Reprieve!

People whom I have interviewed for this book—every single one of them—imagined that they could not be happy without the dream that they had to abandon, yet each one went on to be happier than they imagined they could be. New careers, new relationships, new interests . . . all totally unexpected, and mostly unrelated to the dream. None of them could have imagined how it would turn out for them or what their happy ending would look like, and yet each one of them found a next happy that they hadn't expected.

And all of them, beyond a new happiness, have gone on to find a deeper meaning and lessons that came from the loss of their dream that they might not have found any other way. Also—and I think this is really an important point—all of them shared with me that in answering the questions I asked them (the same ones I ask you to consider), they found greater meaning, insight, and understanding that allowed them to further integrate their feelings, move on, let go, and more deeply embrace their happy ending. I share that with you to tell you that the process you are engaging in through reading this book, answering these questions, and wrestling to find meaning for your dream will make a difference for you, too.

Let's hear about the next happy for some of the people we heard from earlier in the book.

SALLY

Do you love your fate? Are you happy that it all worked out as it did?

Yes! I 100 percent love my life and am very happy I didn't get what I wanted before. It was a tough process for me to truly let go and move on. When I finally gave the old dream up, grieved, and moved on, I felt like a different person. The giving up process was a bit like slowly waking from a vivid night dream so real it took time to sort out sleeping from waking consciousness. After I released that particular dream, I decided not to pursue a partner; I just went about my life focusing on my own growth and priorities. In my core, I still wanted a partner who would value and choose me, but I released the waiting, trying, etc. I vaguely remember saying something like, "If there's a guy out there who wants me badly enough, he's going to have to catch up/ keep up." This view was a transformation in me and I have not regretted it. I am now married to a fantastic man who more than keeps up.

I recently introduced my husband to a close friend who has known me for decades. She initially reflected that it seemed my husband was more "into" me than I am "into" him. I assured her that this is not the case, but upon reflection I think what she saw was the absence of the angst-y, off-balance me who never felt secure with the men I loved. I was always trying to win someone's love by being what they wanted.

Do you see how your hard work in moving on and letting go allowed for this next happiness? What were the benefits of giving up on your dream?

By giving up and mourning my dream, I came into a deeper embodiment of self and the conviction that I would rather live alone as a whole, authentic self than tear myself apart trying to force something that was never going to be. Now I see that what I ultimately gave up was the pain and effort of striving for something that was not right for me.

What guidance do you really want people to have about getting to their next happy after having a dream that they didn't realize?

Striving can have its own lessons, and each person has to decide if/when it's right for them to give up on a dream, but here's what I might say to one experiencing inordinate suffering for a dream that is not coming to fruition: Consider that there might be another, even better possibility waiting for you in your future. You may find yourself incredibly glad you didn't get what you wanted when you see what is waiting for you around the bend.

MARGARET

Do you love your fate?

This is hard to answer because I might have loved my other fate, too. I might have been an art history professor, and that is hard to let go of. But, that being said, I am not unhappy with my current fate. And I do believe everything happens for a reason. I might not have gone on this very personal journey if not for my professor hitting on me as he did. I love who I am right now. I love what I know about myself and the world. And that I wouldn't trade for anything.

Are you happy that it all worked out as it did?

Happy might be too strong a word. As I said above, I do believe everything happens for a reason. Sometimes, those reasons are hard to see when you are in the thick of it. It was a *long* time before I could see why this happened to me. And the journey included help from therapists, friends, healers, and psychics.

I do see how my hard work has led me to this new place of happiness and peace. Throughout this process, I was always striving for a sense of peace. My journals are filled with me trying to find peace of mind. And, I am very happy to say, I have finally found it. It was a long time coming (seven-plus years). But it was definitely worth the struggle.

I was definitely reluctant to dream again. There was a lot of fear. But, the funny thing is, it happened anyway. When I was in the depths of my despair, I watched a lot of British television. Those shows saved my life. They were not only an escape, but they were also the catalyst for the beginnings of a new dream. I would watch *Monarch of the Glen* and *Ballykissangel* and think, I could write this better. I started dreaming about my ideal plot for a series. And that dream is still going today.

As the process of healing became more profound, I allowed myself to take little steps toward dreaming again (like being part of a writers' group). Then I participated in a few writing classes at UCLA. Last summer I did a weeklong writing seminar at Antioch University. I had to apply and send in a writing sample. The fear was definitely there. But I did it anyway. I got in, I loved the class, and I did something similar this winter at UCLA. And, I am happy to report, I applied (and was accepted) to an MFA program that starts this summer.

I am very private about the loss of my dream. Very few people really know what happened and how deeply I was affected by it. So, I don't get a lot of "all's well that ends well" (thank God). I was very aware that people were uncomfortable with my particular loss of a dream. They just wanted it to go away and not be talked about. Even my husband was reluctant to process it with me. This was definitely a lonely journey.

What I think everyone should know is that there is always hope for a happy life. It takes work. It isn't easy. But if you believe in it, if you are open to all possibilities, and if you do the work, it does happen.

Was there a benefit to not getting my dream? Most definitely. If I had breezed through Cal State L.A. and gone on to teach, I might not have taken this incredible journey. I have faced a lot of my fears, I have healed a lot of old wounds, and I am still working on opening my heart. And I feel like this part of my happy ending has just begun. I have a wonderful feeling of hope for the future. And that is my peace of mind. That is my "happy ending."

What I want everyone to know is that if you look inside, if you do the work, the world is a beautiful, giving place. We all have the same opportunities for happiness. In the beginning, I did a lot of asking "why me?" And it gets you nowhere unless you are willing to take responsibility and really hear the answers. I finally started listening, and I am so grateful I did!

The Best Exotic Marigold Hotel is a movie that features the stories of a multitude of characters whose dreams and lives have not worked out as they imagined.[4] There are failures galore: a failed love affair, a failed investment, a failed retirement, a failed marriage. And these weren't twenty-somethings with plenty of time to turn these failures around: The residents of the Best Exotic Marigold Hotel are all senior citizens, and not one of them was living out their Plan A. At best, this was a Plan F for all involved. The new guests come to the B.E.M.H. for a variety of reasons: The narrator and main character, Evelyn, played by Judi Dench, is newly widowed and has just discovered that her husband had blown through their retirement fund and left her with no money. She bravely and courageously seeks a new life in India, with an inspiring spirit of adventure that most in her situation might not muster (myself included). Evelyn surprisingly seems to be in acceptance about her fate as she imagines a new life for herself after losing her spouse, her financial security, and her home.

Another character, Muriel, played by Maggie Smith, is not even close to acceptance. She is pissed off, and only in the way Maggie Smith can be pissed off. She's mad for a lot of reasons, it turns out: First off, she doesn't want to have to go to India in order to have surgery, but it is the only place she can afford to get the surgery she needs. Also, she is extremely xenophobic and the idea of going to India for the procedure is no dream; it is a nightmare. Her anger, we discover, goes deeper: She is grieving being displaced as a nanny.

Douglas and Jean are a couple who lost their retirement fund in order to fund their daughter's Internet start-up. They chose the exotic retirement option over a less-than-lovely retirement community available to them in India. This is a couple in deep crisis.

Madge and Norman arrive independently, but they have the same hopes: They both are there to meet someone. They seek love and relationship.

Graham, a recently retired high court judge who had spent his early life in India, is on a mission; he is going to India for a reason, which he keeps secret, but it is to find the lover he had when he was a young man. We see in Graham

feelings of hope, but also of guilt, regret, loss, and grief. He mourns for hi past and the pain he inflicted on a young man with whom he had a homo sexual relationship that caused the man's family to be shamed.

All these characters, at the end of their rope, have made a decision to retire to India and move to the Best Exotic Marigold Hotel, "a home for the elderly and the beautiful," or says the hyperbolic and highly Photoshopped brochure that promises a luxury retirement in Jaipur, India. The Best Exotic Marigold Hotel is not, however, all it is Photoshopped to be. Sonny Kapoor, the young, chipper, and blindly optimistic host of the hotel is in the midst of his own dream: He wants to turn the dilapidated hotel into a beautiful and majestic retirement hotel—only reality and the dream have yet to meet, and his guests in are in for a harsh awakening once they arrive. The road to the Best Exotic Marigold Hotel is paved with good intentions, but they could use an actual paver, an electrician, a plumber, and a contracting team to bring it up to code.

Sonny is endlessly optimistic as he encourages his disheartened guests: "Everything will be all right in the end. So if it is not all right, then it is not yet the end." Now keep in mind he does not say, "It will all work out as you hoped." No, no such promises. Sonny is saying that it will be all right in the end. I think this is an important maxim to hold on to as you go through this journey. Yes, dear you, it will all be all right in the end, and if you are still grieving, angry, jealous, bitter, and unable to love your fate, then you aren't at the end yet—but you will get there in time. This grief process will not stay where it is; you will get through this, and the loss of the dream will not be the only thing to occupy your mind for all time, forever—that is, unless you refuse to let more happiness sneak in.

Let me just interject that I have a love for working with the elderly. worked in a Japanese retirement hotel, I trained at a center for healthy agin and one of my favorite people in my world and my life was my 101-year-o grandmother. I was particularly inspired when I met someone in this st of life who hadn't let life beat them down and who hadn't let their life cumstances stop them from trying new things, being open to new ideas, taking risks to have new adventures, even after enduring a lifetime of loss couple of instances come to mind. One was a beloved teacher of mine in her late sixties, decided it was time to begin her education to beco

therapist. At eighty, she completed her PhD. Eighty! This story really gets to me, inspires me, and gives me hope that it is never too late to make life rich, meaningful, and happy.

Another woman I met in this milieu was forced into retirement when she still had a whole lot of life in her. She chose to use this formidable loss as an opportunity to reinvent herself and discover how she wanted to spend the rest of her life. She took stand-up comedy courses and a writing course, became a peer counselor, and created a second act that had been richer than the first. It is never too late to have a happy ending. Never. I meet forty-, thirty-, and twenty-somethings who tell me it is too late for them. I always drag out these stories. I want them to know and I want you to know: It is not too late.

As I watched *The Best Exotic Marigold Hotel*, it was the characters who were stuck in the past and who wouldn't be open to new experiences who made me cookaloo. I almost wanted to shout at the screen, "Good God, you are in India. Enjoy it. Make the best of it. Take a risk. Enjoy what is there to be enjoyed. Don't let the past or fear stop you. Move on, lady!" Okay, good advice, and advice I could have benefitted from when I was struggling to move into acceptance. But once I got into acceptance, I was able to do what Judi Dench's character did and start taking risks and enjoy what is and find a totally unexpected happy ending. Her happy ending, I will have you know, brought me to tears. Mine did, too. And, as I am highly emotional about this topic of people finding happiness after letting go of a dream, it is likely that one day if we were to meet and I were to hear your story, I would openly delight in your next happy, too.

SELF-HELP SUGGESTIONS

- ☐ What are your feelings about closure? Do you expect it of yourself? Does it seem absurd to totally feel nothing about what you wanted so much? Can you see how continuing to have some feelings about the loss of the dream is important to you?

- ☐ Can you occasionally make some space for the sadness, a little like visiting a cemetery to honor the loss? Sometimes I visit the journals of when I was trying to conceive or, as I said earlier, visit the American Girl store just as a means of honoring the part of me that wanted that so very much.

- ☐ How might you occasionally visit that dream? How might this experience enhance your capacity to love your life just as it is?

- ☐ What all of a sudden seems interesting that wasn't before?

- ☐ Are you a little scared to allow yourself to dream? What do you think will happen if you dream again? How has your old dream impacted your ability to dream again?

- ☐ Are there moments when you feel almost grateful for how things are right now, even without your dream?

- ☐ Can you see how the dream not realized is important to you and to who you are today?

- ☐ What might you have missed out on if you had gotten the dream?

- ☐ Can you see how far you have come since you began this journey? What has changed for you since you started this process of moving on and letting go?

Postscript

I want to take this moment to thank you for having the courage to let go of what isn't working, to seek support in moving through this pain, and to have hope enough to buy this book and come this far. Please visit www.traceycleantis.com for further support in getting to your next happy.

Notes

CHAPTER 1: NEVER GIVE UP

1. W. R. D. Fairbairn, *Psychoanalytic Studies of the Personality,* reprint ed. (New York: Routledge, 1994), 67.

2. FHA Mortgage, "A Rational Reason to Default on Your FHA Mortgage," January 12, 2012, http://fhamortgagemag.com/2012/01/a-rational-reason-to -default-on-your-fha-mortgage.

3. U.S. Bureau of the Census, 1999, quoted on Widow's Hope, "These Are the Statistics," www.widowshope.org/first-steps/these-are-the-statistics.

4. Rose M. Kreider and Renee Ellis, "Number, Timing, and Duration of Marriages and Divorces: 2009," Current Population Reports, P70-125 (Washington, D.C.: U.S. Census Bureau, 2011), www.census.gov/prod/2011pubs/p70-125.pdf.

5. *Silver Linings Playbook,* directed by David O. Russell (The Weinstein Company, 2013), DVD and Blu-ray.

6. Elisabeth Kübler-Ross, *On Death and Dying: What the Dying Have to Teach Doctors, Nurses, Clergy, and Their Own Families,* reprint (New York: Scribner, 2011).

CHAPTER 2: WHY DID THE CHICKEN PUSH THE ROCK UP THE HILL?

1. Rose M. Kreider and Renee Ellis, "Number, Timing, and Duration of Marriages and Divorces: 2009," Current Population Reports, P70-125 (Washington, D.C.: U.S. Census Bureau, 2011), www.census.gov/prod/2011pubs/p70-125.pdf.

2. Centers for Disease Control and Prevention, National Center for Health Statistics, "Infertility," page last updated February 13, 2014, www.cdc.gov/nchs/fastats /infertility.htm.

3. Richard Vedder, *Twelve Inconvenient Truths about American Higher Education* (Washington, D.C.: Center for College Affordability and Productivity, March 2012), http://centerforcollegeaffordability.org/uploads/12_Inconvenient _Truths.pdf.

4. Richard Vedder, Christopher Denhart, and Jonathan Robe, *Why Are Recent College Graduates Underemployed?* (Washington, D.C.: Center for College Affordability and Productivity, January 2013), http://centerforcollegeaffordability.org/uploads /Underemployed%20Report%202.pdf.

5. Deloitte, "2010 Shift Index: What's New?," www.deloitte.com/assets/Dcom
   -UnitedStates/Local%20Assets/Documents/TMT_us_tmt/Shift%20Index%20
   2010/us_tmt_si_whatsnew_102510.pdf.

6. Casting Frontier, "Your Chances of Becoming a Star," May 11, 2012,
   www.castingfrontier.com/tag/unemployed-actors.

7. Erika Kinetz, "Practice, Practice, Practice. Go to College? Maybe," *New York
   Times,* December 21, 2005, www.nytimes.com/2005/12/21/arts/dance/21danc
   .html?pagewanted=print&_r=0.

8. Heather Robinson, "Athletes Find Booming Business Off the Courts," *Hilltop,*
   vol. 93, no. 13, September 9, 2009.

9. Tyler Lacoma, "How Many New Businesses Fail in the First Year?" eHow.com,
   www.ehow.com/how-does_5212542_many-businesses-fail-first-year_.html.

10. RealtyTrac Staff, "2011 Year-End Foreclosure Report: Foreclosures on the
    Retreat," January 9, 2012, www.realtytrac.com/content/foreclosure-market
    -report/2011-year-end-foreclosure-market-report-6984, quoted in FHA Mortgage,
    "A Rational Reason to Default on Your FHA Mortgage," January 12, 2012,
    http://fhamortgagemag.com/2012/01/a-rational-reason-to-default-on-your
    -fha-mortgage.

11. Gregory E. Miller and Carsten Wrosch, "You've Gotta Know When to Fold
    'Em: Goal Disengagement and Systemic Inflammation in Adolescence,"
    Psychological Science 18, no. 9 (2007): 773–77, http://sites.northwestern.edu
    /foundationsofhealth/files/2013/03/07-Psych-Sci-Youve-gotta-know-when-to
    -foldem.pdf.

12. Camille Peri, "Coping with Excessive Sleepiness: 10 Things to Hate About Sleep
    Loss," WebMD.com, page reviewed February 13, 2014, www.webmd.com
    /sleep-disorders/excessive-sleepiness-10/10-results-sleep-loss.

13. Gregory E. Miller and Carsten Wrosch, "You've Gotta Know When to Fold
    'Em: Goal Disengagement and Systemic Inflammation in Adolescence,"
    Psychological Science 18, no. 9 (2007): 773–77, http://sites.northwestern.edu
    /foundationsofhealth/files/2013/03/07-Psych-Sci-Youve-gotta-know-when-to
    -foldem.pdf.

14. "Classic Mythology/Jungian Psychology," Wikiversity.org, page last modified
    April 11, 2014, http://en.wikiversity.org/wiki/Classical_Mythology/Jungian
    _psychology.

15. Joseph Campbell, "Lecture Details," Joseph Campbell Foundation website,
    www.jcf.org/new/index.php?categoryid=104&p9999_action=displaylecture
    details&p9999_svl=I15.

16. Ernest Becker, *The Denial of Death* (New York: Free Press, 1997).

17. *The Wrestler,* directed by Darren Aronofsky (Fox Searchlight, 2009), DVD.

CHAPTER 3: THE DR. KEVORKIAN OF DREAMS

1. Jack Kevorkian quoted in Andy Rooney, "My Interview With 'Dr. Death,'" www.ihavenet.com/humor/Andy-Rooney-My-Interview-With-Dr-Death.html.

2. Nils B. Jostmann and Sander L. Koole, "When Persistence Is Futile: A Functional Analysis of Action Orientation and Goal Disengagement," draft, August 19, 2008, p. 14, www.researchgate.net/publication/257030818_When_Persistence_is_Futile _A_Functional_Analysis_of_Action_Orientation_and_Goal_Disengagement /file/9c9605243f9ca964cd.pdf; also published in *The Psychology of Goals,* ed. Gordon B. Moskowitz and Heidi Grant (New York: Guilford Press, 2009).

3. Raj Raghunathan, "The Art of Giving Up: The Importance of Disengaging from Goals," *Psychology Today,* April 19, 2011, www.psychologytoday.com/blog /sapient-nature/201104/the-art-giving.

4. "Brain Activity during Transient Sadness and Happiness in Healthy Women," *American Journal of Psychiatry* 152, no. 3 (1995): 341–51, http://ajp.psychiatry online.org/article.aspx?articleID=170877, cited in Daniel Goleman, "The Brain Manages Happiness and Sadness in Different Centers," *New York Times,* March 28, 1995, www.nytimes.com/1995/03/28/science/the-brain-manages-happiness -and-sadness-in-different-centers.html.

5. Gregory E. Miller and Carsten Wrosch, "You've Gotta Know When to Fold 'Em: Goal Disengagement and Systemic Inflammation in Adolescence," *Psychological Science* 18, no. 9 (2007): 773–77, http://sites.northwestern.edu /foundationsofhealth/files/2013/03/07-Psych-Sci-Youve-gotta-know-when -to-foldem.pdf.

6. Ibid.

7. *The Descendants,* directed by Alexander Payne (Fox Searchlight, 2012), DVD.

CHAPTER 4: LET'S ACKNOWLEDGE JUST HOW MUCH THIS SUCKS

1. Jane E. Brody, "Biological Role of Emotional Tears Emerges through Recent Studies," *New York Times,* August 31, 1982, www.nytimes.com/1982 /08/31 /science/biological-role-of-emotional-tears-emerges-through-recent-studies.html.

2. Elizabeth Gilbert, *Eat, Pray, Love: One Woman's Search for Everything Across Italy, India and Indonesia* (New York: Viking, 2006); Frances Mayes, *Under the Tuscan Sun* (New York: Chronicle, 1996).

3. Monica McGoldrick, Joan Marsh Schlesinger, Evelyn Lee, Paulette Moore Hines, Joseph Chan, Rhea Almeida, Barbara Petkov, Nydia Garcia Preto, and Sueli Petry, "Mourning in Different Cultures," in *Living Beyond Loss: Death in the Family,* 2nd ed., ed. Froma Walsh and Monica McGoldrick (New York: W.W. Norton, 2004), 119.

4. Camille B. Wortman and Roxane Cohen Silver, "The Myths of Coping with Loss," *Journal of Consulting and Clinical Psychology* 57, no. 3 (1989): 349–57, cited in Monica McGoldrick, Joan Marsh Schlesinger, Evelyn Lee, Paulette Moore Hines, Joseph Chan, Rhea Almeida, Barbara Petkov, Nydia Garcia Preto, and Sueli Petry, "Mourning in Different Cultures," in *Living Beyond Loss: Death in the Family,* 2nd ed., ed. Froma Walsh and Monica McGoldrick (New York: W.W. Norton, 2004), 119.

5. Monica McGoldrick, Joan Marsh Schlesinger, Evelyn Lee, Paulette Moore Hines, Joseph Chan, Rhea Almeida, Barbara Petkov, Nydia Garcia Preto, and Sueli Petry, "Mourning in Different Cultures," in *Living Beyond Loss: Death in the Family,* 2nd ed., ed. Froma Walsh and Monica McGoldrick (New York: W.W. Norton, 2004), 119–120.

6. Paraphrased from Monica McGoldrick and Froma Walsh, "A Time to Mourn: Death and the Family Life Cycle," in *Living Beyond Loss: Death in the Family,* 2nd ed., ed. Froma Walsh and Monica McGoldrick (New York: W.W. Norton, 2004), 28.

7. American Psychiatric Association, *Diagnostic and Statistical Manual of Mental Disorders, 5th ed. (DSM-5)* (Arlington, VA: American Psychiatric Association, 2013).

CHAPTER 5: THE UGLY STEPSIBLINGS OF EMOTIONS

1. Karla McLaren, *The Language of Emotions* (Boulder, CO: Sounds True, 2010).

2. Naomi Eisenberger, Matthew D. Lieberman, and Kipling D. Williams, "Does Rejection Hurt? A fMRI Study of Social Exclusion," *Science* 302, no. 5643 (2003): 290–92, cited in Lea Winerman, "Talking the Pain Away," *Monitor* 37, no. 9 (October 2006), www.apa.org/monitor/oct06/talking.aspx.

3. Center for Nonviolent Communication, "Feelings Inventory," 2005, www.cnvc.org/Training/feelings-inventory.

4. Ibid.

5. *Merriam-Webster,* online edition, s.v. "fear," www.merriam-webster.com/dictionary /fear.

6. James Hollis, *Finding Meaning in the Second Half of Life: How to Finally, Really Grow Up* (New York: Gotham Books, 2005).

7. Ibid.

8. "Jack Black: Fear Is the Rocket Sauce," CBS News, November 4, 2012, www.cbsnews.com/news/jack-black-fear-is-the-rocket-sauce.

9. Brené Brown, "Shame vs. Guilt," brenebrown.com, January 14, 2013, http://brenebrown.com/2013/01/14/2013114shame-v-guilt-html.

10. "Brené Brown On Shame: 'It Cannot Survive Empathy,'" HuffPost OWN Videos, updated August 27, 2013, www.huffingtonpost.com/2013/08/26/brene-brown -shame_n_3807115.html.

11. *Amadeus,* directed by Milos Forman (Warner Home Video, 2009), DVD.

CHAPTER 6: EVERYBODY NEEDS SOMEBODY TO LEAN ON

1. Tracey Cleantis, "Infertility: 16 Things You Should Never Say to a Woman Who Is Childless but Not by Choice," HuffPost, updated June 25, 2012, www.huffingtonpost.com/tracey-cleantis/infertility-16-things-you_b _1449350 .html.

2. Harold S. Kushner, *Living a Life That Matters* (New York: Anchor Books, 2002), 123–24.

3. Pamela Mahoney Tsigdinos, comment on Tracey Cleantis's Facebook page, used with permission.

4. Michael Blumenfield, "Choosing a Psychotherapist: Should Gender Matter?" HuffPost, updated July 31, 2011, www.huffingtonpost.com/michael-blumenfield -md/choosing-a-psychotherapist_b_868475.html.

5. *Ordinary People,* directed by Robert Redford (Warner Bros., 2001), DVD.

CHAPTER 7: MAN'S SEARCH FOR MEANING

1. Robert Jay Lifton, *Thought Reform and the Psychology of Totalism: A Study of 'Brainwashing' in China* (University of North Carolina Press, 1989), 429.

2. Jiddu Krishnamurti, *The First and Last Freedom* (New York: Harper & Row, 1975).

3. Used with permission from Danielle LaPorte, "When Gratitude Is Harmful," www.daniellelaporte.com/gratitude-harmful.

4. Noam Shpancer, "What Doesn't Kill You Makes You Weaker: A History of Hardship Is Not a Life Asset," *Psychology Today,* August 21, 2010, www.psychology today.com/blog/insight-therapy/201008/what-doesnt-kill-you-makes-you-weaker.

5. Ibid.

6. Barbara L. Ganzel, Pilyoung Kim, Gary H. Glover, and Elise Temple, "Resilience after 9/11: Multimodal Neuroimaging Evidence for Stress-Related Change in the Healthy Adult Brain," *Neuroimage* 40, no. 2 (April 1, 2008): 788–95, published online January 29, 2008, www.ncbi.nlm.nih.gov/pmc/articles /PMC2405811.

7. Viktor E. Frankl, *Man's Search for Meaning,* hardcover ed. (Cutchogue, NY: Buccaneer Books, 1993), 117.

8. Ibid., 85.

9. Ibid., 54–55.

10. Viktor E. Frankl, *Man's Search for Meaning*, hardcover ed. (Cutchogue, NY: Buccaneer Books, 1993).

11. *Harry Potter and the Sorcerer's Stone*, directed by Chris Columbus (Warner Home Video, 2007), DVD.

CHAPTER 8: THE SYMBOLIC MEANING OF YOUR DREAM

1. Adam Phillips, *Missing Out: In Praise of the Unlived Life* (New York: Farrar, Straus and Giroux, 2013).

2. Ibid., xii.

3. Ibid., xi.

4. Raj Persaud and Peter Bruggen, "Does Fame Make You More Suicidal?" HuffPost, updated June 8, 2013, www.huffingtonpost.co.uk/dr-raj-persaud/stephen-fry -attempted-suicide_b_3395012.html.

5. Richard M. Ryan and Tim Kasser, "Further Examining the American Dream: Differential Correlates of Intrinsic and Extrinsic Goals," *Personality and Social Psychology Bulletin* 22 (1996): 280–87, cited in "The Path Taken: Consequences of Attaining Intrinsic and Extrinsic Aspirations in Post-College Life," *Journal of Research in Personality* 73, no. 3 (June 2009): 291–306, www.ncbi.nlm.nih.gov /pmc/articles/PMC2736104.

6. P. Brickman and D. T. Campbell, "Hedonic Relativism and Planning the Good Society," in *Adaptation-Level Theory: A Symposium,* ed. M. H. Appley (New York: Academic Press, 1972), 287–304.

7. Sonja Lyubomirsky, *The How of Happiness: A Scientific Approach to Getting the Life You Want* (New York: Penguin, 2007).

8. *It's a Wonderful Life,* directed by Frank Capra (original release 1946).

CHAPTER 9: THE NEXT HAPPY

1. Sonja Lyubomirsky, *The How of Happiness: A Scientific Approach to Getting the Life You Want* (New York: Penguin, 2007).

2. Haruki Murakami, *1Q84* (New York: Knopf, 2011).

3. Joseph Campbell, *Reflections on the Art of Living: A Joseph Campbell Companion* (New York: Harper, 1995).

4. *The Best Exotic Marigold Hotel,* directed by John Madden (Fox Searchlight, 2012), DVD.

Resources

Memoir

Blue Nights by Joan Didion (Random House / Vintage)

Giving Up the Ghost by Hilary Mantel (Henry Holt and Company / John Macrae Books)

A Grief Observed by C. S. Lewis (HarperOne)

A Heartbreaking Work of Staggering Genius by Dave Eggers (Random House / Vintage Books)

In an Instant: A Family's Journey of Love and Healing by Lee Woodruff and Bob Woodruff (Random House)

Love Is a Mix Tape: Life and Loss, One Song at a Time by Rob Sheffield (Three Rivers Press)

Nothing Was the Same by Kay Redfield Jamison (Random House / Vintage Books)

Perfectly Imperfect: A Life in Progress by Lee Woodruff (Random House Trade Paperbacks)

The Pure Lover by David Plante (Beacon Press)

This Is How: Proven Aid in Overcoming Shyness, Molestation, Fatness, Spinsterhood, Grief, Disease, Lushery, Decrepitude & More—For Young and Old Alike by Augusten Burroughs (St. Martin's Press)

Wonder Women: Sex, Power, and the Quest for Perfection by Debora L. Spar (Picador)

The Year of Magical Thinking by Joan Didion (Vintage)

Feelings/Emotions

The Art of Empathy: A Complete Guide to Life's Most Essential Skill by Karla McLaren (Sounds True)

The Gifts of Imperfection: Let Go of Who You Think You're Supposed to Be and Embrace Who You Are by Brené Brown (Hazelden)

Healing through the Dark Emotions: The Wisdom of Grief, Fear, and Despair by Miriam Greenspan (Shambhala)

The Language of Emotions: What Your Feelings Are Trying to Tell You by Karla McLaren (Sounds True)

On Desire: Why We Want What We Want by William B. Irvine (Oxford University Press)

The Other Side of Sadness: What the New Science of Bereavement Tells Us about Life after Loss by George A. Bonanno (Basic Books)

When Anger Scares You: How to Overcome Your Fear of Conflict and Express Your Anger in Healthy Ways by John R. Lynch (New Harbinger Publications)

Infertility

I'm Taking My Eggs and Going Home: How One Woman Dared to Say No to Motherhood by Lisa Manterfield (Steel Rose Press)

Otherhood: Modern Women Finding a New Kind of Happiness by Melanie Notkin (Seal Press)

Rocking the Life Unexpected: 12 Weeks to Your Plan B for a Meaningful and Fulfilling Life without Children by Jody Day (CreateSpace)

Silent Sorority: A Barren Woman Gets Busy, Angry, Lost and Found by Pamela Mahoney Tsigdinos (BookSurge Publishing)

Grief/Loss

Healing after Loss: Daily Meditations for Working through Grief by Martha Whitmore Hickman (Avon Books)

Heartbreak: New Approaches to Healing—Recovering from Lost Love and Mourning by Ginette Paris (Mill City Press)

How to Survive the Loss of a Love by Melba Colgrove, Harold H. Bloomfield, and Peter McWilliams (Prelude Press)

On Death and Dying: What the Dying Have to Teach Doctors, Nurses, Clergy and Their Own Families by Elisabeth Kübler-Ross (Scribner)

On Grief and Grieving: Finding the Meaning of Grief through the Five Stages of Loss by Elisabeth Kübler-Ross and David Kessler (Scribner)

Transitions: Making Sense of Life's Changes by William Bridges (Da Capo Press)

When Bad Things Happen to Good People by Harold S. Kushner (Anchor)

When Things Fall Apart: Heart Advice for Difficult Times by Pema Chödrön (Shambhala)

Psychology

The Denial of Death by Ernest Becker (Free Press)

Finding Meaning in the Second Half of Life: How to Finally, Really Grow Up by James Hollis (Gotham Books)

Living Your Unlived Life: Coping with Unrealized Dreams and Fulfilling Your Purpose in the Second Half of Life by Robert A. Johnson and Jerry M. Ruhl (Tarcher)

Man's Search for Meaning by Viktor E. Frankl (Buccaneer Books)

Missing Out: In Praise of the Unlived Life by Adam Phillips (Farrar, Straus, and Giroux)

Social: Why Our Brains Are Wired to Connect by Matthew Lieberman (Broadway Books)

Your Next Happy

Authentic Happiness: Using the New Positive Psychology to Realize Your Potential for Lasting Fulfillment by Martin Seligman (Simon and Schuster / Atria)

Bonjour, Happiness! Secrets to Finding Your Joie De Vivre by Jamie Cat Callan (Citadel Press)

The Happiness Advantage: The Seven Principles of Positive Psychology That Fuel Success and Performance at Work by Shawn Achor (Crown Business)

The Happiness Hypothesis: Finding Modern Truth in Ancient Wisdom by Jonathan Haidt (Basic Books)

The Happiness Project: Or, Why I Spent a Year Trying to Sing in the Morning, Clean My Closets, Fight Right, Read Aristotle, and Generally Have More Fun by Gretchen Rubin (Harper)

The How of Happiness: A Scientific Approach to Getting the Life You Want by Sonja Lyubomirsky (Penguin)

The Slight Edge: Turning Simple Disciplines into Massive Success and Happiness by Jeff Olson, with John David Mann (Greenleaf Book Group)

So Good They Can't Ignore You: Why Skills Trump Passion in the Quest for Work You Love by Cal Newport (Grand Central Publishing / Business Plus)

Stumbling on Happiness by Daniel Gilbert (Random House / Vintage Books)

Ten Years Later: Six People Who Faced Adversity and Transformed Their Lives by Hoda Kotb (Simon and Schuster)

About the Author

Tracey Cleantis is a marriage and family therapist with a private practice in Valencia and Pasadena, California. She holds a master's degree in counseling psychology from Pacifica Graduate Institute and has studied at the C.G. Jung Institute of Los Angeles.

Tracey calls herself "The Dr. Kevorkian of Dreams" and is committed to helping people let go of what isn't working, grieve the loss, and get to the other side where happiness waits for them. Through her online writing, workshops, and seminars, she has built a national reputation as an accessible and trustworthy expert with a special expertise in the death of a dream. Her popular *Freudian Sip* blog on the *Psychology Today* website worked to make psychoanalytic thought easy to understand and accessible, one sip at a time, and her internationally known blog *La Belette Rouge* focused on life on both sides of the couch. Tracey also writes for the *Huffington Post* and has published essays, fiction, and poetry in various publications, including the *Sojourner* and *Mode Magazine.* Her interviews and advice have been featured in stories in *Psychologies Magazine, The New York Daily News, Redbook, Yahoo News, Salon.com, Forest and Bluff, Sheridan Road,* and on Fox News Boston.

Tracey lives in Pasadena, California, with her boyfriend, Keith, and her dog, Lily. Visit her at www.traceycleantis.com.

About Hazelden Publishing

As part of the Hazelden Betty Ford Foundation, Hazelden Publishing offers both cutting-edge educational resources and inspirational books. Our print and digital works help guide individuals in treatment and recovery, and their loved ones. Professionals who work to prevent and treat addiction also turn to Hazelden Publishing for evidence-based curricula, digital content solutions, and videos for use in schools, treatment programs, correctional programs, and electronic health records systems. We also offer training for implementation of our curricula.

Through published and digital works, Hazelden Publishing extends the reach of healing and hope to individuals, families, and communities affected by addiction and related issues.

For more information about Hazelden publications,
please call **800-328-9000** or visit us online at
hazelden.org/bookstore

Other titles that may interest you:

The Gifts of Imperfection
Let Go of Who You Think You're Supposed to Be and Embrace Who You Are
— A *New York Times* Best Seller!
BRENÉ BROWN, PHD, LMSW

In *The Gifts of Imperfection,* Brené Brown, a leading expert on shame, authenticity, and belonging, shares what she's learned from a decade of research on the power of *Wholehearted Living,* a way of engaging with the world from a place of worthiness.

Order No. 2545 (softcover)
Also available as an e-book.

Choosing a Good Life
Lessons from People Who Have Found Their Place in the World
ALI BERMAN

In *Choosing a Good Life,* Ali Berman explores what it means to be at peace with ourselves, our choices, and the world around us in all its glorious chaos. She takes us into the lives of people who, despite their vastly different talents, challenges, and interests, have achieved a deep sense of balance in and satisfaction with their lives. Berman pinpoints their common approaches and qualities to reveal how they have found contentment—and how we can too.

Order No. 7538 (softcover)
Also available as an e-book.

Hazelden Publishing books are available at fine bookstores everywhere. To order from Hazelden Publishing, call **800-328-9000** or visit **hazelden.org/bookstore**.